Pass Receiving in
Early Pro Football

Pass Receiving in Early Pro Football

A History to the 1960s

JERRY ROBERTS

McFarland & Company, Inc., Publishers
Jefferson, North Carolina

LIBRARY OF CONGRESS CATALOGUING-IN-PUBLICATION DATA

Names: Roberts, Jerry, 1956–
Title: Pass receiving in early pro football : a history to the 1960s / Jerry Roberts.
Description: Jefferson, North Carolina : McFarland & Company, Inc., Publishers, 2016 | Includes bibliographical references and index.
Identifiers: LCCN 2015036285| ISBN 9780786499465 (softcover : acid free paper) | ISBN 9781476622286 (ebook)
Subjects: LCSH: Passing (Football)—United States—History.
Classification: LCC GV951.5 .R64 2016 | DDC 796.332/64—dc23
LC record available at http://lccn.loc.gov/2015036285

BRITISH LIBRARY CATALOGUING DATA ARE AVAILABLE

**ISBN (print) 978-0-7864-9946-5
ISBN (ebook) 978-1-4766-2228-6**

© 2016 Jerry Roberts. All rights reserved

No part of this book may be reproduced or transmitted in any form or by any means, electronic or mechanical, including photocopying or recording, or by any information storage and retrieval system, without permission in writing from the publisher.

Front cover illustration by John Richards

Printed in the United States of America

*McFarland & Company, Inc., Publishers
Box 611, Jefferson, North Carolina 28640
www.mcfarlandpub.com*

*To my life's football companions:
my late father, Alex Roberts; my brother, Mark Roberts;
the skilled quarterback of my checkered sandlot career, Kevin Morris;
my Sunday Steelers watching partner, Doug List; and
my new favorite receiver, my nephew, Tyler Kolfschoten.*

Table of Contents

Acknowledgments ix

Preface 1

One. Initiating the Forward Pass in American Football 5

Two. College Football in 1906 11

Three. Pop Warner at Carlisle 21

Four. Knute Rockne vs. Army 28

Five. Receiving in Pro Football's Earliest Times 34

Six. The NFL's Fledgling Years 41

Seven. The First Dynasty: Green Bay 52

Eight. The Chicago Bears and the T Formation 59

Nine. The First Receiving Superstar: Don Hutson of Green Bay 78

Ten. Monsters of the Midway 84

Eleven. The Pivotal 1943 Season and After 96

Twelve. Clark Shaughnessy and Offensive Firepower 109

Thirteen. Paul Brown in the AAFC and NFL 124

Fourteen. Between the AAFC and AFL: More Deep Threats Emerge 140

Fifteen. Tight End: Biography of a Position 149

Sixteen. Running Backs as Receivers 175

Table of Contents

Appendix: Individual Honors   207
Chapter Notes   219
Bibliography   228
Index   237

Acknowledgments

Sports writers and editors who helped me along my winding way as a journalist have included Phil Musick, Steve Hecht, Ralph Wimbish, Joe Garvey, Bob Whitley, Phil Axelrod, Sharon Eberson, Gary Tuma, Charley "Pally" Feeney, Vito Stellino, Mark Madden, Mike White, Drew Nelson, Phil Collin, Mike Braham, Rob Fernas, Bill Cizek, Jimmy Johnson, and Jeff Samuels. My friend and former boss, Don Lechman, a sports-book aficionado, provided inspiration. I have to thank such autumn Saturday heroes as Danny Rick, Don Manley, Bill Steig, Steve Stempler, and especially my brother Mark and Kevin Morris as well as any number of other Morrises.

Four former pro running backs gave me time and their memories: Bob Thurbon, John Henry Johnson, Jim Brown, and Gale Sayers. I learned a few things about pro football as a sports editor and writer covering the Pittsburgh Steelers in the 1970s, especially from Chuck Noll, Jim Smith, Andy Russell, L.C. Greenwood, and Joe Greene.

Thanks go to the staff and management of the LA84 Foundation Sports Library in Los Angeles, particularly to Michael Salmon. Special thanks also go to Geoff Strain, who insisted that I visit the LA84 Library.

Ian Allen of South Bay Baseball Cards, Inc., in Lomita, California, deserves no small amount of gratitude. A tip of the helmet goes to Barry Bowen, treasurer of Tootsie Roll Industries of Chicago, for the use of defunct Philadelphia Gum Company and Fleer Corporation vintage football cards. Don Lechman of Torrance, California, lent football cards and friendship to the project. Charles G. Lamb of Louisville, Kentucky, graciously granted the use of the Notre Dame cards from the Collegiate Collection, and Stacy R. Marshall facilitated the connection to Mr. Lamb. Bev Wilson, assistant general counsel of The Topps Company, Inc., allowed permission to use the vintage 1950s Bowman Gum Company cards. Topps® Bowman® football cards are used courtesy of The Topps

ACKNOWLEDGMENTS

Company, Inc. For more information about The Topps Company, please see the web site at www.topps.com. Alexis Melisi of Topps also aided in the permission from Topps.

The staffs and managements of the libraries in the following California cities were also helpful: Torrance, Huntington Beach, Anaheim, Long Beach, Carson, Redondo Beach, Rolling Hills Estates, and Gardena.

Preface

Except for the chapters on tight ends and running backs, which are detailed through the game-altering "Mel Blount rule" prior to the 1979 season, this book ends with the 1960s. The story of pass receiving before television winds down from 1958, when the Baltimore Colts defeated the New York Giants in the NFL championship game, during which the great Raymond Berry caught a then-playoff record 12 passes from Johnny Unitas in an overtime comeback victory. It has been called the greatest game ever played, in part because the nationally televised contest ended in sudden-death overtime and captured the fascination of the American public.

Big TV contracts in the next decade created the Super Bowl in 1966 as well as the 1970 merger of the National Football League with the pass-oriented American Football League. Viewers across America in the 1960s could watch the exploits of AFL receiving stars Lance Alworth, Don Maynard, Otis Taylor, and Fred Biletnikoff on a weekly basis, and half a dozen books now describe that upstart league in detail. By then, too, the more running-oriented NFL had become a popular Sunday viewing ritual across the land.

The purpose of this book is to provide a description of pro pass receiving and its influence on the overall game of professional football before TV. NFL Films began shooting every play in every NFL game in 1965, as the nation avidly added televised football to the weekly day of rest. The visual record exists from then on.

This book contains what's not generally known about the receiving game. I wanted to sift through the facts about pro football's formative and mid-century years to highlight more than just the spectacular career of the legendary Don Hutson; in fact, the Hutson information I considered requisite. I tried to package it as succinctly as possible before writing about people and events on either side of his spectacular career, which is described elsewhere. He has been fittingly remembered as the great player he was.

Part of the impetus to do this book was a boyhood appreciation of receiving that escalated when someone told me, "If you can touch it, you can catch it." There's a recipe for heartbreak, not to mention bumps and bruises. Alworth and Biletnikoff snatching footballs on TV made for particular thrills and often uncommon feats, inspiring appreciation, which later was transferred to many others: Roy Jefferson, Charlie Sanders, Lynn Swann, Drew Pearson, Ozzie Newsome, Jerry Rice, Hines Ward…

Another reason to do this book now has been the transformation of pro offenses into what's called the "vertical" game in the 21st century. The most popular televised sport's most spectacular play remains the long gainer—sometimes a run or interception, kick or punt return—but most often the long bomb. College and professional teams pass much more often than in previous decades. Coaches in the win-now atmosphere of big-time collegiate athletics and under the microscope of media attention in the NFL have emphasized the big play, primarily the downfield throw—the field-stretching heave. This book helps explain the long history that has led to this aerial circus—how we got here.

Names that can stand as signatories to large portions of football history—John Heisman, Pop Warner, Knute Rockne, Curly Lambeau, Red Grange, and George Halas—were all instrumental in the establishment and proficiency of forward-passing techniques, rules, and frequency. Hutson and Tom Fears are, respectively, known as the first great pre-war and post-war receivers, but they weren't alone in talent, style, and success. This book elaborates on benchmark-makers who pulled footballs from flight: Gibby Welch, Johnny Blood, Ray Flaherty, Crazy Legs Hirsch, Mac Speedie, et al.

Unlike other pro sports leagues, the NFL didn't begin keeping individual statistics—except who scored, and occasionally not even how he scored—until 1932, so that the information gathered for earlier seasons has been drawn from early football histories, biographies, periodicals, reference works, NFL publications, and other sources.

Receivers in all eras of football have received less attention than quarterbacks or coaches, even in the modern era of Jerry Rice's unsurpassed supremacy. This book can't avoid the mention of several espe-

Preface

cially influential quarterbacks and coaches, and it certainly gives them their due: Some chapters and their titles emphasize the importance of Pop Warner, Clark Shaughnessy, and Paul Brown, for instance. And the bespectacled, porkpie-topped specter of George Halas hovers over much of the pro history of the forward pass. But the main attraction here is the ends and backs on the completion side of the aerial game.

A point should be made about another strong impetus to write a football book about bygone days. Statistics are manipulated by everyone from architects to school administrators to prove points, and language is then revised to prove just the opposite, all with the same numbers. But one thing both sides too often have in common is a bias in favor of the stats and records from "the Super Bowl era" and the years "after the merger." They have done a disservice to football history, ignoring large swaths of the past and denigrating the sport's pioneers. Stats, sound bites, stories and "historical" assessments that take no account of the early decades provide at best an incomplete view of history.

Total Football, the otherwise excellent statistical reference to the pro game, followed suit by concentrating on the "The Road to the Super Bowl and Super Sunday" *before* it compiled earlier championships and seasons. The NFL Network, owned by the league, began operating in 2003 with some throwback programming and clips, but that dearth of older historical programming soon evaporated. The network underwrites some incisive documentaries and covers the annual Pro Football Hall of Fame enshrinements, but the league's rich history could be mined for much more on-air gold.

Great receiving careers split before and after the first Super Bowl include those of Berry, Maynard, Alworth, Lionel Taylor, Bobby Mitchell, Mike Ditka, John Mackey, and dozens more. Jim Brown's last season was 1965, the year before the first Super Bowl. Johnny Unitas was on two Super Bowl–winning rosters, but he also won two NFL championships in the 1950s. Green Bay claims "Titletown" not on four Super Bowl wins alone but also on nine NFL championships previous to 1965.

Admittedly, football on TV has been terrific, even if it has led some to make a false association between the birth of pro football and the advent of the Super Bowl. But the NFL traces its lineage to 1920, and football has been played professionally since before the turn of the 20th century. Despite the visual dynamics of pro football's heated competition and great athletic feats in the TV era, thousands of passes were completed for hundreds of miles toward important victories before the Super Bowl. The mission here has been to emphasize and remember these achievements.

It is hoped that this book contributes to a better understanding of football's formative years and illuminates overlooked figures, incidents and games, particularly those associated with passing.

Chapter One

Initiating the Forward Pass in American Football

In the United States Centennial year of 1876, Custer's Last Stand was made by the Seventh Cavalry against the Sioux and Northern Cheyenne nations along the Little Big Horn River in Montana Territory. That same year, Mark Twain's *The Adventures of Tom Sawyer* was published, Alexander Graham Bell invented the telephone, Colorado was admitted to the union as the 38th state, and James "Wild Bill" Hickock made the acquaintance of "Calamity Jane" Cannary in Deadwood, South Dakota.

Another meeting took place on Thanksgiving weekend, November 30, at the St. George Cricket Field in Hoboken, New Jersey: The Yale and Princeton football teams played each other for the first time. In the game, Oliver Thompson caught a touchdown pass.

This last item may not have had the impact or the lasting legacy of the other events—at least for some people. The mention of this particular illegal forerunner of the forward pass was described in the 1901-vintage *Athletics at Princeton—A History*: "McCosh was 'snivied on' by Camp who, when tackled, threw the ball forward to Thompson. Princeton at once claimed foul and ceased to prevent the touchdown. Much dissatisfaction was aroused against the referee, who, instead of deciding the question, actually tossed up a coin and Yale was allowed the touchdown."[1] The Princeton protests were against the rules violation of a forward throw, since sideways and backward tosses—laterals—only were allowed in the sport, which was then still played in America by rugby rules. A touchdown was worth two points at that time, and Yale defeated Princeton, 2–0.

American football in those truly formative years between the Civil War and the Industrial Age used the United Kingdom's *Rugby Union*

Code, which enforced the game in its purest form—if that's not an oxymoron for the rough-and-tumble sport—among American colleges. That Walter Camp happened to be the first player to benefit from the unorthodox forward-pass score versus Princeton was ironic. As college football's greatest 19th-century organizer, rules arbiter, judge of talent, and keeper of heritage, Camp opposed passing even after the Rules Committee governing college ball allowed it three decades later. But in 1876, as a frosh pounding for Yale, he took the two points.

Camp resisted a growing pro-passing contingent who became more prevalent and vocal through the turn of the 20th century, and who wanted to develop throwing the football as a way to open up offenses for the good of the increasingly brutal game. Dubbed in *Harper's Weekly* by famed sports writer Caspar Whitney as the "Father of American Football," Camp felt proprietary care for the game he nurtured out of rugby into a wholly American tradition by re-adjusting the rulebook from time to time to streamline a more exciting sport.[2]

Camp's gradual adjusting and oversight of the Americanization of rugby included limiting teams to 11 players on the field, the concept of downs to run plays, the first standardization of the field (110 yards long and 53 yards wide) and the establishment of a scoring system (five points for a field goal, four for a free kick after a touchdown, two for a touchdown, and one for a safety).

Camp held great sway in the football world before and after the turn of the century, when college play dominated the sport, and Yale dominated college play. Camp was captain of the Yale team from 1878 through 1880, and Eli coach from 1888 through 1892, during which the team posted a 67–2 record with three undefeated seasons. In 1888, Camp's 14–0 Elis shut out all opponents, 704–0. Camp also coached Stanford in the 1890s to a 12–3–3 record over three years. A New Haven clockmaker by trade, he returned to his alma mater as not just a commanding figure on the Yale campus, but as a national sporting personality whose game evolved as an increasingly popular—if increasingly roughhouse—autumn campus ritual.

Camp's opposition to throwing the ball forward was rooted in preserving the innovations and traditions that he oversaw in the college game through its evolution from rugby. But his stonewalling of the pass also served the New Haven native's ulterior motive to keep Yale at the top of college football. His big and physical home team didn't require changes, especially through such a potential game-altering innovation as the forward pass. Moreover, in the first decade of the 20th century, the established run-propelled powerhouses feared that the forward pass might give smaller schools successful edges against their staunch defenses.

Caspar Whitney selected the first All-American team, published in 1889 in the New York periodical, *The Week's Sport*, and Camp took over that annual conferring of individual gridiron glory in 1898. That first All-American squad selected by Whitney included Yale's Amos Alonzo Stagg and Harvard's Arthur Cumnock at the ends, and such stars as Yale's W.W. "Pudge" Hefflefinger at guard, and Princeton's Edgar Allan Poe, the grandnephew namesake of the famous writer, in the backfield.

Camp was the official keeper and updater of college football's rules under the umbrella organization he created, the Intercollegiate Football Association or IFA. The IFA rules were commonly viewed as the official rules for all of organized football. For generations into the 1930s, the collegiate rules governed by rote all levels of professional, semi-pro, high school, and club football. In Chapter XIV of *Rules of the Season of 1896*, jointly written by Camp and Lorin F. Deland of Harvard, Rule 20 (a continuance from rugby rules), states, "A player may throw or pass the ball in any direction except toward the opponents' goal. If the ball be batted in any direction or thrown forward, it shall go down on the spot to the opponents."[3]

Upholding the status quo of the game he nurtured, Camp ignored an event of the previous season, brought to his attention by John W. Heisman. During his first decade as a college coach in the South—at Auburn, Clemson, then Georgia Tech—Heisman was intrigued by the possibilities of the forward pass. The event that turned him into a pro-pass enthusiast occurred in a game he scouted, the 1895 Georgia-North Carolina contest. The Carolina fullback, in punt formation, threw the ball sideways and forward to teammate George Stephens, who raced 70 yards for a touchdown.

Georgia Coach Glenn "Pop" Warner protested that the play was illegal, but the referee claimed that he did not see it, according to Heisman, and the TD stood. Heisman began a campaign to convince the recalcitrant Camp of the benefits of throwing and catching the ball. Writing more than three decades later in *Collier's*, Heisman claimed, "I had seen the first forward pass in football. It was illegal, of course. Already Warner was storming at the referee. But the referee had not seen the North Carolina lad, goaded to desperation, toss the ball. And he refused to recall the ball. A touchdown had been made and a touchdown it remained."[4]

Heisman, who had played collegiately at Brown and the University of Pennsylvania, and coached at nine colleges to 1927, became the namesake for college football's greatest prize for individual skill and accomplishment, the Heisman Trophy. He also was one of the most persistent advocates of the forward pass. He wrote several times to Camp in the first years of the 20th century, urging the game's self-styled patriarch to accept the pass as a regular weapon in offensive arsenals.

Pressure from other powers weighed on Walter Camp, issues tarnishing the game of football itself. The sport had developed a very unwanted statistic that doubled as its largest public relations problem: fatalities. The protection of the players and the violence in the sport had become national issues by 1905, when three collegians and 18 players in all levels of organized football died from injuries received on the playing field, according to *The New York Times*. The *Chicago Tribune* reported that 159 players had been "seriously injured" in the same season.[5]

The one fresh casualty who particularly stoked the anti-football bias in the media center of New York was Union College player Harold Moore, who died in a pile-up during the New York University game in November. NYU Chancellor Henry MacCracken, on a mission to better safeguard players, convened a meeting in December of 13 representatives of athletic departments at New York area learning institutions that fielded football teams. Each school became charter members of the Intercollegiate Athletic Association of the United States or IAAUS, which, five years later, renamed itself the National Collegiate Athletic Association or NCAA.

President Theodore Roosevelt, who once insisted that he would "disinherit a boy if he were to weigh the possibility of broken bones against the glory of playing football for Harvard," met with 60 college delegates after the MacCracken meeting to discuss the public outcry following the gridiron deaths and injuries.[6] The Rules Committee of the IAAUS, had which absorbed the Camp-organized IFA, took up the mission of safety on the field during its January 1906 meeting in New York.

Historically, many injuries through the 1890s were incurred during mass-attack running plays using battering-ram-style assemblages of players. In these plays, ball carriers were escorted by phalanxes of blockers, occasionally interlocked together by arms and special belts with handles to hold on to each other. During mass-attack plays, head injuries and broken arms resulted as much from friendly collisions as from oppositional hits. The pass, some reasoned, would send plays and players wide and downfield, spreading them out, and contribute to the contraction of plays such as the "flying wedge."[7]

The flying wedge was developed at Harvard in 1892 by Lorin F. Deland, Camp's co-writer on the rule book. Deland designed the Roman Legion–like play specifically to neutralize Yale's marauding end, Frank Hinkey. Never having been in a football game didn't stop Deland from tinkering with the sport's strategy. As an aficionado of military and chess maneuvers, Deland devised the flying wedge, according to authors Bernard M. Corbett and Paul Simpson, "based on decidedly warlike precepts."[8]

The V-like formation positioned the ball carrier, in this case, All American fullback Charlie Brewer, inside the vortex, and was incorporated into Harvard's game plan by co-coaches George A. Stewart and George C. Adams. The flying wedge was only one of a number of mass-escort plays throughout Eastern football. The "mass plays" and the belts with handles, because of the resulting injuries, were outlawed in 1894 by the Rules Committee. But teams still congregated blocking gangs on many plays, skirting the rules. Wedges, with grouped blockers escorting ball carriers, had been used since the 1880s when Princeton and Lehigh were credited with devising them. Camp used the "shoving wedge" at Yale.[9]

Through the turn of the 20th century, the black mark earned by the sport's roughhouse tactics turned scandalous. "At the beginning of 1906, the wider football public, which included women as well as men, had the fresh hope that the rules committee would devise a new, safe, sportsmanlike, and orderly game to replace the thoroughly discredited spectacle of the 1890s," historian John Sayle Watterson wrote.[10]

Three influential men on the Rules Committee with Camp believed that the forward pass would open up the game with new dimensions of exciting play. Two had connections to the high-profile service academies:

Dr. Harry Williams, who had coached the West Point squad in the 1890s, and the former Lehigh University coach and then (1905–1906) U.S. Naval Academy coach, Paul Dashiell. The third advocate was a former University of Pennsylvania player and one-time Pennsylvania Attorney General, John C. Bell, the father of then future Pennsylvania Governor John C. Bell, Jr., and future National Football League Commissioner De Benneville "Bert" Bell. These three—Williams, Dashiell, and Bell, Sr.—Heisman wrote in 1928, "deserve the main credit for the pass being in the game today."[11]

Their votes on January 12, 1906, during the IAAUS Rules Committee meeting, held at the Murray Hill Hotel in New York City, legalized the forward pass in college play. J. William White, a Philadelphia surgeon, was among those who helped re-write the rule book during the 10-hour session. Afterward, Walter Camp and others of his "old guard" still held reservations that passing could irrevocably change the game in a detrimental manner. This is why the committee placed certain restrictions on forward passing[12]:

- The ball had to cross the line of scrimmage five yards outside where it was received from the center, or the offense lost possession.
- Only players lined up at the end of the line could catch the ball. If any of the nine other offensive players touched the thrown ball, loss of possession would result.
- A forward pass could not cross a goal line. If it did, it was a touchback and the ball was awarded to the opposition. The ball had to be run across the goal line after the catch.
- An incomplete pass resulted in loss of possession at the point where the ball hit the ground.
- If a pass went out of bounds, any player could recover it from either team, leading to what a rules maker of a later era, David M. Nelson, called "many a cinder burn when players scrambled for the ball on running tracks surrounding the fields."[13]

Chapter Two

College Football in 1906

"Like the invention of the airplane, the forward pass turned out to be the most revolutionary gridiron change of the early 1900s," historian John Sayle Watterson wrote in the long view of history.[1] But that autumn, few teams used the option right away, at least in Walter Camp's purview of the eastern elite schools.

One impediment to passing was that most players could not control the trajectory of the large and pumpkin-shaped, rugby-styled pigskin. The ball, often called a "blimp," usually had only seven laces. The average-sized hand couldn't really gain much purchase on the pigskin with the thumb and the index and ring fingers, even over the laces. Throwing was awkward. Some players heaved it end-over-end. Some used a flat-handed method in a windmill-like catapult. Others threw it two-handed, from the chest, in the basketball manner. It wasn't until 1912 that the official college pigskin became more elongated, and passers could better get a one-handed grip on the ball.

Throughout the early decades in the 20th century, the notion prevailed, particularly among the long-established teams at Yale, Harvard, Princeton, Dartmouth, and Pennsylvania, that running the ball still was not only the most effective mode of advance, but—nearly equal in importance—it was also the sound, manly, and honorably sporting way of proving dominance. Teams resolved to march down the field in military style, incrementally gaining ground, muscling the opposition back into its own territory until victory was achieved over the goal line.

An incompletion, according to the new rules, was tantamount to an interception—a turnover. Some coaches never embraced the pass. Some prejudice against passing prevailed not only through the first decades of the 20th century in both college and the pro leagues, and persisted even after an incompletion simply became a wasted down. Various coaches considered passing unsound, even through the World

War II era, when George Halas' Chicago Bears threw from the T formation and dominated the NFL. As late as the 1970s, Ohio State's Woody Hayes, who had been coaching since 1946, at Denison University, still operated under the often-repeated credo, "There are three things that can happen when you pass, and two of them ain't good."[2]

The same sentiments were shared among many coaches in the early 20th century, especially in the New England and Mid-Atlantic regions, where the sport became established at colleges as an autumn weekend ritual, and in Western Pennsylvania and Ohio, where it was sowing the seeds of semi-professionalism. Big-time football in those years, prior to radio, meant especially the powers that *New York Herald-Tribune* sports editor Stanley Woodward dubbed in 1933 the "Ivy League"—Harvard, Yale, Princeton, Pennsylvania, Cornell, Brown, Dartmouth, and Columbia (and, at the time, West Point Academy).[3]

Collegiate teams from New England through Virginia were covered by the newspapers in Boston, New York, Philadelphia, and Washington: Navy, Rutgers, Wesleyan, Lafayette, Lehigh, Tufts, Fordham, New York University, Villanova, Bucknell, and others. Sports writers of the day often tended to reinforce the attitudes of the local coaches in stories that usually supported the hometown team. Run-oriented coaches didn't cozy up to the pass. Regional coaching giants, such as John Heisman at Georgia Tech, Amos Alonzo Stagg at the University of Chicago, and Fielding "Hurry Up" Yost at the University of Michigan, were only just establishing traditions, and were far removed from the media center of New York.

The pass had been used in an experimental manner during the very end of the 1905 season, or a month shy of the IAAUS rules changes. In December, two Kansas schools, Washburn and Fairmont (now Wichita State), tangled for the second time that season to try out prospective safety measures, testing them for adoption by IAAUS teams at large. These included using three downs instead of four to make a first down. That, ostensibly, would cut down on inside running plays by including more punts—an idea that never caught on. The forward pass was used in the game, as Washburn completed three and Fairmont two—in a scoreless tie.[4]

After the changes in 1906, passing was utilized as a major portion of one team's offense—with alacrity and success. While the eastern elite continued running nearly 100 percent of the time, the passing game became a fascination in westerly locales. The aptly named Eddie Cochems at St. Louis University was the first coach to build his offense around the forward pass. "E.B. Cochems is to forward passing what the Wright brothers are to aviation and Thomas Edison is to the electric light," was the epic-scale comparison declared by historian David M. Nelson.[5] A native of Sturgeon Bay, Wisconsin, Cochems had been a halfback on the University of Wisconsin teams from 1899 to 1901, and arrived in St. Louis after coaching stints at North Dakota State and Clemson.

On September 5, 1906, against Carroll College in Waukesha, Wisconsin, Cochems' St. Louis squad ran up against stiff opposition. Even though the Missouri Jesuit school had thrown a pass early in the game and it had resulted in a turnover to Carroll, Cochems ordered again what he referred to as the "air attack."[6] End Jack Schneider was on the receiving terminus of a 20-yard touchdown pass heaved by halfback Bradbury Robinson.

Both teams were stunned. St. Louis kept on throwing the football with success, and won the game, 22–0. St. Louis passed its way to an undefeated season, 11–0, and led the nation in scoring, 407–11. The season capper was a 31–0 victory over the University of Iowa, in which eight of 10 passes were completed for four touchdowns, and an average of 20 yards a reception. To follow that up, Cochems led St. Louis to a 7–3 record in 1907, including a stunning 34–0 victory over the Nebraska Cornhuskers on Thanksgiving Day at Sportsman's Park in St. Louis.

"I was sports editor of the *St. Louis Globe-Democrat* during Cochems' three-year period as St. Louis University coach ... and viewed many games," wrote J. Edward Wray in a 1954 letter to historian Allison Danzig. "There is no doubt that Cochems was the first coach to exploit the forward pass thrown overhand, both long and short, approximating closely the methods used today. I have a mass of correspondence from [Amos Alonzo] Stagg and other old-time coaches on the subject, letters from Bradbury Robinson and Cochems and other St. Louis University officials, and assure you, from observation and correspondence, that Cochems was the only man to effectively use any type of forward pass approaching the forward pass of today."

"Cochems had a powerful team besides having a secret weapon," Wray wrote. "He took his men to Lake Beulah, Wisconsin, in the summer of 1906, and there had a wonderful two months developing the long-throwing ability of Bradbury Robinson, with Jack Schneider receiving."[7] Cochems ensconced his team at a Jesuit retreat southwest of Milwaukee and drilled his players on the mechanics of throwing and catching the "blimp" football. As Harold Keith later wrote in *Esquire*, Cochems instituted "the first, forward pass system ever devised."[8] Wray wrote that Cochems used the pass judiciously with the ground game, and the Robinson-to-Schneider combination used a mix of short and long throws.

"The really wonderful part of the passing lay not only in its being an unknown weapon, but in the fact that the team was powerful enough to gain ground by straight football and then shift to the long, long pass [often of 50 or more yards' carry] and then to a fast 'bullet' shot just over the forward line," Wray wrote.

"The enemy's ignorance was pitiful, not knowing when to close ranks or spread out its defense," Wray continued. "The passing, considering that they used a 'blimp' football, not the streamlined, slim one of today, was out of this world.... Cochems was really a man of ideas and surely deserves all the credit for first development of the forward pass as we know it today."[9]

The St. Louis offense amazed aficionados. "It was the most perfect exhibition of the new rules in this respect that I have seen all season and much better than that of Yale or Harvard," former Army player Horatio B. "Stuffy" Hackett said after refereeing the St. Louis-Iowa game. "The St. Louis style of pass differs entirely from that in use in the East. There the ball is thrown high in the air and the runner who is to catch it is protected by several of his teammates forming an interference for him. The St. Louis players shoot the ball hard and accurately to the man who is to receive it, and the latter is not protected. With the high pass, protection is necessary ... [because] the ball requires some time to reach its goal, time enough for the defensive side to run in. The fast throw by St. Louis enables the receiving player to dodge the opposing players, and it struck me as being all but perfect," Hackett related.[10]

Both Robinson and Schneider passed and caught the ball in Cochems' offense. The former was the long-ball thrower, heaving it distances of 50 yards and more in an "overhand spiral—fingers on the lacing," according to an illustration of Robinson accompanying a chapter written by Cochems in editor Walter Camp's 1907 edition of *Spalding's How to Play Foot Ball*.[11]

While Cochems' St. Louis team is generally regarded as the first team to successfully use the forward pass, other teams and players claim other pioneering firsts regarding the aerial game. Figuring out who did what *first* regarding the throwing and catching of blimps in football's sketchily chronicled halcyon days is less important than marking the early times when the forward pass made an impact. Unlike baseball or even 20th century basketball, football received scant statistical coverage and/or interpretation until the 1930s.

The first pass to startle the East was Sammy Moore's 18-yard toss to Irvin Van Tassell for Wesleyan University on September 29, 1906, against Yale. Since the Wesleyan aerial was heaved in a 21–0 Yale win, it might be said to have been insignificant. Still, it was a shocking development in the midst of "Big Three" play—that trio in the first decade of the 20th century being Yale, Harvard, and Princeton.

Moore had been shown the overhand spiral pass by his coach, Howard Rowland "Bosey" Reiter, an All American at Princeton in 1899. Reiter claimed to have invented the overhand spiral while he was a player-coach for Cornelius McGillicuddy's Philadelphia Athletics of the single-season 1902 National Football League, the first American professional football league. The claims of others to mastery of the overhand spiral would come several years later after the forward pass became legalized for college play by the IAAUS.

But Reiter's contention was that he developed the overhand spiral in his year with the Athletics. McGillicuddy, who also answered to "Connie Mack" as his baseball-managing legend grew, was in his second year of a half-century of managing the Athletics baseball club in the American League. Mack had ignited contretemps in the City of Brotherly Love by trying to raid the National League's Philadelphia Phillies of baseball players. Phillies owner John I. Rogers filed a lawsuit to protect his team, and while that was brewing, decided to field a football team. Ben Shibe, the Athletics owner and namesake of the former Shibe Park in Philadelphia, asked Mack to field a better one, simply to one-up the cross-town rivals. Mack was joined in the gridiron effort by former University of Pennsylvania All American tackle Charles Edgar "Blondy" Wallace, a figure of later controversy in pro football annals.

(As captain of the Canton Bulldogs in 1906, Wallace was accused by the *Massillon [Ohio] Independent* of trying to fix the biggest game in the formative years of pro football, the Canton-Massillon contest. This never-proven charge was a byproduct of the paper's hometown cheerleading for the Massillon Tigers—city editor Edward J. Stewart managed the Tigers—a conflict of interest in a later era's definition of journalistic comportment. The scandal curtailed semi-pro play for several years in Canton, and sullied Wallace's reputation.[12])

In 1902, Mack and Wallace called Dave Berry, editor of the *Latrobe Clipper* in Westmoreland County, Pennsylvania, east of Pittsburgh. Berry had organized previous semi-pro and pro games in Western Pennsylvania, where the better and more experienced players were found. While Yale's Pudge Hefflefinger was the first known professional football player, paid $500 for his services by the Allegheny Athletic Association of Pittsburgh in 1892 for a game against the Pittsburgh Athletic Club, Berry fielded the first all-professional team, the Latrobe club in 1897, which forged strong local rivalries with the neighboring town teams in Greensburg and Jeannette.

Berry was installed as president of the 1902 National Football League and organized its third team, the Pittsburgh Stars, which was bankrolled by the Pittsburgh Pirates baseball team owner, Barney Dreyfuss, and starred former Bucknell fullback and future Baseball Hall of Famer Christy Mathewson, who had just finished his third season pitching for the New York baseball Giants.[13]

Playing in this loosely organized, three-team league, which actually gave the baseball team owners a rein on their players during the off-season, Bosey Reiter and Hawley Pierce, a Native American former star for the Carlisle Indian Industrial School, tinkered with more efficient ways of tossing the lateral. Pierce showed Reiter an underhand spiral pass. But Reiter, citing short arms, was unable to throw for any distance from an underhand delivery. Reiter worked on an overhand pass by trying one of Connie Mack's specialties as the former catcher for the Pittsburgh Pirates—a baseball backstop's throw to second base. Reiter found that by throwing overhand, he had better distance and accuracy than underhand.[14]

Wesleyan hired Reiter as football coach in 1903, before the forward pass was permitted. When the pass was admitted into college ball in

1906, Reiter introduced the overhand spiral technique to Sammy Moore. Receiver Van Tassel explained his 1906 catch against Yale to the United Press: "I was the right halfback, and on this formation played one yard back of our right tackle. The quarterback, Sam Moore, took the ball from center and faded eight or 10 yards back of our line. Our two ends angled down the field toward the sidelines as a decoy, and I slipped through the strong side of our line straight down the center and past the secondary defense. The pass worked perfectly. However, the [Yale] quarterback coming up fast nailed me as I caught it. This brought the ball well into Yale territory, about the 20-yard line."[15] Van Tassel was actually an illegal receiver, according to the rules. At the time, only ends were allowed to catch passes, not backs, which proves that the refereeing in the era was as proficient or deficient as many receivers have believed it to be in any decade.

The football season opened for most schools in those years during the first week of October—after the St. Louis win over Carroll, and mostly far from big-city paper scrutiny. But the impact of passing was immediate. The *Des Moines Daily News* reported on October 3, 1906, that "probably the first use" of the "long forward pass" was by Missouri in a 23–4 win over Kirksville Normal School (later Northeast Missouri State University, and now Truman State University).[16]

The October 4, 1906, reports in the *Trenton Times* included Princeton defeating Stevens Tech (Institute of Technology), 22–0, as "old-time football gave way to the new game"; the Carlisle Indian Industrial School beating Susquehanna University, 40–0, as "the forward pass was used for a number of good gains" in the hinterlands of Pennsylvania; Harvard blanking Bowdoin, 10–0, "in a hard-fought contest that was featured by a newfangled and daring forward pass that Crimson worked in the closing minutes of play"; and Williams College defeating the Massachusetts Agricultural College (later the University of Massachusetts) by scoring the game's only TD on a forward pass thrown by a player named Waters.[17]

Yale All-American Paul Veeder has often been cited as throwing the "first forward pass in a major game," meaning, in the elite spirit of Corbett and Simpson's book title, *The Only Game That Matters*, the Yale-Harvard fray.[18] On November 24, 1906, Veeder completed a pass of about 30 yards to R.W. Forbes as the Elis once again defeated Harvard, 6–0, before 32,000 fans in New Haven. But that was three weeks after St.

Louis completed 45- and 48-yard passes versus Kansas before a crowd of 7,000 at Sportsman's Park in St. Louis.

The prevalence of passing in its inaugural year was supported by the testimony gathered in the 1950s by Allison Danzig, the *New York Times* sports writer, who compiled *The History of American Football* (in 1956), much of it from correspondence solicited from the great coaches.

Amos Alonzo Stagg, coach at the University of Chicago, claimed that "I personally had sixty-four different forward pass patterns" in 1906,[19] and that he remembered Pomeroy Sinnock "throwing lots of passes for the University of Illinois in 1906."[20] Many passes were reportedly thrown in the Illinois-Wabash game, none to much avail in a scoreless tie. Stagg felt that the pass was pandemic, and the spiral form was well known and used consistently. Stagg's Chicago team passed frequently in its final game, a 63–0 victory over Illinois.

"I have seen statements giving credit to certain people originating the forward pass," Stagg said. "The fact is that all coaches were working on it. In 1906 all of us coaches were teaching the spiral forward pass. I know that I had [star Chicago back Walter] Eckersall practicing it."[21]

Stagg was another of the early coaches whose work on honing the spiral has been described as equally integral to the game as the pass-throwing experimentation of Eddie Cochems, Pop Warner, and Bosey Reiter—people working independently yet simultaneously to solve problems to use the new weapon in different regions of the nation. Stagg biographer Ellis Lucia explained Stagg's approach to the process.

"Players hurled the ball end over end, firing it from the crook of the wrist or grasping the end in the palm of their hand," Lucia wrote. "Sometimes they flipped it underhand. The underhand motion often gave the ball a slow spiral effect. Stagg noticed this. He began experimenting with a smoother flight. The spiral spin, with one end pointed dead ahead, enabled the ball to 'sail' smoothly and more accurately in an easy floating motion, like a bird. In the parlor of his home, Alonzo experimented with the ball, using Stella as a receiver. When he nearly knocked over her favorite vase, she banished him to the backyard."

"Lonnie tried several different holds, striving to get the proper spin on the ball without making it flip-flop end over end, and also to throw it with force and deadly accuracy," Lucia continued. "He resorted to his old pitching techniques for the arm motion, and hung a blanket on the clothesline to throw into. He noticed that when he laid the ball in his palm, with his hand and fingers gently curling around it, feeling the seams and center lacings, he got the best results firing it point-first."[22]

He showed the grip to the Maroons' backfield star, Eckersall. "The ball neatly cut the air and bucked the wind," Lucia wrote. "Stagg sent the receiver out farther and farther, zigzagging to different points on the gridiron. The pass worked, and taking to the air could get a team over the biggest, toughest line of beef in the world. It would also provide fans with spectacular new thrills."[23]

Stagg at first was a true-blue, Yale-trained, "old-guard" follower loyal to Camp's camp and the master's attitudes about football. But Stagg developed as a great coach and innovator in his own right and was a huge backer of the forward pass. Stagg went from playing All American end at Yale to coaching football at Springfield College in Massachusetts. Beginning in 1892, and for 40 years after, Stagg coached the University of Chicago team. This was followed by 14 more seasons as head coach at the College of the Pacific, in Stockton, California. Stagg spent five more seasons as an assistant coach to his son at Susquehanna University in Selinsgrove, Pennsylvania. He retired at age 91, and died in 1965 at age 103 in Stockton.

The laundry list of inventions credited to Stagg, many of which have had direct impacts on the passing game, were tallied in 1976 by Tom Bennett of NFL Properties, and included " the direct pass [hike] from center [later perfected by Clark Shaughnessy], end-arounds, fake handoffs, flankers, the hidden-ball play, huddles, laterals, man-in-motion, numbers on jerseys, onside kickoffs, pivots, placekicks, quick kicks, quarterback keepers, shifts, spiral passes, a standing not a squatting quarterback, unbalanced lines...."[24]

In the early years of the 20th century, Stagg was appointed to the Camp-guided IFA Rules Committee while he coached at Chicago, and was converted into an "energetic champion of the forward pass, an offensive tool that had worked so well for him at Chicago," John Sayle Watterson wrote.[25] Stagg saw the benefits of the pass for opening up the game and making it more exciting for the spectators and, above all, using it as a winning strategy. In the process, Stagg went against his old benefactor, Camp, and joined others who wanted to renovate football away from brute strength, and take advantage of plays that used strategy, speed, and finesse.

Carl Snavely, who spent 32 years as a head coach—at Bucknell, North Carolina, Cornell, and Washington University in St. Louis—corroborated Stagg's memories, telling Danzig that Larry Voorhis, the Penn State quarterback in 1906, shifted to tailback and threw forward passes to an end named Burns. "They threw a spiral pass," Snavely wrote.[26] Pop Warner wrote, "Many coaches and passers began experimenting with the spiral early in 1906."[27]

Overwhelmingly, though, the run still dominated the East. "Eastern elevens are using nothing but the old-style formations," Eddie Cochems wrote, a bit puzzled, in his chapter, "The Forward Pass and the On-Side Kick," in Camp's *Spalding's How to Play Foot Ball*. But his prognostication was a bit off: "It will be a matter of a season or two until the coaches throughout the country come around to my way of thinking or I will be badly mistaken."[28] He wasn't badly mistaken, just mistaken. It took a lot longer for most teams to warm up to using the pass as much as he did.

CHAPTER THREE

Pop Warner at Carlisle

Knute Rockne was 18 when the pass was legalized, eight years away from his pharmacy degree at Notre Dame and on the verge of a greater decade as a ringer, selling his services as a mercenary end to teams in the loosely organized Ohio League. St. Louis University's passing success in 1906, Rockne wrote years later, was attributable to the enrollment of "a few boys with hands like steam shovels who could toss a football just as easily and almost as far as they could throw a baseball.... One would have thought that so effective a play would have been instantly copied and become the vogue. The East, however, had not learned much or cared much about Midwest and Western football. Indeed, the East scarcely realized that football existed beyond the Alleghanies [sic]."[1]

One team in the Allegheny Mountains that used the forward pass with alacrity was the Carlisle Indian Industrial School. This was the first off-reservation boarding school designed for Native Americans, created by the federal government, operated by the Army, and located in the old Carlisle Barracks in Cumberland County, Pennsylvania. The same Glenn Scobie "Pop" Warner, who guided Georgia in 1895 when Auburn coach John Heisman witnessed an illegal forward pass that went for a touchdown, coached Carlisle in 1907 to an 10–1 record.

"At first, Warner opposed the forward pass," wrote Lars Anderson in 2007. "He didn't believe that it belonged in the game. But, gradually, the notion of flinging the ball through the sky to gain yardage began to preoccupy him. Ever since his first practice at Cornell, the strategy of football had fascinated Warner. The forward pass was like a new tool in his shed. That he could use to devise plays to confuse the other team. In virtually all of his conscious hours, the questions rushed at Warner: *How can I use the forward pass to my advantage? Will the speed of my boys make it easier to complete the forward pass? What's the best way to throw a football? How can the pass help me deceive the opponent?*"[2]

Warner's gambling mien combined in the autumn of 1907—Jim Thorpe's first season on the Carlisle team—with the notion, according to Anderson, that the coach was "more intrigued by the forward pass than was any coach in the nation," despite the testimony of Stagg, Snavely, Cochems, and Reiter, which pointed to Stagg's contention that many coaches were experimenting with the pass.[3]

However, the innovative and risk-taking Warner may have evolved the spiral pass with more precision than any of them. He also was unique in his attitude toward the weapon in eastern football circles. Warner, wrote David M. Nelson, "was the leading proponent of throwing the ball in the East and was to that region what Eddie Cochems was to the Southwest."[4] Nelson also countered Rockne's notion that it took extra-large hands to grab a football from flight: "[Warner] accomplished his team's success without any evidence that the Carlisle Indians had bigger and bonier hands than their opponents on the Eastern Seaboard or anywhere else."[5]

Warner tested a theory before the season started. "Instead of having a thrower hurl the ball down the field end-over-end, or lob it, or push the ball shot-put style in the direction of the receiver—as many other teams were doing—he taught his boys how to fling a spiral," Anderson wrote. "Gripping the ball on its laces, he showed them how to let it roll off their fingertips with a spiraling motion as they released the ball. This type of throw, Warner instructed, would allow the [throwing back] to wing the ball with accuracy thirty to forty yards down the field."[6]

Thorpe and all the Indian backs practiced the spiral, but halfback Frank Mount Pleasant "quickly became proficient at the deep pass," Anderson wrote.[7] The target usually was the speedy, gifted end, Albert Exendine, who was notable in profiles and portrayals of Thorpe as the more famous man's academic tutor. Exendine was named All American in 1906 and 1907.

"During scrimmages, Mt. Pleasant would receive the snap and run around in the backfield, dancing nimbly and avoiding tacklers," Anderson wrote. "Then, when Albert Exendine ... broke free thirty yards down the field, Mt. Pleasant would heave the ball with all his might. Exendine would run under the arcing rainbow of a pass and cradle it into his arms for a long gain."

"After each successful forward pass in practice, Warner became more convinced that no team on their 1907 schedule could stop Carlisle's potent offense," Anderson wrote.[8] Years later, Warner told Allison Danzig, "Frank Mount Pleasant of Carlisle was using the spiral pass expertly in 1907."[9] The Indians crushed Lebanon Valley, 40–0, in the opener; then blanked Villanova, 10–0, and destroyed Susquehanna, 91–0. The Indians defeated Penn State, 18–5; Syracuse, 14–6; and Bucknell, 15–0.

"Five 1907 games involving Carlisle illustrate the extent of the forward pass and its effectiveness when integrated into a system of play," Nelson wrote. "Regardless of the severe penalty for incomplete passes, the rewards were worth the risk. Carlisle played in five of fifteen representative games reported on in the *Football Guide*"—the era's important annual digest of the collegiate season—"and was the only team to use the forward pass as a regular part of its offense. In the other ten games, the forward pass was only mentioned twice."[10]

The Indians' undefeated skein set up the game of the collegiate year against the likewise 6–0 University of Pennsylvania. Carlisle and Penn would end the season as the two top winners in college football, the only teams with double figures in victories. The Quakers' only loss was to Carlisle before 20,000 fans at Franklin Field in Philadelphia. "Carlisle defeated Pennsylvania, 26–6, and the game report stated that the Indians had perhaps reached the top of their execution of the forward pass," Nelson wrote, interpreting the *Football Guide*, which also stated that "the season had not developed far enough for Pennsylvania on their side to have their defense properly perfected," meaning to thwart the Indians' passing proficiency.[11]

The very next week, on November 2, Princeton did what Penn could not. The Tigers defeated Carlisle, 16–0, on a wet and slippery field in New York City. The *Football Guide* reported, "It was an especial triumph for Princeton in that they had made a study of the Indians' ... game and particularly the effectiveness of Carlisle's forward passing for scoring. Hence Princeton's blocking of forward passes practically put out of commission anything like a scoring play for the Indians."[12]

Pop Warner's team then beat Minnesota, 12–10, in Minneapolis. "The Indians' two touchdowns were scored after Albert Exendine made long runs after catching passes from Pete Hauser," Nelson wrote.[13] The Indians also defeated Harvard, 23–15, scoring all its touchdowns through the air, and wound up the season by beating Stagg's University of Chicago team, 18–10.

Warner and Thorpe became, of course, icons of sports culture. Warner won three National Championships at the University of Pittsburgh and one at Stanford while his name has lived on across America beyond his 1954 death at age 83—via the nationally-scoped Pop Warner leagues, which train youngsters in football fundamentals.

However, Mount Pleasant and Exendine excelled, too, against the grain of racism to become multiple-time head coaches in college ball, spreading the gospel of the passing game. Born on the Tuscarora Reservation in Niagara County, New York, in 1884, Mount Pleasant was an Olympic athlete in 1908 and later coached football at Franklin & Marshall College, Indiana Normal School (now Indiana University of Pennsylvania), West Virginia Wesleyan, and the University of Buffalo.

An 1884 native of Bartlesville, Oklahoma, Exendine was inducted into the College Football Hall of Fame in 1970. He was head football coach at Otterbein, Georgetown (55–21–3 from 1914 to 1923), Washington State, Occidental, Northwestern Oklahoma, and Oklahoma A & M. A Dickinson College law graduate, Exendine became an attorney with the Bureau of Indian Affairs in Oklahoma.

The passing success of the Carlisle Indians demanded attention, and other teams warmed to the forward pass. Football historian Parke Davis wrote in 1928 that Yale successfully used the pass to set up touchdowns by fullback Ted Coy in the 1907 Princeton game. In turn, that led to the judicious use of the pass play by Yale and other teams as a decoy. "The tacticians now awoke to the possibilities of the play," Davis wrote, "and in 1908 every team carried numerous variations of forward pass plays. But they were employed principally as threats to compel the defense to spread its backfield defenders."[14]

By 1908, many coaches believed that they had better become proficient at the forward pass rather than have it pass them by. Hugo Bezdek, a Czechoslovakia-born former fullback who played for Amos Alonzo Stagg at the University of Chicago, was the coach of the University of Arkansas in 1908, when it lost to Cochems' St. Louis team. At Bezdek's request, Stagg came to Fayetteville, Arkansas, to teach Bezdek's players the forward pass. Little by little, college by college, the proficient use of the pass spread across the nation. Bezdek's later offensive dexterity led three teams to the Rose Bowl—the University of Oregon, the Mare Island Marines of San Francisco Bay, and Penn State. (A multisport maverick of the early 20th century, Bezdek also was manager of the Pittsburgh Pirates baseball team from 1917 to 1919, and coached the NFL's Cleveland Rams in their first season, 1937.)

Still, the pass play was a work in progress. The IAAUS Rules Committee amended in 1908 the stipulation governing a pass that was touched but not caught. The new rule said that only the first player of the offense touching an incomplete pass was entitled to recover it if the pass was not completed, deterring offensive shenanigans that must have been similar to the infamous "Holy Roller," the 1978 touchdown by Dave Casper of the Oakland Raiders (covered in the later chapter on tight ends).

The idea that the forward pass was a partial solution to stem injuries and fatalities did not come to pass. The game hadn't "opened up" much at all with passing. In fact, the fatalities increased after 1905. In 1909, Eugene Byrne, an Army cadet, suffered spinal injuries in the Harvard game, and died the next day, prompting even the cancellation of the increasingly popular Army-Navy game. Archer Christian, a University of Virginia player, suffered a concussion in the Georgetown game, resulting in a cerebral hemorrhage and his death. Reports and tallies varied, but at least 33 deaths in 1909 were related to organized football injuries. The campaign for football's abolishment was renewed.

"Football is not a sport in any sense," wrote Bat Masterson, the former buffalo hunter, frontier marshal, hired gunslinger, and roving gambler. He had left the Wild West to be the sports editor of the *New York Morning Telegraph*. His brand of law in Dodge City was more effective than his pen against the popular tide of collegiate football. He famously described football as "a brutal and savage slugging match between two reckless opposing crowds. The rougher it is and the more [players who are] killed and crippled, the more delighted are the spectators, who howl their heads off at the sight of a player stretched prone and unconscious on the hard and frozen ground."[15]

Football in the early 20th century was just as controversial as it has become in the early 21st century, when lawsuits against the NFL for concussions have made NFL Commissioner Roger Goodell into more of a safety legislator than a sports league boss. The consensus in the early

1900s still wanted to find an even-handed way of toning down the sport's violence. As the president of Princeton, Woodrow Wilson was tactfully in charge of an esteemed institute fielding a gridiron power. Prior to ascending to governor of New Jersey, president of the United States, and creator of the League of Nations, Wilson said, "Football is too fine a game to be abolished offhand." The future Nobel Peace Prize winner added, "I do think, however, that it should be modified to some extent in order to obviate these fatal accidents as far as possible."[16]

Another series of sweeping changes were in store for the sport, some of which adjusted previous rules. The Rules Committee in 1910 included a fourth down per offensive set to gain a first down, and four 15-minute quarters of play. The committee again abolished interlocking interference for ball carriers, and any aid for the ball carrier by other offensive players. But the hotly contested forward pass also saw the lifting of restrictions on throwing the ball as well as more protection for receivers.

Historical descriptions recall a bitter fight that lasted all spring at several meetings in New York and Philadelphia among committee members, some of whom wanted to abolish the forward pass altogether, including Walter Camp of Yale and Edward K. Hall of Dartmouth. But a pro-passing contingent prevailed, including collegiate sports administrators Crawford Blagden and Percy Haughton of Harvard, Howard Henry and Bill Roper of Princeton, and Carl Williams of the University Pennsylvania.[17]

"It was not until the sweeping reforms of 1910 that the forward pass began to blossom," wrote football official Mike Thompson in the *Saturday Evening Post* in 1931.[18] These 1910 changes to the passing rules included the following:

- Defensive players were forbidden to interfere with a pass receiver after the offensive man had crossed the line of scrimmage—except in efforts to deflect or catch the ball.
- The pass could now cross the line of scrimmage at any point, dispensing with the five-yard restriction.
- The ball had to be thrown from at least five yards *behind* the line of scrimmage, and was limited to 20 yards downfield.
- Backs as well as ends could now be eligible receivers.

- One back could go in motion on each offensive play, either laterally or toward his team's goal.[19]

Fed up with not only the changes that were altering the game he nurtured for generations, Walter Camp walked away from the Rules Committee. Yale's undefeated 1909 edition was loaded, as ever, with physical bruisers. Percy Haughton of Harvard and Bill Roper of Princeton both bitterly criticized Camp in the committee meetings and afterward for only looking out for Yale's interests.[20]

Two years later, other changes were made by the Rules Committee, including the reduction of the field from 110 to 100 yards, the inclusion of end zones behind goal lines, and the increase of the touchdown from five to six points. With these changes came other alterations for the forward pass:

- The 20-yard limitation was lifted and the ball could be thrown for any distance downfield.
- Passes could now be caught in the end zone, resulting in touchdowns.[21]

In other words, the long bomb, a term that had yet to enter the football lexicon, would become a factor. As well, a receiver could use the opposition's end-zone real estate, which would also have to be covered by defensive backs, who previously had not had to worry about any ground beyond the goal line. These new freedoms for ends and players releasing out of the backfield were not lost on the Norwegian-born and Chicago-bred Knute Kenneth Rockne, who entered Notre Dame at age 22 in 1910 and became team captain for the 1913 season.

CHAPTER FOUR

Knute Rockne vs. Army

A key figure in the evolution and use of the forward pass, Knute Rockne was a 5-foot-8, 165-pound end on the Notre Dame Fighting Irish. When the 1912 rule changes were initiated, the future legend resolved to become a better pass receiver. That summer, he and his best friend, Irish halfback Gus Dorais, went to Cedar Point Amusement Park on Lake Erie in Sandusky, Ohio, to be lifeguards and waiters for the summer, and to perfect their use of the forward pass on the beach. Rockne particularly wanted to learn to better catch the ball with his hands. Most players gathered in the ball with their arms against their bodies and often from a fixed position.

Reaching for, and snatching, passes out of flight with open hands, using athletic finesse, timing, and dexterity on the run, hadn't yet been perfected in the techniques of receiving—or hadn't yet been translated with any detailed descriptions by the sporting press of the times. Not much description of the receiving styles of Jack Schneider of St. Louis or Albert Exendine of Carlisle appeared in the press.

"What Rockne learned was that if there was an art in throwing, there was also an art in receiving," interpreted Harry Stuhldreher, who played for Rockne as a three-time All American quarterback from 1922 to 1924, and was immortalized as one of the "Four Horsemen of Notre Dame" that last season (in the *New York Herald-Tribune* by sports writer Grantland Rice). "[Rockne] saw that it wasn't finished work to have the ball bounce against his arms and chest when he caught it."

"There were too many chances for fumbles that way. It cut your stride and didn't look neat. So Rockne patterned himself after a baseball player and caught it with his fingers. Each day at Cedar Point they worked seriously on perfecting their respective jobs. They learned that the pass had infinite possibilities and could be incorporated into a system of play," Stuhldreher wrote.[1]

Four. Knute Rockne vs. Army

Rockne said that the painstaking preparations on the Cedar Point beach led to a new way of catching the football. "In the early days the players threw it and caught it much like a medicine ball," Rockne wrote in 1930. "We mastered the technique of catching the football with hands relaxed and tried to master the more difficult feat of catching it with one hand."[2]

Jesse Harper, Notre Dame's coach at the time, emphasized in a 1954 letter to Allison Danzig that the Cedar Point summer adventure had everything to do with improving Rockne's receiving techniques. "They took a football with them to teach Rock to catch the ball in his hands instead of his stomach, the way many coaches taught at that time," Harper wrote. "If you will check the 1912 team of Notre Dame you will not find anything startling about their forward passes."[3]

Under Harper, the Fighting Irish used the forward pass to upgrade the team to the status of a national powerhouse. The legacy of Notre Dame football didn't begin in 1913, but the team's emblematic gridiron prominence as a defining national institution of autumn Saturdays can be traced to that season. Specifically, on the afternoon of November 1, the small Roman Catholic school out of the Midwest, which was so unknown that *The New*

Jesse Harper coached football and served as athletic director at Notre Dame University from 1913 to 1917 and oversaw the Fighting Irish's increased use of the forward pass. He later resumed his AD role at South Bend (1931 to 1933) after Knute Rockne died in a plane crash (Collegiate Collection, courtesy Charles G. Lamb).

York Times wrote that it was from South Bend, *Illinois*, provided the upset of the college year, defeating the Army Cadets, 35–13, at West Point, New York.

It was the first meeting of the two teams. Yale had dumped Army off its schedule because the Cadets took a cavalier attitude toward the rule specifying four years of collegiate playing eligibility; to the Army, there was no eligibility on any battlefield. Plus, Army reasoned that it could use a breather—knock around the Midwestern upstart for an afternoon. At first, the larger Army team pushed the Irish all over the field. Dorais, according to Rockne's account, told the huddle, "Let's open up."[4] Dorais hit right halfback Joe Pliska with a few passes for first downs, startling Army's defense. Rockne feigned an injury by limping back to the huddle three consecutive times.

"The Army halfback covering me figured I wasn't worth watching," Rockne wrote. "Even as a decoy, he figured I was harmless. Finally, Dorais called my number, meaning that he was to throw a long forward pass to me as I ran down the field and started out toward the sidelines. I started limping down the field and the Army halfback covering me almost yawned in my face, he was so bored. Suddenly, I put on full speed and left him there, flat-footed. I raced across the Army goal line as Dorais whipped the ball and the grandstand roared at the completion of a forty-yard pass. Everybody seemed astonished. There had been no hurdling, no tackling, no plunging, no crushing of fiber and sinew. Just a long-distance touchdown by rapid transit. At the moment I touched the ball, life for me was complete."[5]

Notre Dame led at the half, 14–13. Harper and Dorais changed tactics in the second half, returning to the running game with fullback Ray Eichenlaub. In the fourth quarter, Army closed its ranks again to stop the run, and Dorais opened up the passing game again with tosses to Pliska and ends Rockne and Fred Gushurst. The Black Knights of the Hudson were shocked.

"The Westerners flashed the most sensational football that has been seen in the East this year, baffling the Cadets with a style of open play and a perfectly developed forward pass which carried the victors down the field 30 yards at a clip," sports writer Harry Cross emphasized in *The New York Times*. "Football men marveled at this startling display of open football."[6] Bill Roper, the former head coach at Princeton, was one of the officials of the game. He told Cross that he had never before seen the forward pass developed to such a state of perfection.⁷

Coach Jesse Harper's decision that day to tell Dorais to pass and keep on passing was declared by several aficionados decades later the greatest single coaching decision in college football during the twentieth century.⁸

Rockne and Dorais helped establish the pass under eastern purview as an integral tool for victory, a method that could be used by physically small and speedy teams to outfox and outplay the behemoths. "Press and football public hailed this new game, and Notre Dame received credit as the originator of a style of play that we had simply systematized," Rockne wrote in reaction.⁹

"The Dorais-to-Rockne forward passing combination wakened the East to the possibilities of the new open game on the gridiron," columnist John Kieran wrote in *The New York Times*. "Others had used the play before and used it well but it so happened that the Dorais-to-Rockne tandem was the inspiration and example for a new system and a new spirit in football over a wide territory."¹⁰

A galvanizing moment in forward-passing history occurred on November 1, 1913, at West Point, New York, when Notre Dame defeated Army, 35–13. The Midwestern upstart football school startled the Cadets with passes to Knute Rockne, memorialized on this 1990 Collegiate Collection card (Collegiate Collection, courtesy Charles G. Lamb).

The popular 1940 Warner Bros. movie, *Knute Rockne, All American*, starring Pat O'Brien in the title role, engendered second- and third-hand interpretations of the film's portrayal of the advances in the use of the forward pass, expanding Rockne's role from increased proficiency to the outright invention. (The film co-starred Ronald Reagan as halfback George Gipp, who died at age 25 after contracting streptococcus virus. Rockne, via O'Brien's portrayal and Robert Buckner's screenplay, urges in a locker room speech, "Win one for the Gipper!"[11])

Rockne also evolved different receiving routes. "On one occasion going down the field, with the defender playing him deep, Rockne fell down," Dorais remembered in a 1951 correspondence with Allison Danzig. "I threw it to him and he got up and came back; and we decided to put it into the repertoire."[12]

This was the earliest known devising of the buttonhook or curl pattern. Several decades later, Don Hutson was given credit for developing different patterns and variations of them. But there's every reason to believe that the same basic routes were in use in the 1910s as were used in the 21st century: slant, curl-in, curl-out, square-in (down-and-in), square-out, fly, hitch-and-go (down-out-and-down), post (fly and angle toward the goal posts) and flag (corner route). Nearly every route from Rockne's day through Hutson's to Jerry Rice's era is the same or a slight variation on the same.

One exception perhaps is the back-shoulder dart near the sideline as 21st-century QBs such as Peyton Manning, Tom Brady, Drew Breese, and Ben Roethlisberger have refined accuracy. Diagrams of "passing trees," depicting varying routes, were published in 1923 by Illinois coach Bob Zuppke, and in 1971 by Paul Zimmerman, author of *A Thinking Man's Guide to Pro Football*.[13, 14] Seemingly different at first glance, and with different nomenclature, they illustrate most of the same general basic routes.

"Rockne was the first end that to my knowledge developed the pass lanes as they still are today," Dorais wrote, although Stagg claimed that he earlier developed the basic routs and their variations, and Hutson is given credit for this later. "All the other ends I threw to and all I saw in those days depended on sheer speed ahead to just get behind the defender. [Rockne] worked on cuts and angles to get loose and on a change of pace," Dorais wrote.[15]

Rockne's role in the saga of the forward pass, if not as significant as his hallowed coaching career at Notre Dame, was prescient and substantial. As the Irish coach, he posted a record of 105-12-5 from 1918 to 1930, including five undefeated and untied seasons. His .881 winning percentage remains the highest among major college head coaches.

Four. Knute Rockne vs. Army

Rockne rose to celebrity status as American sons and daughters of the Old Sod, Roman Catholics, and sports fans everywhere became lifelong Notre Dame fans. When Rockne was killed in a 1931 plane crash near Bazaar, Kansas, President Herbert Hoover called it a "national loss."[16]

The decisive Notre Dame victory over Army not only made the football world pay attention to the Fighting Irish, it made them pay more attention to the pass. Teams began throwing the ball throughout the nation, particularly in the Southwest, as a weapon of choice in the manner of St. Louis, Carlisle, and Notre Dame—as a fully mastered or at least much-used part of the offensive arsenal. The Universities of Oklahoma and Texas embraced the pass, and the state of Texas, particularly, became a hotbed of the aerial attack, where Texas Christian University, Southern Methodist University, Texas A & M, and Baylor all passed regularly.

Collegiate receivers who emerged as top scoring threats between world wars included Roger Kiley of Notre Dame, catching tosses from Gipp, under Rockne's watchful eye; Bennie Oosterbaan of Michigan, catching balls thrown by Benny Friedman; Jerry Dalrymple of Tulane; Paul Moss of Purdue; Don Hutson catching the throws of Dixie Howell at Alabama; Yale's Larry Kelley, who won the Heisman Trophy, and Forest "Evy" Evashevski of Michigan.

Only some of these young men turned pro in the NFL, most notably Hutson for the Green Bay Packers. Many of them did it for fun, not for the money, which couldn't support a family in those days. Players needed offseason jobs to sustain their families and pay the mortgages. Better pay in a year-round "real job" often pulled them away from the game they loved after a year or two. Collegiate ball was still by far the most popular version of the sport.

CHAPTER FIVE

Receiving in Pro Football's Earliest Times

In the years before the NFL, the pro game was much more catch-as-catch-can. Some of the great receivers, such as Albert Exendine and Knute Rockne, became coaches. But before Rockne took over the reins at Notre Dame, he spent the latter 1910s as a ringer in the rough-and-tumble Ohio League. Under his own name in different seasons, Rockne played end for the Akron, Ohio, Indians; Fort Wayne, Indiana, Friars; and Massillon, Ohio, Tigers. He used aliases when he moonlighted for Notre Dame's hometown semi-pro club, the South Bend Silver Edges. The opposition of the Silver Edges and other teams playing against notable ringers often just winked back, because they usually had their own ringers, and any game of one-upmanship to expose illegal players did neither team any good.

Forward-passing tandems often didn't live in the towns for which they played, and had to develop chemistry on the fly, so to speak, during the games. Team chemistry and practice sessions were often not possible as ringers arrived on Sunday mornings, often on night trains after college games the day before in other states. The semi-pro and pro game of football in the decades prior to the NFL's forerunner, the American Professional Football Association, which was formed in 1920, was a cobbled-together arrangement in almost all aspects. Teams, like uniforms, often were patched together on a weekly basis. Travel was by train or jitney at a time when nearly every road in Pennsylvania, Ohio, and Indiana was a back-road that often became a mud track in autumn weather.

The evidence gathered by Keith McClellan for his 1998 book about pro football's earliest days, *The Sunday Game: At the Dawn of Professional Football*, showed that the forward pass was used quite often by the town and city teams playing in various conferences or alliances that historically has loosely become known as the "Ohio League." Instead of being a desperation move as a last resort, the forward pass was integral to offenses and crucial to scoring among the teams scattered from Davenport, Iowa, and Rock Island, Illinois, across Indiana and Ohio to Buffalo, New York, and Altoona, Pennsylvania—clubs as far north as the Minneapolis Marines and as southerly as the Cincinnati Celts.

These semi-pro and later pro teams used the college rule book as their own and adjusted to the forward passing rules accordingly. While pro teams existed in such major cities as Detroit, Cleveland, and Cincinnati, and two (the McKeesport Olympics and Pitcairn Quakers) were near Pittsburgh, the Canton Bulldogs and Massillon Tigers became the most famous, notable for their rivalry—14 miles apart—in Stark County, Ohio. Canton and Massillon stacked their rosters with ringers and former All Americans from the East and Midwest, including such enduring names as Knute Rockne, Jim Thorpe, Greasy Neale, and Indian Joe Guyon. Canton's importance to the development and history of the professional game helped lead to its selection in the 1960s as the home of the Pro Football Hall of Fame.

A lion of the national sporting scene by the time of his death in a plane crash in 1931, Knute Rockne had been a mercenary "ringer" on Sundays in the loosely organized Ohio League during the 1910s, for teams in Akron and Massillon, Ohio, and Fort Wayne and South Bend, Indiana (Collegiate Collection, courtesy Charles G. Lamb).

"The first authenticated pass completion in professional ball occurred on October 27, 1906," according to the Professional Football Researchers Association. Bullet Riley of the Massillon Tigers caught a pass thrown by Peggy Parratt in a 61–0 victory over the combined Benwood and Moundsville teams from the West Virginia side of the Ohio River. "The toss was good for only a few yards and played no decisive part in the game's outcome," according to the *PFRA Annual*, "but—so far—it's the earliest documented completion by the pros. The receiver was a young man named Dan Policowski who saved proofreaders countless headaches by playing under the name of 'Riley.' The passer was quarterback George 'Peggy' Parratt. Understandably, no one got excited about Peggy's short pass; his 65-yard run from scrimmage and 100-yard kickoff return got the headlines."[1]

Operated by "buccaneer businessmen" in McClellan's words, the Ohio teams were stocked with factory workers and other locals as well as hired players from everywhere and collegiate players sometimes playing under aliases.[2] These teams engendered local loyalties and became a readymade basis for the wagering racket.

College football administrators, such as Walter Camp, and sports writers, such as Caspar Whitney, were very much prejudiced against the pro leagues. "At certain times," wrote historian Tom Bennett, "the paying of men to play football has been termed heresy and the throwing of passes dismissed as the lazy man's way of making yardage."[3]

However, the Ohio League gave former and sometimes enrolled college players a chance to earn cash at the game they loved. Ohio teams were no strangers to the aerial attack. The Dayton, Ohio, Gym-Cadets threw as many passes as any team in the pre-NFL era. "The Gym-Cadets capitalized on the forward passing wizardry of Alphonse H. Mahrt, who had recently graduated from St. Mary's," McClellan wrote, referring to the Catholic school that became the University of Dayton.[4]

The Gym-Cadets defeated the Dayton Oakwoods and the Cincinnati Celts in 1913 to claim a generally unofficial Southern Ohio championship. In both games, all of the Gym-Cadets' touchdowns came on Mahrt's forward passes. "Mahrt is a small cuss," the *Cincinnati Enquirer* quipped, "probably weighing no more than 138 pounds, but he has the nerve and gets away with many a great play that some less strong hearted warrior would not attempt. He evaded one Celt charge after another, and then when satisfied that the time was ripe, deliberately stepped in the midst of a bunch of huskies and tossed. The rest was easy."[5]

McClellan uncovered an astonishing fact: "Indeed, three out of every four Dayton plays were forward passes."[6] After many of the Gym-

Cadets went on to play for the Dayton Triangles, the *Toledo Blade* described a 1916 game won by the Triangles, 12–0, over the Toledo Maroons: "Mahrt picked his man and shot the ball, like a bullet, into his hands. Pass after pass was successful, netting long gains."[7]

McClellan wrote that in the first nine games of Dayton's season in 1916, the Triangles sustained 33 scoring drives, and that "forward passes played an important role on fifteen of those scoring drives."[8] As usual at all levels of football, in all eras, the passers, such as the obviously talented Mahrt, received the lion's share of the media's coverage, but McClellan noted, "Norb Sacksteder was one of the primary targets in Al Mahrt's passing game."[9] Sacksteder later played in the NFL for the Dayton Triangles, Detroit Tigers, and Canton Bulldogs, and caught a TD pass in 1922 for Canton.

The *Toledo Blade* reported shenanigans surrounding a faked forward pass during the 1916 Columbus Panhandles game with the Cleveland Indians: "On one of the formations in which [Cleveland back Lorin] Solon smashed outside left tackle for a 15-yard gain, Meyer [sic] fooled the bruisers by tossing a black headguard in the air to a player on the right side of the line. The feint pulled four of the Pans away from Solon."[10]

(While most college players wore leather helmets by the 1920s, only some such protection was used in the turn-of-the-century years, even as crude head protectors were developed. One of the first was crafted from moleskin specifically for the Army-Navy game in 1893 by George M. "Bull" Reeves, a player for the U.S. Naval Academy. Further football injuries could lead to brain damage, Reeves was told. He averted that to become an admiral and the "Father of Carrier Aviation." Another helmet was devised by an eventual Major League Baseball player. It was cut from leather at an Easton, Pennsylvania, saddle-maker in 1896. The future St. Louis Cardinals and Boston Beaneaters outfielder, George "Deerfoot" Barclay, claimed the "head harness" prevented cauliflower ears while he played football for Lafayette College. By the 1910s, flap-eared or "dog-eared" style helmets were in use. Various machine-shop nose-guards and shin-guards were used by players protecting injuries. Sewn-in shoulder pads were in use in the 1890s, and rules about protection materials were nonexistent or so lax that by the time Jim Thorpe was playing the NFL, he was accused—perhaps falsely—of lining his shoulder pads with sheet metal.[11])

Among the rovers in the Ohio League was Alfred Earle "Greasy" Neale, a Parkersburg, West Virginia, native who, in 1917, played end for coach Jim Thorpe's Canton Bulldogs while he also coached West Virginia Wesleyan College. Greasy once claimed that he caught six touchdown passes in his first game for Canton, against the Columbus Panhandles.[12] The Methodist friars operating WVW in the boondocks of Buckhannon would have frowned upon Greasy's professional activities up north on the Sabbath. So, the future Washington & Jefferson, Virginia, West Virginia, Yale, and Philadelphia Eagles coach played for Canton under the alias of Foster. Greasy also led the Cincinnati baseball Reds with 10 hits and a .357 average in the 1919 World Series—which was thrown to the Chicago White Sox, rigged by racketeers in the infamous "Black Sox Scandal."[13]

The Youngstown, Ohio, Patricians fielded a tough team in 1915, defeating McKeesport and Pitcairn before playing the Columbus Panhandles to a scoreless tie. Youngstown's star player, Busty Ashbaugh, caught a 17-yard pass in the Pitcairn game to set up a score. The anticipated big game that year in the Ohio League was between Youngstown and Massillon, and it contained significant passing.

"Massillon ... hired Russ Goodwin to play quarterback," McClellan wrote. "Goodwin and Red Fleming played together at Washington and Jefferson College and were familiar with one another and the offense that Red had brought to Massillon from his college experience. Fred Heyman, Goodwin's favorite receiver at college, was also on the Massillon roster, so Goodwin had two familiar passing targets."[14] The college partners prevailed. "Passes from Goodwin to Heyman broke the game wide open,"[15] McClellan wrote. Massillon completed 12 of 14 passes and won, 27–0.

Perhaps the two most notable Ohio League games of all occurred in 1915 between the Canton Bulldogs and the Massillon Tigers. The standard rivalry that two such large towns in close proximity engender on a normal basis was increased to incendiary levels by professional football. The wagering that accompanied the games recalled the accusations against Blondy Wallace a decade earlier.

For the first game, Canton famously secured the services of the former Carlisle Indians great and Olympic decathlon winner, Jim Thorpe. Although ringers have been paid more, Thorpe's single-game fee of $250

Five. Receiving in Pro Football's Earliest Times

put him in the elite class. Despite Thorpe, Massillon defeated Canton, 16–0, at Massillon Driving Park. The Tigers' Gus Dorais, who had starred with Knute Rockne at Notre Dame, was reunited with the star end at Massillon, and completed seven of 19 passes for 119 yards, and kicked three field goals.

The rematch on November 28 was billed as the championship of the Ohio League, something like the virtual Super Bowl of the Jazz Age in the Buckeye State, attended by an uncontained, overflow crowd that spilled onto the field at League Baseball Park, just outside Canton. "Dorais now began to pass the ball," McClellan wrote. "He threw an arching, 'fluffy' pass that was deflected by Carp Julian but was nevertheless caught on the rebound by Red Fleming, who made another first down."[16]

The stars who were supposed to shine did. "Dorais then threw a twenty-five-yard pass to Knute Rockne, who caught the ball over his shoulder with two men defending—one attempted to intercept the ball, and the other tackled Rockne as soon as he caught the ball," McClellan wrote. "However, on the next play, Thorpe intercepted a Dorais pass and returned the ball to midfield, thereby halting the Massillon drive."[17]

With Canton up, 6–0, McClellan wrote, "Dorais started the fourth quarter by throwing a pass to Rockne, who deceived the defender with his acting, sidestepping, and change of pace. The pass

Gus Dorais was notable as the Notre Dame All American QB who refined the forward pass with end Knute Rockne to defeat Army in 1913. He also starred in the Ohio League in the 1910s for the Fort Wayne Friars and Massillon Tigers. Dorais coached the Detroit Lions in the 1940s (Collegiate Collection, courtesy Charles G. Lamb).

covered thirty-three yards, and Rockne ran for an additional twelve yards."[18] The drive ended with a Dorais incompletion in the end zone intended for Rockne. At that time, according to the rule book, an incompletion in the end zone meant turning the ball over to the opposition on its own 20-yard line.

Regaining the ball at midfield, Massillon drove through the rainy, late-afternoon gloom as Dorais completed passes to the Bulldogs' pair of ends from Ohio State—a 12-yard toss to Windy Briggs, and two connections netting 19 yards to Boyd Cherry. "On the next play," wrote McClellan, "Dorais threw a pass to Windy Briggs, who caught the ball on his outstretched fingertips as he dove for the end zone, but in doing so he disappeared into the crowd."[19] Moments later, Charlie Smith, a Canton tackle out of Michigan Agricultural College (now Michigan State University) and one of the first African American pros, emerged from the crowd with the ball. Briggs insisted that a policeman had kicked the ball from his arms after he had crossed the goal line. The apparent score would have tied the game.

The Bulldogs argued that no police were there—the ballpark was outside city limits. With perhaps more money wagered than on any football game of the times, the crowd was unruly to say the least. People streamed onto the field, arguing. The officials were threatened with lynching by both sides. After 20 minutes of indecision, and eight minutes left on the game clock, the contest was called because of darkness.

It was decided that the winner would be announced at 12:30 a.m. in a statement to be read at the Courtland Hotel in Canton. This singular decision was for safety—it would give the officials time to sneak aboard the midnight train out of town. The overflow crowd at the hotel after midnight was informed that Briggs' touchdown was disallowed. Canton won the most controversial pre–NFL pro game, 6–0. Years later, Canton Bulldogs manager Jack Cusack chanced to speak with a railroad conductor who claimed to have won the game for the city. He had $30—two weeks' wages—bet on Canton, and was so angry when he saw Windy Briggs make the catch, that he kicked the ball out of the receiver's hands. Because of his conductor's uniform, Briggs mistook him for a policeman.[20]

CHAPTER SIX

The NFL's Fledgling Years

The National Football League traces its lineage to the upstart American Professional Football Conference or APFC, consecrated on August 20, 1920, among team owners from four Ohio cities. They met in Ralph Hay's Hupmobile showroom on the ground floor of the Odd Fellows Building in Canton. The participants from Akron, Canton, Cleveland, and Dayton sought to stabilize a reasonably solvent plan to administrate a pro football league as the nation settled to normalcy two years after the First World War.

The famous Nesser brothers of the Columbus Panhandles had complained that they had played against Knute Rockne five or six times in 1919. In his second year as head coach of Notre Dame, the scrappy 165-pound end was still selling his services on Sundays to the highest bidders in the Ohio League. High per-game payments to team-hopping ringers were driving some clubs to the brink of bankruptcy. The APFC seemed to have a sane and business-like approach in an era when barnstormers and ringers were out for top dollar across the sporting landscape. A second APFC meeting on September 17 brought other reconstituted and new teams into the APFC fold—from Massillon, Ohio; Decatur and Rock Island, Illinois; Muncie and Hammond, Indiana; Buffalo and Rochester, New York, and elsewhere.

Some continuity from pre-war pro football came right from the top. Joe Carr, a great organizational wizard of pro sports history, succeeded figurehead Jim Thorpe as APFC president in 1921. A sports writer and assistant sports editor for the *Ohio State Journal* in Columbus, Carr had organized the Columbus Panhandles semi-pro baseball and football teams. He became president of the first pro American Basketball Association (from 1925 to 1928), and was the Major League Baseball executive who helped build the minor league system from 12 leagues in 1933 to 41 at the time of his death in 1939—which also was his 19th consecutive year as president of the NFL.[1]

Carr was succeeded as president by an original member of the Dayton Gym-Cadets of the 1910s, Carl "Scummy" Storck, who was, in turn, succeeded by Elmer Layden, the head coach and athletic director at Notre Dame, and a former member of Rockne's "Four Horsemen" backfield of 1924.

At least 15 pre–World War I pro players eventually became head coaches in the NFL, including Jim Thorpe of the Canton Bulldogs (1920) and Oorang Indians (1922–23), Ted Nesser of the Columbus Panhandles (1920–22), Paddy Driscoll of the Chicago Cardinals (1921–22) and Chicago Bears (1956–57), Tommy Hughitt of the Buffalo All-Americans (1921–24), Scummy Storck of the Dayton Triangles (1922–25), Al Nesser of the Akron Pros (1926), William Lone Star Dietz of the Boston Redskins (1933–34), Greasy Neale of the Philadelphia Eagles (1942–50), Dutch Bergman of the Washington Redskins (1943), and Rockne pal Gus Dorais of the Detroit Lions (1943–47).

Leadership in football continuity helped the NFL get rolling in many communities. The ragtag pro sport in the Jazz Age still took time to establish loyal fan bases, regular stadiums and fields, consistent styles of play, refereeing and rules—all of which influenced the character and success of the fledgling league as it struggled to play before attendances that were less than a fourth of college-game crowds. The passing techniques that had worked up until 1920 were used, if sparingly, in the new league, as dozens of teams joined or dropped out of the NFL in its first two decades—many initially as the league's growing pains were obvious, but also in the years through the Great Depression to World War II.

Early stars helped establish both teams in their cities and the NFL on the sports landscape. Player-coach Paddy Driscoll, a native of Evanston, Illinois, and an All American at Northwestern, had played halfback for the Hammond, Indiana, Clabbys (named for prizefighter Jimmy Clabby, a welterweight champ) in the pre-war semi-pro leagues, and was on the Great Lakes Naval Training Station team with George Halas that won the 1919 Rose Bowl over Hugo Bezdek's Mare Island Marines. Along with Thorpe and ends Halas, Dutch Thiele, Bob "Rube" Marshall—one of the early game's African American players—and oth-

Six. The NFL's Fledgling Years

ers, Driscoll was a star player and coach from the pre–NFL era whose exploits helped the NFL survive.

A dynamic field leader and kick scorer who led the NFL in field goals four times, Driscoll was integral to all of his teams' passing attacks. He tied for the NFL lead in touchdown receptions (two) in 1921 for the Cardinals, and led in touchdown passes (six) in 1926 for the Bears—statistical categories that barely registered among fans, coaches, or players in the days when football, the most unsentimental of team sports, had none of the historical framing of numerical accountability that marked baseball.

Driscoll was enshrined in the Pro Football Hall of Fame in its third year of existence, 1965. He was atypical in overall talent and career longevity in those years, but he was a Chicago star whose popularity helped both the Cardinals and Bears survive the lean years. Playing for the astronomical sum of $300 a game for the Cardinals, Driscoll scored the only touchdown in the 1920 game between the Cards and the Chicago Tigers, in which the loser agreed to disband and allow the other team the city's main APFC franchise. The Cards won, 6–3. But the next year, Halas invaded the Cardinals' turf, bringing his Decatur Staleys, named for a starch company, to Chicago and, a year later, re-naming them the Chicago Bears. Driscoll played until he was 33, and later coached for his old nemesis and pal, Halas.

Despite some gathering fan bases, the NFL still had to fight the stigma attached to the pre-war pros, that the players were mercenary ringers, like Rockne, seeking big paychecks wherever they could, and damn city loyalty. Or they were college players using aliases on Sunday, and getting paid under the table. Or they were nothing more than crude mud-wallowing brawlers, muscle-bound gym rats, or college loafers who never opened a book—mugs who helped big-city gamblers wager on games. Purists such as Walter Camp and Amos Alonzo Stagg, and some sports writers still claimed that professionalism tarnished the ideals of the sport that they had nurtured collegiately for generations.

Historian Dr. L. H. Baker claimed that the first banner newspaper headline—one running across eight columns at the top of a page—regarding pro football had as much to do with the pro sport's ill repute as with simple recognition. It appeared in the *Chicago Herald and Examiner* of January 30, 1922: "Stagg Says Conference Will Break Professional Football Menace."[2]

The college game, meanwhile, was becoming entrenched as a wildly popular Saturday afternoon rite, and not just on the East Coast. Football traditions were increasingly becoming established west of the Allegheny Mountains. In 1920, Rockne, building his glory years, coached Notre Dame to its second consecutive 9–0 record, him none the worse for wear after Saturday night trains into the Ohio hinterlands for pro Sundays.

Refinements to passing attacks occurred at all levels of football. Bob Zuppke, famous as coach of the University of Illinois, developed the screen pass during early assignments—as early as 1908 at Muskegon High School in Michigan—then at Oak Park High School in Illinois. Coach Bob Folwell in 1912 at Washington & Jefferson College in Pennsylvania refined the screen, during which a back caught a short toss behind a timed escort of blockers collecting just after the hike behind the line of scrimmage.[3]

The pro teams were often less organized than the schoolboy squads. The APFC changed its name to the National Football League in 1922, and labored in the 1920s to simply survive, as corporate sponsors and the gate take were used to underwrite the next week's travel plans to Detroit, Buffalo, or Akron. The NFL used college rules as their own de facto strictures to establish continuity, both from year to year, and for college stars entering the league. Its team owners often barely had the foresight to envision any specific future for the league. Many of its teams only just met payroll and travel expenses, and getting through to the next game and the next season consumed owners and coaches.

Greasy Neale, who was player-coach of West Virginia Wesleyan, played on Sundays for the Canton Bulldogs. He was among the many sporting rangers who had full autumn weekends with lots of travel. Arda Bowser was an assistant coach at his alma mater, Bucknell University, in Lewisburg, Pennsylvania, and rode trains to Harrisburg and Philadelphia to play on Saturdays. From there, he rode trains across Pennsylvania to Cincinnati or Canton for Sunday games, got paid with checks that most of the time didn't bounce, and rode return rails back to Lewisburg on Sunday nights. On Thanksgiving weekend, 1922, he played four games in four days, one in a rock quarry in Northumberland County, Pennsylvania.[4]

The 1920s are often referred to as the "Golden Age of Sports," the heyday of Babe Ruth and the New York Yankees, Man o' War, Jack

Six. The NFL's Fledgling Years

Dempsey, and the Galloping Ghost of Illinois, Red Grange. But as college football stadiums were built or enlarged across the country to accommodate the growing gridiron fandom, the pro game was still trying to glom onto that trend by trying to hire graduating stars.

Some college stars as well as the pro teams they joined were only in the league for a year or two, and the foggy memories of such NFL clubs as the Tonawanda Kardex, New York Brickley Giants, and Duluth Kellys remain only on newspaper clippings and in the sports encyclopedias that cite them. Unlike the tidily maintained game of baseball, where every major league pitch was recorded from the late 19th century forward, statistics to the football world meant the final score. The NFL did not keep stats until the 1932 season, and the only pass receiving numbers that have been scraped together before then come from variable news reports and offer a very incomplete picture.

Receptions and receiving yards weren't kept on any consistent basis—only touchdowns. In many ways, the stats couldn't be streamlined. In 1924, for instance, the Frankford Yellow Jackets from suburban Philadelphia played 14 games and went 11–2–1, but the Cleveland Bulldogs played nine games and went 7–1–1 and won the NFL title via a better winning percentage (.875). Frankford placed third (.846) because the Chicago Bears went 6–1–4 (.857) for second place. Ties were thrown out of the equation in those days instead of counting as half a win and half a loss as they do today. Comparable stats of any kind were impossible in 1924, when the Kenosha, Wisconsin, Maroons played five games in the NFL, the Kansas City Blues participated in nine, and the Green Bay Packers played 11.

The NFL rules in its first decade were hand-me-downs from the NCAA's Rules Committee. Thus, as football historian John Maxymuk wrote, "The deck was stacked against passing in the early pro game."[5] The passer had to throw the ball from at least five yards behind the line of scrimmage. An incomplete pass in the end zone was a touchback and turnover. Two thirds of all games in the 1920s were shutouts, and scoreless ties were not unusual. Three times as many interceptions resulted as touchdown passes. Punting on third down was considered a sound strategy in your own territory, since conventional wisdom dictated that advantageous field position led directly to scoring.

In the Roaring '20s, passing attacks generally receded, not only in professional football, but in the college game as well, in which the shifty and exciting halfback, Red Grange, was the greatest star, and the Four Horsemen were immortalized at Notre Dame, when *running* backs grabbed the headlines: Ernie Nevers out of Stanford, Swede Oberlander at Dartmouth, Wildcat Wilson at Washington, Johnny Mack Brown at Alabama, Gibby Welch of Pittsburgh, and Chris Cagle of Army.

The biggest boost that the NFL received in the 1920s came from Galloping Ghost's barnstorming tour in 1925 with the Chicago Bears. The 73,000 fans who attended the Bears-Giants game at the Polo Grounds saved the New York team from folding. Similar post-season tours occurred in 1926 and 1927, when the Duluth Eskimos, touting Ernie Nevers (and featuring Johnny "Blood" McNally and Walt Keisling) from city to city, toured for 16 post-season games, earning the nickname "Iron Men of the North" from legendary *New York Herald-Tribune* sports writer Grantland Rice.[6]

It was an era when every player did everything. Even Red Grange blocked when he wasn't the ball carrier. Lou Smythe, a tailback for the Canton Bulldogs in 1923, became the first player to lead the league in rushing touchdowns (seven) and TD passes (six) in the same season. Tailbacks were expected to punt, throw, and block. The quarterback position was then also known as blocking back. Only years later, with the advent of the T formation, did that position evolve into the field general and most protected position on the field. Ends were expected to mostly block, and were sparingly deployed on pass patterns. Everyone played both ways—offense and defense—and played with injuries. The term "special teams" was decades away from entering football parlance.

In the 1920s, the passing game was still being refined in the college rule book, which the pros then used, as well as on the field. In 1924, the intentional grounding penalty was increased to 15 yards while the screen pass was discouraged as players who were ineligible as receivers were required to not obstruct defenders. In 1926, a five-yard penalty was imposed on all incomplete passes after first down. In 1928, no offensive player who had crossed the line of scrimmage could interfere with a defender until the pass was touched. In 1929, pass interference was further tightened on defenses trying to disrupt screen passes.[7]

The one end who stood out among all others in the 1920s was Guy

Six. The NFL's Fledgling Years

Chamberlin. He and LaVern Dilweg of the Packers were named to the NFL's All-Decade Team of the 1920s in retrospect by the league. Early-NFL historian Richard Whittingham named Chamberlin and Halas as the league's best ends over the same decade. Chamberlin was voted into the Pro Football Hall of Fame in 1965, its third year of existence.

Born in 1894 in Blue Springs, Nebraska, Chamberlin became an All-American halfback at the University of Nebraska. He participated in—and shared some responsibility for—the Cornhuskers' legendary mid–1910s 29-game unbeaten streak. In Nebraska's 20–19 victory over Notre Dame in 1915, Chamberlin ran for two touchdowns and passed for the third. In the Army during World War I, he became the athletic director at Camp Kearney in San Diego. Jim Thorpe, who had been Chamberlin's boyhood idol, recruited the end onto the Canton Bulldogs in 1919, the year before the APFA, the NFL's forerunner, began.

At 6-foot-2 and 196 pounds, Chamberlin was tall and fast for the era, and Halas lured him onto the Decatur Staleys in 1920. The two ends together were the best pair in the league, as the next year they led the 9-1-1 big-city re-branded Chicago Staleys to the NFL Championship. The "Great Chamie," as Chamberlin was nicknamed at Nebraska Wesleyan prior to his Cornhusker years, was, according to Halas, "the best two-way end I've ever seen. He was a tremendous tackler on defense and a triple-threat performer on offense."[8]

In 1922, Chamberlin began a stint as a player-coach, one in which the coaching aspect overshadowed his apparently peerless field prowess as a great pass receiver. In six years as a head coach, from 1922 through 1926 and 1928, Chamberlin guided two teams to four NFL Championships in three different cities. His Canton Bulldogs, sans Thorpe—who had moved on to coach and play for the Native American club, the Oorang Indians—won NFL titles in 1922 and 1923. Only a few members of the same team traveled north with Chamberlin to capture the top spot again in 1923 as the 7-1-1 Cleveland Bulldogs.

In 1925, Chamberlin took over the Frankford Yellow Jackets in suburban Philadelphia and led them to a 14–1–2 record and the 1926 NFL Championship. In 1927, he played for the Chicago Cardinals without coaching. He coached the Cards without playing in 1928, loyally bringing Thorpe back to the game at age 41 for the former Carlisle legend's final NFL season. Chamberlin finished his coaching career with a 58-16-7 record for a .759 winning percentage. It's the highest winning percentage of any coach in NFL history, ahead of Vince Lombardi (.740), John Madden (.731), and George Allen (.684).

Some citations call Chamberlin one of the first great pass catchers without much elaboration. Pro-Football-Reference.com credits Chamberlin with 17 career TDs, eight of those on receptions. Chamberlin's finest season was probably 1922, when he scored seven TDs, one on a reception. He returned to Blue Springs in 1932 and spent the rest of his years as a farmer, businessman, and state livestock inspector. He occasionally worked as a football analyst on sports broadcasts and was inducted into the College Football Hall of Fame in 1962. He died in 1967 in Lincoln, Nebraska, at the age of 73.

In 1924, the bar for touchdown passes in a season was raised as wingback Bob Rapp of the Bears and end Tillie Voss of the Packers caught five apiece. Voss hailed from Detroit Mercy College, and alternated duties at tackle as well as end. He was one of the larger players of the 1920s at 6-foot-3 and 207 pounds. He was a recognizable star in league circles, making All-Pro teams four times in a nine-year career from 1921 to 1929—playing on 10 different teams. This career is as illustrative as any of the vagabond player's fate in those volatile NFL times, when teams folded sometimes in mid-season.

Halas managed to keep Voss on the Bears for two years. The big end logged a season for the two-year-old New York Giants in 1926. But Voss also had three seasons split between two teams: the Detroit Wolverines and the Buffalo All Americans in his rookie year; the Rock Island, Illinois, Independents and the Akron Pros in 1922, and the Dayton Triangles and Buffalo Bison in his last campaign. Voss' finest season was his one in Green Bay, during which one of his best moments came against the Racine, Wisconsin, Legion, according to the *Milwaukee Journal* of November 3, 1924.

"A sensational catch of a forward pass by Tillie Voss, after he had been knocked to the ground behind the Racine goal line, allowed the Green Bay Packers to defeat the local Legion eleven, 6–3, here Sunday in a thrilling game before a huge crowd," reported the *Journal*. "The touchdown came on the opening play in the fourth quarter. Capt. [Curly] Lambeau, standing on the 45 yard line, zipped the pigskin to Voss, who collided with [Bill] Glaver. Tillie went down on his knees, but

Six. The NFL's Fledgling Years

lunged forward and grabbed the oval, just inches off the ground."[9] A great catch was a great catch in any era.

The record for TD receptions was upped once again in 1928 when rookie back Gibby Welch caught six for the New York Yankees. A 5-foot-11, 178-pound halfback, Welch was an All American at Pitt, where he broke Red Grange's single-season college record in 1926 with 1,964 total yards (from scrimmage and returns). The following year, Welch led the Panthers to the Rose Bowl (a 7–6 defeat by Stanford), and established school marks for rushing and scoring that weren't broached until Tony Dorsett arrived at Pitt in the 1970s.

If Voss was representative of the football "lifer" of the era, Welch was typical of the star who briefly tested the NFL waters, only to decide on another line of work. The Yankees were 4–8–1 during his one season, and he played another year, in 1929, for the 4–6–2 Providence Steam Roller, which touted the notion in the year of the Wall Street crash that Welch was the NFL's all-time highest paid player.

Welch caught four TD passes that year, good for third in the league, and exited the pro game for the real estate market in his native West Virginia. Headlines about him didn't cease with his gridiron career; Welch was publicly accused of trying to kill his third wife, Gladys, in 1948, two months after the nuptials.[10] This postwar scandal, when Americans liked their heroes as squeaky clean as everything else, eventually disappeared from the papers, as these cases often do. Welch never enjoyed legendary Grange treatment as a giant of sports, and died in Pittsburgh in 1984 at age 80.

The bar in receiving touchdowns was raised again in 1929, when one of the more transcendent characters of the pre–World War II game, end Ray Flaherty of the New York Giants, grabbed eight. One of the reasons for Flaherty's and the Giants' success was the addition of the most mercurial passer to have yet entered the game. As pure throwers go, Benny Friedman belongs to that lineage of bombers whose sheer talent was obvious above and beyond won-loss success: Sammy Baugh in the 1930s, Norm Van Brocklin in the 1950s, Sonny Jurgenson in the 1960s, and Terry Bradshaw in the 1970s.

In the period from the NFL's beginning in 1920 through 1932, after which rule changes helped passers and receivers, Benny Friedman threw more passes (782) for more yards (7,040) and more TDs (63) than any other quarterback. He only played in six of those seasons, beginning in 1927. A rookie All American out of Michigan, Friedman became the first player to throw for more than 1,500 yards and for TDs in double figures (12), leading the Cleveland Bulldogs to a league-best 209 points and an 8–4–1 season or fourth-best in the NFL. The Bulldogs folded after the season, and Friedman went back to Michigan the following year to lead the newly formed Detroit Wolverines to third-best in the NFL with a 7–2–1 record. Again, a Friedman team led the league in points (189). Friedman and halfback Tiny Feather led in rushing TDs with six apiece, and Friedman led in TD passes (10).

Friedman's value in a ramped-up passing attack wasn't lost on Tim Mara, owner of the Giants. He bought the Wolverines, folded the team, and brought Friedman to the Giants. In 1929, Friedman doubled his previous year's TD output with 20, a record that stood until 1942. Flaherty joined the Giants that season after his former team, the New York Yankees, folded. Friedman's and Flaherty's talents helped the Giants set a new league scoring record with 312 points, but their 13–1–1 record wasn't enough against the 12–0–1 Green Bay Packers.

In the year that the NFL decided to keep copious play-by-play stats, Flaherty was the first receiver to lead the league in all three major pass-catching categories in the same season with 21 receptions for 350 yards and five TDs in 1932. The yardage was a single-season record up to that point. "Ray Flaherty was another of our favorites on the team," Tim Mara's son, Wellington Mara, recalled. "He was a tremendous competitor. We had two of the toughest players ever at our two ends in those days—Flaherty and Red Badgro—and at the same time they were two of the nicest guys you'd ever meet."

"I recall one particular incident regarding Flaherty," Wellington Mara continued. "He hurt his hand in one game, really didn't hurt it badly but the doctor put a big bandage on it. Ray held it like it was broken in a sling, and he was pretending to be in great pain. Everyone was very solicitous toward him. I don't remember who the player was but it was one of Ray's particular friends and he was helping Ray over to the bench on the sideline. 'Are you all right, Ray?' he asked. 'Yeah, I'm all right,' Flaherty said, and then punched his friend in the stomach with the supposedly broken hand."[11]

With Flaherty and Badgro, two eventual Hall of Famers, at either

Six. The NFL's Fledgling Years

end, the Giants became one of the stronger NFL teams of the 1930s. "The bulk of [Badgro's] career ... was spent with the Giants, a team that participated in the first three NFL championship games," Whittingham recalled.[12] The league went to postseason play in 1932, splitting into East and West Divisions to create a playoff game for the NFL title.

"With Badgro and Ray Flaherty at ends and Benny Friedman and later Harry Newman passing the ball to them," Whittington assessed, "the Giants had one of the first truly effective passing games in NFL history."[13] Badgro and Joe Carter of the Philadelphia Eagles tied for the NFL lead with 16 receptions apiece in 1934.

"Playing offense and defense equally well, he was one of the best half-dozen ends I ever saw," another Red, Grange, said of Badgro.[14] Johnny Blood of the Packers remembered Badgro as "a tireless competitor, big strong, fast, and injury-proof."[15]

When Flaherty retired as a player, he was the first player to have racked up as much as 600 yards receiving, based on known records from 1932 onward. Flaherty was elected to the Pro Football Hall of Fame in 1976 and Badgro in 1981.

Chapter Seven

The First Dynasty: Green Bay

With some teams barely making it to games in the 1920s, practices were up to the discretion of owners and coaches. Ringers still showed up only on the weekends. Developing strategy and especially passing strategy was tough indeed if your best receiver was arriving on a night train from having played a college game the previous afternoon three states away. But one player-coach of the era not only embraced the passing game, he made it an integral part of his offense. Earl Louis Lambeau, known to his players and the town of Green Bay, Wisconsin, as Curly—for his headful of wild blond locks—was a local high school star who played a year at Notre Dame under Knute Rockne. Lambeau played in the same backfield as the legendary George Gipp, who died of strep throat at age 25 in 1920.

After a bout of tonsillitis sent Lambeau home from South Bend to the western shores of Lake Michigan the same year, Curly formed his own team, borrowing Rockne's main offensive formation, the Notre Dame box, as well as $50 to buy a franchise in the APFC in 1921, the league's second year of existence.

Lambeau played mostly tailback, positioning himself several yards behind the center, with the quarterback, fullback and halfback aligned with him in an uneven trapezoid-like "box" to his right (or left) in the Notre Dame box. Taking the center's hike on many or most plays, Lambeau was probably one of three players from 1920s to throw at least 600 passes according to the partial stats available, which were cobbled together by researcher John Maxymuk to provide some semblance of the passing game of those times.[1] The other two players to throw at least 600 passes were the Giants' Benny Friedman and Red Dunn, who also played for Lambeau in Green Bay (from 1927 to 1931).

Seven. The First Dynasty: Green Bay

Lambeau's team originally was underwritten by the Indian Packing Company, a leader in the then relatively new canned meat industry. Prior to its entrance into the APFC in 1921, Indian was bought out by the Acme Packing Company—thus, "Packers." The team was suspended by the NFL in January 1922, because Lambeau used two Notre Dame players with collegiate eligibility during the 1921 season. Other teams had also used collegiate players, but the league made an example of Green Bay. Lambeau apologized at a league meeting, paid a fine, and bought a new franchise, named it the Blues, then renamed it the Packers.[2]

Lambeau was one of the first coaches to conduct daily practice sessions. Passing and catching the blimp-like football were regular portions of those practices. In 1922, Lambeau transferred the team administration to the ownership of a city-based nonprofit organization selling stock and season tickets, so he could concentrate on coaching and playing—and passing. "Lambeau was the first coach to use the forward pass as a basic offense," said Clarke Hinkle, the Packers fullback of the 1930s. "His running game was a threat, but he introduced the passing as a major part of offensive strategy. He's one of the first to pass from behind his own goal line on a first down, for example."[3]

The speed-oriented Packers posted winning records every year from 1921 through 1932, going 92-33-15 in that

The namesake for Lambeau Field in Green Bay, Wisconsin, Curly Lambeau had played tailback at Notre Dame. He used the forward pass with alacrity as coach of the Packers, who went 226-132-22 in his 33 years. He was inducted into the Pro Football Hall of Fame in 1963 (Collegiate Collection, courtesy Charles G. Lamb).

stretch. Green Bay contended for league supremacy each autumn, and won the NFL title an unprecedented three years in a row at the outset of the Great Depression, from 1929 through 1931 with a collective record in that time of 34–5–2 and consecutive records of 12–0–1, 10–3–1, and 12–2.

The Packers collected three later championships during the Don Hutson era of the late 1930s and early 1940s. The unassailable dominance of the Vince Lombardi epoch of the 1960s, including the first two Super Bowl wins, has been justifiably immortalized in sports culture. And the facts of the Super Bowl championships under Mike Holmgren in 1996 and Mike McCarthy in 2011 are fresher in memory. But Curly Lambeau's Packers of the early Depression era formed the NFL's first true dynasty.

In most of those years, Lambeau or his other passing backs in the 1920s and early 1930s—Red Dunn, Bo Molenda, and eventually Arnie Herber—were among the NFL leaders in TD passes. Until 1924, the league standard for receiving touchdowns in a season was three—attained by ends George Halas of the Chicago Staleys and Heinie Miller of the Buffalo All Americans in 1921, and wingback Bob Rapp of Halas' 1923 Bears.

Stats prior to the Depression carried very little currency for fans, coaches, or players. It wasn't until the mid-1930s, when Don Hutson arrived in Green Bay, that an awareness of individual league leadership or big receiving and touchdown numbers described a player's value—one player's value. The NFL between world wars was comprised of football players who did everything, and were expected to do everything, with little specialization or concessions.

Lambeau's Packers deviated from the standard only in the development and keen acquisition of players who could pass and receive. Red Dunn came from the Chicago Cardinals, and Tillie Voss matriculated from the Toledo Maroons. Halfback Marty Norton, who had played for the Minneapolis Marines in 1922 and 1924, became the first Green Bay player to lead the NFL in touchdown receptions—four in 1925, tied with Hal Erickson of the Cardinals and Charlie Berry of the Pottsville Maroons.

Verne Lewellen, a 6-foot-1, 180-pound halfback out of Nebraska, joined the Packers in 1925, when he caught three TD passes. In 1926, Lewellen led the league with four TD grabs, tied with end Duke Hanny

Seven. The First Dynasty: Green Bay

of the Bears. Lewellen's feel for paydirt was as strong as any player of the 1920s. He led the NFL in total TDs in 1928 and 1930—nine each year—and was an integral member of the 1929, 1930, and 1931 title teams.

When he retired after the 1932 season, Lewellen had scored a remarkable 51 career touchdowns in nine years. This was a time when scoring was practically the only consistently kept football stat, and when there were precious few scores at all—two thirds of all games in the 1920s were shutouts. Lewellen scored more touchdowns, 35, than any other player in the NFL's first decade, more than the illustrious names: Grange, Nevers, Thorpe, et al. Lewellen, famous in his era for booming 60-yard punts, caught a total of 83 passes, according to reconstructed records from newspapers and broadcasts, for 12 touchdowns—better stats than most starting ends of his era. He played three games on loan to the New York Yankees in 1927 and all 102 of his other games were in a Packers uniform.

While he was still playing, Lewellen passed the bar exam and ran successfully against Packers teammate and fellow receiver, end LaVern "Lavvie" Dilweg, for District Attorney of Brown County, Wisconsin, where Green Bay is the county seat. In 1950, Lewellen joined the governing board of the Packers, and, in 1954, was named general manager. He stepped back into the role of business manager when Vince Lombardi became both head coach and GM in 1959. Lewellen retired in 1967, having been aboard for 10 Packers NFL titles in all. Lewellen was named All Pro from 1926 through 1929, and not just by the *Green Bay Press-Gazette*, which began making NFL All Pro selections in 1923.

Lavvie Dilweg, a 6-foot-3, 200-pound end out of Marquette, who had played his first NFL season with the Milwaukee Badgers, also was a major contributor to Lambeau's first three championship teams. He caught three TD passes in 1929, two in 1930, and four in 1931, for second place in the league behind his mercurial Packers teammate, halfback Johnny "Blood" McNally. Dilweg has been called the best all-around player at end from his era, and was named All Pro nine times.

Dilweg was one of the Packers' most consistent players on offense and defense, for eight stellar seasons, from 1927 through 1934. Dilweg was selected to the NFL's all-1920s team after playing only four years in that decade. His misfortune was to have been the star end of the Packers directly before Hutson's arrival. The loss to Lewellen in the DA race didn't slow him down politically: Dilweg was elected to the U.S. House of Representatives during the 1940s, and was a foreign relations appointee of the Kennedy Administration. The coincidence of two All Star receivers on the same team having political success makes for an odd counterbalance to their exclusions from the Pro Football Hall of Fame.

There are only so many players elected to the hall each year, and the Packers have seen many of their players enshrined. However, both the top TD scorer, Lewellen, and occasionally cited best end, Dilweg, of the NFL's fledgling decade, never even were finalists for the Hall. Lewellen's surpassing tendency to score is just as obscured today as the fact that Dilweg remains one of two players selected to the NFL's all-1920s team who isn't in the hall (the other is guard Heartley "Hunk" Anderson).

From that era, the one Packer whose legend is never neglected is Johnny Blood. A charter member of the Pro Football Hall of Fame in 1963, Blood was born John McNally in New Richmond, Wisconsin, in 1903. He took the name Blood from a Rudolph Valentino movie, *Blood and Sand*, when he saw it on a marquee on the way with a fellow St. John's College player to break the rules that preserve college eligibility by signing contracts with the semi-pro East 26th Street Liberties in Minneapolis in 1922, three years prior to his first NFL contract with the Milwaukee Badgers. "My name is Blood, and this guy is Sand," he said, introducing himself to Liberties management.[4]

Blood played in the same backfield as Ernie Nevers on the "Iron Men of the North," the Duluth Eskimos, in 1926 and 1927. For the 1928 season, he and pal Walt Keisling—both of them future head coaches of the Pittsburgh Pirates/Steelers—matriculated to the Pottsville Maroons in Eastern Pennsylvania. In 1929, Blood, whose rounder's reputation preceded him in NFL circles and practically everywhere else—found that his running and receiving skills were valued by Curly Lambeau in Green Bay. Lambeau offered Blood one of two contracts, either $110 a week if Blood stopped drinking on Tuesdays during season, or $100 a game if he didn't. "I'll take the $100," Blood wired to Lambeau.[5]

Shenanigans were part of the pro game's reputation between world wars. While pro ball became respectable in the 1960s with big television contracts for both the NFL and AFL and escalating salaries, sports writ-

Seven. The First Dynasty: Green Bay

ers such as Allison Danzig, Myron Cope, Murray Olderman, Richard Whittingham, and others began investigating the league's checkered past. Often what came to the fore were stories of camaraderie and antics. One player, the legendary Blood, who was the inspiration for Dodge Connolly, played by George Clooney in the film *Leatherheads* (2008), accumulated more rover-boy lore than any of them.

"His reputation off the field was even larger, and if there were a rogue's Hall of Fame he surely would be a charter member of that, too," wrote Richard Whittingham in *What a Game They Played*. "One writer of the time referred to the mercurial Blood as 'a Peter Pan who would never shed his eternal youth.' Johnny Blood broke as many training rules as he did tackles, and ignored team curfews just as he did Prohibition. His carousals, antics, and insatiable appetite for life provided an endless stream of amusing and ribald stories throughout the NFL circuit from the mid-1920s through the 1930s."[6]

Former Packers fullback Clarke Hinkle told Myron Cope that Blood would buy out entire brothels for an evening.[7] Passing a tavern or a poker table or a house of ill repute without stopping just wasn't in his lifeblood. And yet he was a closet intellectual and something of a Renaissance man. He once stood in the audience of a John Barrymore performance in a Pittsburgh theatre and traded Shakespearean lines with the master—which may or may not have been prearranged. Blood, who often wintered on Catalina Island, was lucky in his family security—the McNallys were heirs to the *Minneapolis Star-Tribune* fortune.

As a receiver, Blood was possessed of sure hands and surpassing speed. He was the first player to log double figures in TD receptions in a season when he caught 11 in 1931 on the 12–2 Packers, who won their third consecutive NFL title. He also claimed the scoring title with 14 total TDs for 84 points, besting his former Duluth backfield mate, Ernie Nevers, who tallied 66 points. Blood played on four NFL championship teams, including the 1936 Packers, which by then had acquired the only player, Don Hutson, the "Alabama Antelope," who was deemed faster than the aging halfback.

"I never saw a fellow who could turn a ball game around as quickly as Johnny Blood," said Hutson, who arrived in Green Bay in 1935. "When he came into a game, the whole attitude of the players changed. He had complete confidence in himself and a tremendous football sense."[8] Down by six points with five minutes left in a crucial late-season 1936 game against the Detroit Lions, Blood, who had been benched for defying Lambeau by calling passing plays in the huddle, was inserted back into the game and immediately did so again, telling tailback Arnie Herber, "Zoom it, Arnie. Number 3—as far as you can."[9]

Blood sprinted under a deep Herber arc. "Three men from the Lions' defensive secondary converged on Blood, and in one scrambling group they all went up in the air, groping for the ball," Murray Olderman wrote. "They fell in a tangle over the goal line. When the referee unpiled them, Blood on the bottom had the ball and the Packers had the game and eventually an NFL title."[10] Blood's defiance or football sense or both prevailed. "For 67 yards there," Blood said, "I guess I was unemployed."[11]

As player-coach of the Pittsburgh Pirates in 1937 and 1938, Blood missed one of his team's games. "On most teams, the coach worries about where the players are at night,'" Pirates owner Art Rooney once said. "Our players worry about the coach."[12] Blood spent the war years in the Air Force as a cryptographer in the China-Burma-India theatre. He was another Packer with political ambitions. He ran for sheriff of St. Croix County, Wisconsin, on a platform of "honest wrestling."[13] The result was something that happened much more rarely when he was on a football field: He lost.

Thirty-seven of Blood's 49 touchdowns came on pass receptions. He was one of the first players to play as many as 14 seasons. Between his playing days and his charter membership in the Pro Football Hall of Fame in 1963, Johnny Blood tended bar in San Francisco, illegally rode boxcars and was nicknamed the "Vagabond Halfback," dabbled as a sportswriter, feed salesman, hotel clerk, sailor, and refractory maker.[14] "In between all this," Gerald Holland wrote in *Sports Illustrated*, "he played some football—a lot of extraordinary football."[15]

With Blood as its greatest star and such superb receivers as Lewellen and Dilweg, Lambeau's Packers were the first team to ride the passing game to NFL Championships in an era when most other teams still slugged it out on the ground. Some teams had passed with success—the Cleveland Bulldogs and New York Giants among them—but only the Packers up that time had used passing as a means to top success.

Chapter Eight

The Chicago Bears and the T Formation

The most dynamic change in offensive football and in the life of the forward pass wasn't a fad that lingered. It wasn't an upsweep that pushed the running game into the background. It wasn't the result of one season or even five. And it wasn't the design of one man. It was, however, the efforts of one organization that made the difference in gradually creating wide-open offenses that, in the post–World War II era, included much more passing. The Chicago Bears of the 1930s and 1940s deserve the most credit for the midcentury sea-change in all levels of organized football to the T formation.

The evolution, establishment, and proficiency of the T formation in the hands of the Bears started with dabbling in the early 1930s, became a concerted effort in transition by 1939, and reigned as the team's normal offense through the 1940s and ever after. The supremacy of four NFL titles by the Bears in the 1940s—1940, 1942, 1943, and 1946—convinced most professional and college teams to switch to the T formation from the run-dominated offenses of the Depression Era and earlier, such as the single wing and double wing. The T formation, as used by the Bears, provided a balanced attack for speedy athletes, and ushered in a new era of exciting offense, circumstances dovetailing to the upswing in the popularity of spectator sports following the Second World War.

But prior to that, pro football games were still run-dominated slugfests, not much different in tone or nature than the organized chaos of bygone eras, when brawn was infinitely more integral to the game than brains. Teams still tore up midfields in clouds of dust or slippery mud-bowls, with limited scoring and a paucity of breakaway plays. Excitement beyond a carted-off body was occasionally hard to find.

These lawn-ripping, body-piling spectacles were what historian

Robert Smith characterized as "the thralldom of tradition that seemed to have doomed [football] to remain, especially if the field were wet, a slam-bang, grunt-groan, pull-devil, pull-baker affair that was occasionally less fun to watch than an honest wrestling match."[1] But, then, the Bears dusted off the T formation and slowly changed the game of football.

By the late 1940s, the T was the rage on gridirons everywhere. But it was far from anything new. The Bears precision-tooled an old scheme—actually the oldest offensive formation in American football. The T was so old that it was the brainchild of the sport's first great proprietor, legendary Yale University coach Walter Camp, the "Father of American Football." One of his Yale players, end Amos Alonzo Stagg, who later coached at the University of Chicago from 1892 to 1932, when Clark Shaughnessy took over, wrote that the T dates to a rules change in 1888, when linemen were prohibited from extending their arms to protect ball carriers. In that era, orchestrated bunches, such as the human wedge, were used to escort ball carriers, and often led to injuries.

In 1894 Stagg coached Chicago quarterback Frank Hering to play behind the center "and receive the ball on a lift-up snap."[2] That, Stagg wrote, "was the start of the present position of the quarterback in the T formation." This direct transfer of the ball from center to quarterback, Stagg told the *Saturday Evening Post* in 1926, "not only saved the moment lost in rising from a stoop, but it minimized fumbles by permitting the quarterback to use his body as well as his hands in taking the ball from center."[3] Prior to this, the center bounced the ball off the turf, and the quarterback had to field the blimp from that carom for the play to start. By the time the NFL was established in 1920, the bounced ball had become a short toss from the center, a "hike," and usually to the tailback or fullback and not the quarterback.

Among the things that the T formation brought into sharper focus was the essential importance of the snap from the center directly into the hands of the quarterback and the establishment of the QB position to that of field general. Before the Bears established and exploited the T with Sid Luckman switched from tailback to quarterback, the game certainly was a running game, and the runners were the stars, especially in Chicago, which had ridden on the fortunes of Red Grange, Bronko Nagurski, and Beattie Feathers.

Eight. The Chicago Bears and the T Formation

Through the 1950s via the T formation, the quarterback position became elevated in importance on the pro and college levels. The game, every game, and nearly every play in every game, was literally in the QB's hands, and often under his command. Previously, in the single wing, the quarterback was occasionally called the blocking back, and he often lined up behind a guard or tackle while the ball was snapped to either a tailback (or halfback) or fullback for a run that might go in any direction. The evolving specialization of the quarterback as the definite field general and the definite passer in the T also led to the dropping of various standard pan-football-player capabilities from the position's repertoire. Quarterbacks weren't expected to block as much and then not at all.

The direct handing of the ball from the center to the quarterback cut down on mistakes and expedited every play to an immediacy that demanded quicker and faster players at every position, linemen included. It also made the center more effective, since his head was up from the beginning of the snap count, and he didn't have to predetermine where he was going to hike the ball. In effect, his involvement as a participant in the schemes and ruses of plays was very much reduced if not eliminated. Only in the later years—1970s and after—because of sophisticated defenses, the center returned to the role of line sergeant, often barking blocking orders as the linemen set at the line of scrimmage.

Penn State, Michigan, and Dartmouth were among the teams using the T formation regularly in the first decade of the 20th century, with Notre Dame and Boston College following suit. Other teams throughout the country used the T to some extent, including Coach Bernie Bierman's Minnesota Golden Gophers, who won five national championships from 1934 to 1941. Clark Shaughnessy's 10–0 Stanford team of 1940, the "Wow Boys," who had one win the previous year, remains the great turn-around example of what can happen when the T is installed. As the game progressed through the initial decades of the 20th century, the single wing, double wing, Notre Dame box, and other offenses were prevalent, and the T became reserved to an oddity out of the bag of tricks for a gadget play.

But the Bears stayed with the T. Halas had grown accustomed to it when he played at the University of Illinois, where coach Bob Zuppke used it. Similarly, Curly Lambeau used the single wing and Notre Dame box at Green Bay, mainly because he had played in a similar collegiate system for Knute Rockne at South Bend.

Teams stayed with what they knew, experimented with what worked against them, and nominally scouted other clubs until Halas and Greasy Neale and other coaches began the surreptitious exchanging of game films in the 1940s, leading to a league policy of regular film exchange, which became a requisite ritual under Paul Brown. "I kept it all through the twenties with the Bears," Halas said of the T, "although I cannot recall how often the critics denounced the Bears as an old-fashioned team."[4]

The idea's germination for the Bears to implement the man in motion came from Halas' attendance at a college game. "I first saw the man-in-motion worked beautifully from the single wing by Judge Walter P. Steffen at Carnegie Tech," Halas told Joe King, the football writer of the *New York World Telegram & Sun*, in a discussion of the origins of the Bears' resuscitation of the T formation for the 1958 book, *Inside Pro Football*. "Steffen lulled Notre Dame to sleep and then surprised and won with the man in motion."[5] Halas' attendance was on November 27, 1926, amid the standing-room-only crowd at Forbes Field in Pittsburgh to watch the 8–0 Irish have the national championship vanish via a 19–0 victory by Carnegie Tech in one of the college game's greatest upsets.

Halas' thoughts of better utilizing the man in motion were shared with an old University of Illinois crony, Ralph Jones, the longtime assistant to head coach Bob Zuppke. The Bears increased their tinkering with the T after Halas determined that he had better tend more to the business side of professional football. He had quit playing end for the Bears in 1928, and two years later decided the coaching post needed fresh blood. Halas ran the Bears through the 1920s partnered with his old University of Illinois teammate, Dutch Sternaman. Through the NFL's first decade, "Halas and Sternaman feuded often," according to NFL historian Tom Bennett, creating a team morale problem, which led directly to both men stepping aside for a former mentor.[6] The Bears hired Zuppke's former backfield coach as head coach. Jones promised Halas that if he and Sternaman stayed out of his way, he would lead the Bears to the NFL championship within three years.

Halas turned over the reins to Jones from 1930 to 1932, a time when many pro and college teams searched for offensive innovations to

Eight. The Chicago Bears and the T Formation

increase scoring and make the game more exciting. Among the experimentations credited to Jones was splitting the receivers wide in the T to spread the defenders across the field.

Jones sent a back in motion to force defensive adjustments on pass and run plays. "To speed up action in the backfield and add diversity, Jones began applying a little-used rule which allows one man to move as soon as the signals begin and continue moving," Halas recalled. "The one-second halt after the shift does not apply to him."[7] Because of the conspicuousness of the man in motion to defenses and the fans alike prior to the snap, this tip-off portended a passing play. Of course, this wasn't always the case, but it forced defenses to spread out and cover the man in motion.

The notion persisted in football from the 19th century through the initial ragtag pro leagues and into the early NFL years that power running was the best and safest strategy for winning, even if was not the safest, health-wise, for the players. What also persisted with that strategy was the idea that football was a test of strength. Passing, shifts, decoys, and deception had nothing to do with the base notion that our guys can whip your guys. There had never been anything against the man in motion. It's just that any man sent out wide was considered at the time wasted in the prevalent run formations. Why not send that man to block someone? Why not use him to aid the running play instead of making him a decoy?

Halas credited Jones with putting additional refinements into the T, including variations on the man in motion, who usually was the Bears' most famous player, Red Grange, the former University of Illinois All American who Halas used to front a nationwide barnstorming tour in 1925—the most significant early event boosting the NFL in the national spotlight.

The Chicago backfield also included the player who succeeded Grange as the team's most iconographic, the former University of Minnesota All American fullback from Rainy River, Ontario—Bronislau "Bronko" Nagurski, whose very name still personifies the rough-and-tumble game itself during the Depression Era. At quarterback was the former University of Florida star, Carl Brumbaugh, whose ambidextrousness added another dimension.

Gridiron historian Allison Danzig made the distinction that Stagg's use of the man in motion at the turn of the century—and Halas' claim that the Bears under Jones were the first team to run a man in motion from the T—was that Stagg's backfield was in a trapezoid formation while the Bears later used a traditional T.[8]

The T was often or always in flux—a work in progress. Aside from the man in motion—to either side behind the quarterback—shifts by the backs have been a constant in T deployment and deception. As the years evolved, a backfield player, often a halfback, and called the flanker, more often than not lined up in the slot between the wide end and tackle. This formation became known as the Slot T. When the T was used with two tight ends, it was called the Power T. When both ends were split wide, the formation was known as the Flex T. "Flex" in football parlance of the 1930s meant the end was split apart from the tackle or "flexed." This gave the end a better angle at blocking in the defensive end or linebacker on an end run. It also usually allowed the end the advantage of a quicker lead into a pass pattern. If a back lined up just outside and a step behind an end in tight formation or next to the tackle, this alignment was the Wing T. Most of these secondary names for variations on the T formation came into use after World War II. Whether these alignments and realignments started from, or morphed into, a T or a box or a trapezoid arrangement of the backs prior to the snap, it was still a play out of the basic T formation, what Pop Warner called the "regular formation."[9]

The T formation as the Bears used it emphasized dexterity, precision, and speed instead of brawn. It required split-second timing between the center and quarterback, and the quarterback and the running backs. Instead of waiting on holes, the backs were at full speed forward out of their three-point stances on the go-count, faking a handoff or scraping the ball from the pivoting QB's grasp, knifing to holes between widely spaced linemen. The back often could choose another hole if his first option was plugged by a defender. While the T facilitated the passing game, it also opened up the running game. It was a boon for both types of play, and it led to the often-quoted adage that says that a successful running game sets up the passing game, and vice versa.

Play-action fakes to one or more backs were possible on eventual passing plays. When one of the backs went in motion, it often forced a defensive adjustment, weakening the area vacated by the defender, often

Eight. The Chicago Bears and the T Formation

a linebacker or defensive back, making the defense vulnerable to the run. The wider the linemen lined up and the more spread out the ends were, conventional wisdom suggested a pass play. That, in turn, might set up an unexpected run. These runs were often counter or misdirection plays designed by Clark Shaughnessy, who joined the Bears as a Halas assistant in the late 1930s. As time went on, any widely split backfield player became known as a flanker, and his identity was more of a receiver than a backfield runner. Eventually, the flanker was identified almost exclusively as a receiver as the mystery of what he was about to do on any play evaporated.

To advance the story of the T for a moment—a bit after the Bears refined it—the formation evolved throughout the NFL and in college and eventually high school and changed the nomenclature of positions. As the duties of the split end and the flanker became practically the same, even though one was on the line of scrimmage and one was a step back in the backfield, both positions by the 1970s were known as wide receiver. Through the same evolution, the distinctions of the duties of the end that often stayed on the line to block on passes or runs became clearer, creating by the 1960s the tight end, a hybrid of offensive lineman and receiver, epitomized by the play of Mike Ditka for the Bears, John Mackey for the Baltimore Colts, and Jackie Smith for the St. Louis Cardinals.

Because of these changes to the receiving corps, the T also warped into the general "pro set" of the postwar era, consisting of backfields using two runners or setbacks, the fullback and the halfback, both of whom ran and blocked. From the 1970s onward, many teams sought to exploit one gifted star running back, and the fullback position in the ever-evolving T formation morphed into mainly a blocking back.

Coach Paul Brown of the Cleveland Browns adapted the T for unadorned passing plays in the late 1940s when his team was still in the All American Football Conference. Where Chicago's version of the T depended on quick and immediate play action and fakes, Brown had his quarterback, Otto Graham, take the snap and back-peddle immediately. The multifaceted Graham dropped straight back to pass without play-action fakes, protected as he was by a "pocket" of blockers. The Browns' line and backs would form a semicircle of protection, from where Graham could spot downfield receivers.

A widely split man in motion was used by the Bears for long pass plays to isolate a defensive back one-on-one in the 1930s. "What the Bears did," Halas wrote in 1953, "was to put the T and the man in motion together and then gradually add refinements, such as the signal system [used by the majority of college and professional teams today] and counter plays and *spreads*. This was a period of evolution spanning almost twenty years and was the product of the Bears' organization rather than of one individual."[10]

A booklet about the T, *The Modern T Formation and the Man-in-Motion*, and the formation's uses was published in 1941 by the three Bears coaches most responsible for its success: Clark Shaughnessy, Ralph Jones, and George Halas.[11]

By counter plays, Halas referred to those that initially develop to appear as if they go one way, such as to the left side, to key the defense into leaning that way. Often the offensive linemen and backs feint a step or two that way on the snap to get the defenders instinctively leaning. Occasionally, the offensive players decoy through what appears to be a full play. In any case on a counter play, the quarterback's handoff to the ball carrier is back the other way, occasionally on a pivot, against the grain, or, in a case in which the play is "sold" as if it is going left, back to the right side. The counter might include a split-second delay for the ball carrier to accept the ball.

By spreads, Halas meant a line with more than what had been the usual space between linemen, with often one or both ends and/or the flanker split way wide. This alignment forces the defense—linemen, linebackers, and backs—to spread wide as well. Ralph Jones increased the distance between offensive linemen from a foot to a yard, according to Halas. "The change gave the defense new opportunities to enter our backfield," Halas said. "To remove this gift, Jones needed to speed action in the backfield, to improve the blocking, and to open holes in the line quickly. For plays coming through the line, the blockers should not try to bring down the assigned defense men, but merely to deflect them ... for a few seconds but long enough for our back to get through with the ball."[12]

During Ralph Jones' tenure, the league hadn't yet created divisions or a title game, and the team with the best record was named the champion. When Jones signed on as head coach, he promised Halas that the

Eight. The Chicago Bears and the T Formation

Bears would win an NFL championship within three years. The Bears went 9–4–1 in 1930 and 8–5 in 1931 for third-place finishes during the Green Bay Packers' championship years.

Jones fulfilled his promise in 1932 after one of the weirdest team starts in NFL history. After four games, the Bears logged three scoreless ties and a 2–0 loss to the Packers on a safety. The Bears eventually went 6–1–6 on the season, tying won-lost records with the Portsmouth Spartans, who ended the season at 6–1–4. Ten games or one fifth of the NFL's 50 contests that year ended in ties. Chicago or Portsmouth played in nine of those, including 13–13 and 7–7 ties against each other. Despite 13 years in business, the league lacked uniformity and standards as teams didn't have to play the same number of games.

The Bears and Packers played 14 games apiece; the Spartans, New York Giants, Brooklyn Dodgers, and Staten Island Stapletons played 12 each, and the Boston Braves and Chicago Cardinals played 10. At that time, ties in the league were thrown out, and the winning percentage determined teams' ranks, not the number of wins. This rankled coach Curly Lambeau and his Packers, who had gone 11–3–1 on the season, winning almost double the games that Chicago won, yet missing their fourth straight league title.

Reform for the standings arrived decades later. Since 1972 in the NFL, ties have counted as half a win and half a loss, which obviously created different won-lost percentages than in the years when the ties were simply erased. Had the league's 1932 won-lost-tie records have been judged under the 1972 rule change, Green Bay would have won the league outright—and won an unprecedented fourth NFL title in a row.

League President Joe Carr and team owners Halas and Harry Snyder of Portsmouth decided that a final, added game would crown the league's winner. Portsmouth was one of the last of the NFL's holdover "town teams," located in southern Ohio, about 110 miles up the Ohio River from Cincinnati. Not everyone was enthused about the added game. Future Pro Football Hall of Fame tailback Dutch Clark of the Spartans was scheduled to coach the Colorado College basketball team, so he skipped the contest. However, 9,683 paying fans turned out for what the *Portsmouth Times* called "a sham battle on a Tom Thumb gridiron."[13]

A blizzard hit Chicago before game time and left drifts three feet deep. The game scheduled for Wrigley Field was instead played indoors at Chicago Stadium on December 18, 1932. A circus had just vacated the premises, conveniently leaving behind trucked-in dirt, in which were buried a few leftover surprises from the animal acts. They were discovered once the football game got underway on an 80-yard-long floor, which was narrower than the regulation gridiron by five yards. To compensate for the short "field," each offense regressed to its own 30-yard line after it crossed midfield to simulate 100 yards.

This indoors contest was scoreless for more than three quarters, as if it might confirm the fact that the two teams' previous meetings were correct—the Bears and Spartans were dead-even clubs, and this time sans any scoring punch at all. With 11 minutes to play, Chicago's Dick Nesbitt intercepted an Ace Gutkowsky pass and returned it to the Portsmouth 13-yard line. Two Bronko Nagurski plunges gave the Bears a first down on the two. The Spartans stopped the Chicago fullback for no gains on the next two consecutive tries. On third and goal, Nagurski, got the snap again, and improvised, according to him. He stopped, retreated, and leaped, completing a jump pass to Red Grange for a touchdown.

A longstanding rule dictated that all passes had to be thrown from at least five yards behind the line of scrimmage. Nagurski, by most accounts, was right behind his own offensive line when he made the throw. "I took a step or two forward as though to begin the plunge everyone expected," Nagurski said. "The defenders converged and there was no way I could get through. I stopped, moved back a couple of steps, and Grange had gone around and was in the end zone, all by himself."[14]

The referee called nothing, and the TD stood. Portsmouth coach Potsy Clark's chagrin propelled him onto the field as fast as he could run. Clark protested the play to the referees, the league, and for years afterward to anyone who would listen, to no avail. The Bears added a safety for a 9–0 victory. Halas prevailed.

Chicago won the championship with an .875 winning percentage, based on its 7–1 record after the third Portsmouth contest of the season. Green Bay placed second with a .769 winning percentage. And Portsmouth ended up third with a .750 percentage, based on its final 6–2 record after being defeated by the Bears.

Halas' 1932 indoor championship was a watershed event in pro foot-

Eight. The Chicago Bears and the T Formation

ball history. The success of the game led the NFL to split the league into East and West Divisions (or conferences as the terminology changed through the years) and schedule a championship game from that point forward.

The crucial winning play of the season came on a pass play—Nagurski hitting Grange—however dubious that play was, rules-wise, and it issued from a team that used the pass increasingly through its employment of the T formation. That year, the Bears' Luke Johnsos and Red Grange were among the league's top five receivers with 19 and 11 receptions respectively. Four of Grange's league-leading seven touchdowns were through the air. Nagurski threw three TD passes. And the Bears won their second NFL Championship, following the crown won by player-coach Halas' Chicago Staleys in 1921.

Ralph Jones' use of the T formation was singular and successful. "*Football became a game of brains*," Halas wrote, using italics for emphasis. "Instead of knocking men down, Jones tried to entice the defense into doing something helpful for us." Halas also found that the fans liked the swifter and more wide-open play, fulfilling his own wishes to make the game and the league more accessible to a wider fan base. "Best of all," he remarked, "the public found our brand of football exciting."[15]

A 5-foot-7, 135-pound Indianapolis native, Ralph Jones coached large, as they say. He coached football and basketball at Wabash College just after the turn of the 20th century. His 1910–11 Purdue basketball team went undefeated (12–0) and his overall hoops record at the University of Illinois was 192–9, including two Big Ten championships. He also was an assistant to Illinois' great Zuppke, before he moved on as head coach of Lake Forest Academy in suburban Chicago. Zuppke and Jones had coached Halas, who relied on his Illinois connection through the years to secure the signing of Red Grange when every team, including the Giants, were after the All American—and to also tap the talented Jones. The mission of a Bears championship accomplished, Jones returned to Lake Forest in 1933 as athletic director and football coach, and stayed there through 1948. He retired to Colorado and passed away in Boulder in 1951 at the age of 71.

At the winter league meeting in February 1933, Halas successfully campaigned to get the five-yard rule eliminated from the pro game, so that any back could throw the ball from anywhere behind the line of scrimmage. Even Potsy Clark agreed that the change was a sound decision. Halas had already pocketed the championship, but Clark and the other owners or team representatives reasoned that abolishing the five-yard restriction would free up the passing game for more and exciting offensive play. Halas, of course, understood that the jettisoning of the rule would certainly benefit the Bears in the T formation.

He was the savvy "Papa Bear" to be sure—without question as cunning and resourceful a coach as his reputation maintains. But he needed a league for the Bears to dominate, and he was determined to make it successful. His rule changes to improve the game itself ultimately were for a better NFL, and none of the enmity that had, for instance, been ascribed to Walter Camp for changing or not changing rules to greedily benefit his Yale team, followed Halas for his rule advocacy. Of the men who navigated the shoals in the name of the league—Joe Carr to Bert Bell, Wellington Mara to George Preston Marshall, Pete Rozelle to Dan Rooney—George Halas did more to drive and improve the NFL than any of them. "As a player, coach, and executive, Halas was a thundering presence in the NFL for sixty years, the individual most responsible for the league's survival and ultimate prosperity," Stephen Fox wrote in *Big Leagues: Professional Baseball, Football, and Basketball in the National Memory*.[16] Halas knew that a more refined passing game certainly aided his team, but it was also for the good of the league and for the very game that he nurtured through the century.

Also at the February 1933 meeting, Halas successfully advocated for bringing the goal posts in from the end lines to the goal lines, to facilitate kick-scoring to help break the preponderance of ties that plagued the NFL. As well, the Chicago icon successfully convinced the league to adopt inbound lines—the forerunners of hash marks—10 yards from, and parallel to, the out-of-bounds lines. This allowed offenses whose last play ended up out of bounds to start the next play toward the middle of the field, inside the inbound lines, rather than at the point where the previous play's ball carrier exited the field of play. Formerly, offenses were hemmed against the out-of-bounds lines, where defenses could, and did, bottle up attempts to move downfield from those cramped positions.[17]

The hash marks also meant more operating room for the receivers. The real estate between the hash marks and the sidelines became the

Eight. The Chicago Bears and the T Formation

receiver's backyard, unless he was going up against a superior defensive back. Talent, speed, and shiftiness were emphasized even more in this operating space, as several receivers in the late 1930s used it to their advantage, including the Packers' Don Hutson, the Washington Redskins' Wayne Millner, the Cleveland Rams' Jim Benton, and the Chicago Cardinals' Gaynell Tinsley.

All three of the 1933 league decisions were designed to help offenses, boost scoring, and make the game more exciting to draw more fans. As well, these rules were the first concerted departures from collegiate rules, which the pros had generally used. With Halas' advocacy, these changes represented independent governance by the league as it became more established in spite of low salaries, uneven attendance, and the vicissitudes of the Great Depression. The college game was still by far the more popular brand of football among fans, and would remain so for another two decades, garnering the lion's share of newspaper coverage and growing the stars who might later possibly play in the pros.

The NFL, however, was growing in both independent character and number of teams, as it expanded in 1933 when the Commonwealth of Pennsylvania relaxed its Blue Laws that applied to the Sabbath. That finally enabled professional football to be played on Sundays in the Keystone State, traditionally the breeding ground for great high school and college players, and the birthplace

A Notre Dame All American and eventual Pro Football Hall of Famer, end Wayne Millner was a main target for Sammy Baugh on the Washington Redskins. In the 28–21 defeat of the Chicago Bears for the 1937 NFL title, Millner caught nine passes for 160 yards and two TDs (Collegiate Collection, courtesy Charles G. Lamb).

of pro ball in the 1890s at athletic clubs in and around Pittsburgh. Thus, the pros returned. Joining the league were the Pittsburgh Pirates, owned by racetrack operator Art Rooney, and the Philadelphia Eagles, owned by a syndicate fronted by DeBenneville "Bert" Bell, a future NFL commissioner and the son of a one-time Pennsylvania Attorney General.

With the five-yard restriction lifted for the 1933 season, passing increased throughout the league—even if individual receivers seemed to not make the same strides as the passers. The league leaders in receptions—Shipwreck Kelly of the Brooklyn Dodgers and Roger Grove of Green Bay—grabbed 22 and 17 balls, respectively.

Arnie Herber of the Packers was the only player to throw more than 100 passes in 1932. He threw 101 and completed 37—14 to Johnny Blood and nine to Roger Grove, each of whom scored three times. Teams ran the ball not exclusively, but they usually threw only in spot situations, as a surprise or when they fell behind and needed to play catch-up. The average offense of the eight-team league in 1932 threw a dozen times a game and completed four. In 1932, 1,044 passes were thrown, and 372 completed for 5,300 yards and 42 touchdowns—compared to 3,238 rushes for 10,549 yards and 55 TDs. Despite their potential as a big play or to ignite a scoring spark, passes failed two thirds of the time.

In 1933 with the passing zone being anywhere behind the line of scrimmage, NFL teams completed more than 200 more passes than they did in 1932, with, of course, the addition of the Pennsylvania franchises and the short-lived Cincinnati Reds. Passing made an incremental stride, benefiting offenses more, since the average team threw about two more times a game, 14, and completed, on average, two more passes, six. Whereas passing yardage amounted to a third of the offense in 1932, it represented about two fifths in 1933. The pros completed 576 of 1,631 passes for 8,878 yards and 57 TDs—compared to running totals of 4,118 rushes for 13,792 yards and 69 TDs. The league became accustomed to passing.

The rule changes in 1933 opened the way for the rollout, sprint-out, and bootleg. After the Bears played an exhibition game in Los Angeles, influential syndicated columnist and film star Will Rogers wrote, "I came away raving about it, especially the rules under which they play, where you can pass anywhere, anytime. You college fellows better open up your game for this pro game was just made for an audience."[18]

Eight. The Chicago Bears and the T Formation

With Halas returned to coaching, the Bears won the NFL West Division again in 1933 with a 10–2–1 record. They faced the 11–3 East Division-winning New York Giants at fogged-in Wrigley Field in the first ever pre-scheduled NFL championship game. Bears' end Bill Karr scored two second-half touchdowns to lead a come-from-behind victory, 23–21. Karr's first score came on an eight-yard pass from Bronko Nagurski, and the winner came on a lateral from fellow end Bill Hewitt after Nagurski had hit Hewitt with a 14-yard jump-pass.

The game was much more exciting and unpredictable than most NFL contests. On the final play of the game, the Giants' great end, Red Badgro, caught a pass and had one man to beat, as he planned a similar lateral play to trailing teammates Mel Hein and/or Dale Burnett. But Badgro was tackled by Red Grange, who specifically pinned the receiver's arms to his torso. Badgro has said that Grange's wrap-up prevented him from performing the lateral, and ensured the title for the Bears.

When the going gets tough, the great talents have a tradition of doing what they have to do, as Grange did. Players of the times, and especially on Halas' talent-deep squads, were total football players. The 6-foot-3, 238-pound Nagurski's legendary prowess as literally a bone-breaking ball carrier, superior blocker, and devastating tackler usually hasn't extended to any discussions of all-around athletic finesse. But he was the passer on the crucial plays that won back-to-back NFL titles.

The Bears threw more than any team that year, 212 times, completing 74 for 1,229 yards, 11 TDs, and 29 interceptions—second highest in the NFL after Pittsburgh's preposterously high 40 picks (against 60 completions), which the Pirates matched in 1935. Instead of developing a specialist as a thrower, as the Bears later did with Sid Luckman, and as most teams did after switching to the T formation, Chicago had everyone throwing and everyone catching. Halas' philosophy was always to have plenty in reserve, to deploy a phalanx of complete football players, and have interchangeable backups ready for action. This way, too, the frugal-minded Halas didn't have to pay star-caliber salaries to overachievers.

Eleven players threw the ball for Chicago in 1933, and five of them threw more than 25 passes. Keith Molesworth completed 19 of 50 for 433 yards, four TDs, and four interceptions. Nagurski was the only Bear to complete more than 50 percent, with 14 of 27 for 233 yards. Bill Hewitt led the Bears' receiving corps with 14 balls for 273 yards and two TDs.

Freed up to throw the ball from anywhere behind the line of scrimmage, Bears backs threw 24 TD passes compared to their 20 rushing TDs. Two Bears receivers were among the seven receivers tied for the NFL lead in TD receptions with three—Luke Johnsos, and Bill Karr, the Bears' rookie end from West Virginia University.

The other teams that employed the pass with increasing frequency and efficiency used players of natural aptitude for both throwing and receiving, such as Green Bay with Arnie Herber throwing precision passes to Johnny Blood. In 1933, Herber was joined by two other pro throwers, also tailbacks, also operating mostly out of the single wing or double wing, in throwing more than 100 passes and completing 50 or more: Harry Newman of the New York Giants and Glenn Presnell of the Portsmouth Spartans. Herber completed 50 of 124 for 656 yards and three TDs, along with 12 balls to the opposition. In a subpar 5–7 Packers season, Roger Grove caught 17 passes, Lavvie Dilweg grabbed 13, and Johnny Blood collected eight for a 26.9 average per catch as one of those three-TD leaders.

Newman of the East Division-champ Giants completed 53 of 136 passes for 973 yards, 11 touchdowns, and 17 interceptions. His backfield mates excelled as wingback Dale Burnett caught 12 passes, future Pro Football Hall of Fame end Ray Flaherty caught 11, and fullback Kink Richards added seven. Both Burnett and Richards scored three TDs apiece on receptions, and Richards also tied for the overall TD lead (with Shipwreck Kelly of the Dodgers and Buckets Goldenberg of the Packers) with seven.

The football itself underwent a transformation in 1934. To facilitate passing, the ball was slimmed down. The oval-shaped football that we know today, officially defined as a "prolate spheroid," was reduced from a short axis of between 22 inches and 22 and a half inches to between 21 and a quarter inches and 21 and a half inches. This made it easier to grasp, and easier to throw a spiral. The amount of air that could be pumped into the ball was set at between 12 and a half and 13 and a half pounds. This development followed previous reductions in 1912 and 1929 of the original soccer-like sphere that was used in the late 19th century. The NFL's official ball since the league's 1920 inception was the steerhide-covered Spalding J5-V, called the "Duke"—a boyhood nickname for Giants owner Wellington Mara. The brand name "Duke" was

Eight. The Chicago Bears and the T Formation

sold in 1941 to Wilson Sporting Goods, which manufactured the official ball as the "Duke" until 1969, when the ball's official name became, simply, "NFL."[19]

"The 1934 season was a tumultuous one," historian Tom Bennett wrote. "It ended an era."[20] Until then, football had been essentially a running game. The greats to that time had been runners: Thorpe, Grange, Nagurski, and Nevers.

The Bears went undefeated in 1934 with a 13–0 record. Offense and scoring were on the rise, and it appeared as if the Halas-backed rules adjustments prior to the season helped his club to become the first of four NFL teams in history to complete regular seasons without a loss or a tie (the others were the 1942 Bears at 11–0, 1972 Miami Dolphins at 14–0, and the 2007 New England Patriots at 16–0—with Miami the only one to persevere to an NFL title).

The Bears in 1934 were a completely oiled machine. They outscored opponents 286–86, and their commanding ground game was led by the first 1,000-yard rusher in professional football history, Beattie Feathers. A 5-foot-10, 185-pound halfback from Tennessee, Feathers almost averaged a first down per carry with 8.4 yards every time he took a handoff, often escorted through the line by Nagurski. Feathers gained 1,004 yards on 119 carries and scored eight TDs. Nagurski also enjoyed his finest year, gaining a career-high 586 yards on 123 carries for seven TDs. Feathers and Nagurski were one-two in rushing TDs in the league and Feathers led the NFL with nine total TDs.

With this kind of ground game—halfback Gene Ronzani added 485 yards—there wasn't much call to go to the air, but the Bears did anyway, 192 times (or five off Green Bay's NFL-leading 197 throws), for 955 yards and 16 TDs or only four less than the 20 total they scored on the ground. Bill Hewitt was the only Chicago receiver in double figures with 11, but five of those were for TDs, and that led the NFL. Red Grange was along for the ride in his final season as a backup to Feathers, and the Galloping Ghost caught only two passes, but both of those were for touchdowns.

The Giants won the East Division with an 8–5 record, and were severe underdogs against the mighty undefeated Bears. But a frozen field at the famous Polo Grounds and an enterprising equipment manager were the two great influences in the outcome of another legendary championship contest in NFL lore, the "Sneakers Game," on December 9, 1934.[21] Having been foiled in 1933 by Nagurski, Hewitt, and Karr, the Giants sought revenge. How they got it also owes to another sport and the memories of two players.

A freezing Saturday night rain in New York solidified the icy turf as the temperature plunged to nine degrees Farenheit. By kickoff, the mud was virtual tundra. As both teams skated through a first-half adventure, Ray Flaherty suggested that the team wear basketball shoes. He remembered a 1920s game in which his alma mater, Gonzaga, used basketball shoes on an icy field against the University of Montana. Bill Morgan, a Giants tackle from Oregon, also recalled the ploy aiding the University of Washington.

Abe Cohen, a tailor who was the Giants' equipment manager, improvised. Stores were closed in New York on Sundays, but Cohen had access to the Manhattan College sports equipment room. He borrowed nine pairs of basketball shoes, and hustled back to the Polo Grounds. Laced up by most of the Giants' starters, the basketball shoes provided a better grip onto the ice than did the cleats. The Giants were able to feint and make cuts on the Polo Grounds' impromptu rink and put up 27 points in the fourth quarter. Two of the Giants TDs came on runs of 42 and 11 yards by sneakers-equipped fullback Ken Strong. And end Ike Frankian scored on a 28-yard toss from Ed Danowski. The Bears, meanwhile, continued to fall all over themselves.

"We were helpless," Nagurski said after the Giants prevailed, 30–13.[22] "Helpless" would rarely be a word uttered about the Bears, and almost never about Halas or Nagurski. But in the late 1930s, Chicago's powerhouse, stocked with talent, contended for the title only once, in 1937, as Green Bay again emerged as the most formidable pro club. The Bears managed to win the West Division with a 9–1–1 record in 1937, but they lost to the 8–3 East Division-winning Washington Redskins, 26–21, in the title game.

In their maiden season in the nation's capitol after owner George Preston Marshall had moved the franchise out of Boston because of tepid fan support, the Redskins relied on rookie sensation "Slingin' Sammy" Baugh, who had operated coach Dutch Meyer's "aerial circus" at Texas Christian. He led the NFL by completing 81 of 171 passes for 1,127 yards, and threw for eight TDs. Baugh's main targets were ends

Eight. The Chicago Bears and the T Formation

Charley Malone, who caught 28 passes for 419 yards and four TDs, and Wayne Millner, who gathered 14 balls for 216 yards and two TDs.

With a strengthened passing attack that relied on the accuracy of Arnie Herber's arm and the speed and phenomenal hands of Hutson, the West Division-champion Packers won NFL championships over the 7–5 East-champion Boston Redskins in 1936 by a score of 21–6, and over the 9–1–1 Giants in 1939, 27–0. The Packers went to three title games in that period, losing the 1938 contest to the Giants, 23–17. Curly Lambeau opened up the Packers offense even more than it had been in 1936, when Don Hutson became the first NFL receiver to both catch more than 30 passes in a season and gain more than 500 yards with them—34 catches for 538 yards and eight touchdowns. Hutson led the league with nine total TDs.

Working with him, refining him into the deep threat he became, was Packers tailback Arnie Herber. In 1936, Herber officially became the first passer to throw for more than 1,000 yards in a season. He completed 77 of 173 passes for 1,239 yards, and 11 TDs. Unwittingly at first, Hutson was the definition of the receiving specialist, who then redefined the end position. A speed merchant, he worked on precision routes, providing pro football with a game-breaking, championship luster.

Through 1934, no NFL receiver had been credited with gaining at least 300 yards on receptions in any one season. But in 1935, four receivers logged more than 400 yards: Charley Malone (433 yards) of Boston, Tod Goodwin of the Giants (432), and two Packers: rookie Don Hutson (420), and Johnny Blood (404).

After Hutson elevated his game to championship caliber, he caught passes for more than 500 yards for three straight years, leading the league in TD catches each time. He upped the single-season yardage total to 846 yards in 1939.

CHAPTER NINE

The First Receiving Superstar: Don Hutson of Green Bay

The most amazing big-play artist in pro football's developing decades was also the first man to score 100 touchdowns. Sports writer Peter King has contended from a 21st-century vantage point that a case can be made for Don Hutson qualifying as the best player among all National Football League players throughout history.[1]

Not until Jerry Rice arrived was the same sort of appreciation accorded another receiver. But Hutson was the first such superlative-inspiring game-breaker. Between Hutson and Rice were many electrifying and productive receivers, from Crazy Legs Hirsch to Raymond Berry, Lance Alworth to Lynn Swann, Steve Largent to Terrell Owens. But none were as dominant in their eras as Hutson and Rice were in theirs. The Packers' Buckets Goldenberg characterized Hutson as the "Babe Ruth of football."[2]

Hutson wasn't just a pioneer. He was *the* pioneer, and the greatest practitioner of what he evolved on the field. "Hutson invented modern pass receiving," claims the Pro Football Hall of Fame web site. "He created Z-outs, buttonhooks, hook-and-gos, and a whole catalog of moves and fakes."[3] Philadelphia Eagles coach Greasy Neale, a former end whose teams couldn't stop Hutson, once remarked that the deft Packer was "the only man I ever saw who could feint in three different directions at the same time."[4]

He was an All-American at Alabama in 1934, nicknamed the "Alabama Antelope" for his speed, moves, and spare frame. Speculation was that he was too skinny and slight for pro football, an often used misconception that a hundred successful receivers—from Hutson con-

Nine. The First Receiving Superstar: Don Hutson

temporary Ray McLean to Mark Clayton to Wes Welker—have countered on the field of play. "But it wasn't long before his mere presence on the field had changed the defensive concept of the game," says the Hall of Fame profile. "Don could outmaneuver and outrace virtually every defender in the league."[5] No contemporary receiver came close—in style, technique, statistics, accomplishments, scoring, and winning.

Hutson scored 99 touchdowns on receptions and 102 TDs in all from 1935 through 1945, playing all his 11 seasons with the Packers. Not until the 1960s when running backs Jim Brown and Lenny Moore both scored their 100th TDs was Hutson's pay-dirt mark broken. Not until Steve Largent caught his 100th TD pass—in 1989, his 14th NFL year of mostly 16-game seasons—did a receiver catch 100.

Rice played nine more seasons than Hutson during the years when teams played four or five more games each season than in Hutson's time. Rice's numbers are astronomical in the sense that he played at a magnificent level, and the distance between himself and all other receivers of his era is wide. Still, after the Rice era, Hutson still holds the records for most seasons leading the league in pass receptions (eight), most consecutive seasons in pass receptions (five), most seasons in receiving yards (seven), most consecutive seasons in receiving yards (four), most seasons in receiving touchdowns (nine), most consecutive seasons in pass receiving touchdowns (five), most seasons in scoring (five), and most consecutive seasons in scoring (five).

In 1936, his second year in the league, Hutson became the first player to catch more than 30 passes and gain more than 500 yards in a season. In 1937, he became the first receiver to catch more than 40 balls, and in 1939 he was the first to gain more than 800 yards on receptions. He was the first to catch 50 passes in a season, in 1941, and the first to go over 1,000 yards in receptions the following year.

Hutson played on the Packers' NFL championship teams of 1936, 1939, and 1944. During his career, the Packers finished first in the West Division five times and placed second five times, contending nearly every season with George Halas' tough Bears. In retrospect, one aspect of the Depression-era and wartime editions of this longest-standing rivalry in pro football history was the fact that Halas never did figure out how to defend against Hutson, who burned every club in the league.

"I just concede him two touchdowns a game and hope we can score more," Halas once allowed.[6] The Packers were 9–13–1 against the Bears during Hutson's reign. Those 13 losses figured for nearly half of the Packers' total losses during the same years, when they posted an overall record of 97–29–6. The Packers and Bears met twice each year, and three times in 1941, when they both posted 10–1 records, losing to each other, necessitating the first divisional playoff in NFL history, won by Chicago, 33–14. Overall, Green Bay went to five NFL championship games during Hutson's time and won three.

Hutson retired the year before the Packers installed the T formation, which facilitated the passing game, opening up football to more exciting plays and increased scoring. Had Packers coach Curly Lambeau used Hutson in the T, there's no telling how much greater Don's numbers or Green Bay's success would have been.

Donald Montgomery Hutson was born on January 31, 1913, in Pine Bluff, Arkansas. Jim Benton, whose pro career as a receiver was, like every other receiver in the 1930s and early 1940s, played in the shadow of Hutson, remembers his rival on the schoolboy fields of Arkansas. Benton was a freshman on the same 1930 Fordyce team as senior end Paul "Bear" Bryant. "That 1930 Fordyce team beat Pine Bluff and Don Hutson, 50–12," Benton recalled. "Hutson scored both of Pine Bluff's touchdowns that day and he played the game with a broken hand."[7] Both Hutson and Bryant were recruited by Alabama. Hutson teamed with Crimson Tide thrower Dixie Howell, capping their college careers with a 10–0 record and a 29–13 victory over previous unbeaten Stanford in the 1935 Rose Bowl.

Green Bay coach Curly Lambedau coveted the "Alabama Antelope." But so did Shipwreck Kelly, the player-coach and star receiver of the Brooklyn Dodgers, in the year prior to the first NFL draft. Had it not been for a unique decision by NFL President Joe Carr, Hutson might never have become a landmark pass-catcher. The Alabama star signed contracts with both the pass-minded Packers and the NFL's Dodgers, a team that rarely passed. Carr ruled the contract with the earliest postmark would be honored. The Packers' contract was postmarked 8:30 a.m., 17 minutes earlier than the Dodgers' pact. By such logic, Hutson became a Packer.

Hutson cut down the size of his shoulder pads for the pros and removed his hip pads: "It gave me a little more speed, a little better maneuverability, it gave me a little edge, I believe," he once recalled. "We were always working to invent things to give us a hand up. I worked pretty closely with [eventual Pro Football Hall of Fame tailback] Arnie Herber and Lambeau to develop some new and different pass patterns. A lot of them that we came up with are the same kind of things that are run today by the pro teams.... I was fortunate in having a creative coach like Curly Lambeau, one who really saw the merits of the passing game at a time when just about no one else did."[8]

In his second pro game, against the Bears, Hutson set the tone for his career. "On the first play of the game, I caught a pass for a touchdown, an 83-yard play," he remembered. "They double-teamed Johnny Blood on the play and I got ahead of Beattie Feathers, the Bear defender on the other side of the field, and Herber was right on target with the pass. I caught it somewhere near midfield and ran it in. We beat them 7–0 that day. It was a great start for me, gave me a great deal of confidence. After that I didn't spend a lot of time thinking about other ways to make a living."[9]

Hutson remained relatively free of injury and seemed to only get better, frustrating especially the Bears. Fed up with losing to Packers, Chicago was down, 38–0, in the fourth quarter of their second 1942 Packers game. Embarrassed, the Bears still fought to snap Hutson's TD-catch streak, and triple-teamed him with three great athletes: halfbacks George McAfee, Harry Clarke, and Dante Magnani.

Green Bay tailback Cecil Isabel had thrown three incompletions from the Bears' 20-yard line. "Then came the most incredible premeditated play I ever saw on a football field," wrote Pat Livingston of *The Pittsburgh Press*. "Lining up as a flanker, harassed by three Bears, the cagy old Alabaman ran a simple post pattern, diagonally in on the twin-poled uprights, Bears convoying him, stride by stride. As the four men raced under the bar, Hutson hooked his elbow around the upright, stopped abruptly, flung his body sharply left, and left the red-faced Bears scrambling around in their cleats. He stood alone in the end zone as he casually gathered [Cecil] Isabel's throw to his chest."[10]

Hutson explained his own favorite game to Dick Whittingham: "The game I remember most, however, was against Detroit in 1945. We set a bunch of records that day. I caught four touchdown passes and kicked five extra points in one quarter alone. As a team, we scored 41 points in that quarter. We ended up winning the game, 57–21. It all happened because of the winds. I remember vividly how it was blowing straight down the field, like maybe thirty or thirty-five miles an hour. It was all a matter of judging the ball in the air and we were much better at it that day than the Lions."

"With the wind with us, we'd throw these long passes and I was able to get down there under them," Huston went on. "I think their defensive backs didn't think the ball would travel as far as it did. And sometimes, when we were throwing into the wind, I'd have to circle back, like I was going for a lazy fly ball as I did when I played center field. There was never another game quite like that, at least one that I played in."[11] Detroit coach Gus Dorais said the game could be summed up in three words, "Too much Hutson."[12]

Historian Matthew Algeo recounted Hutson slamming his hand in a taxicab door days before the Packers' final 1943 game with that year's wartime combination of the Philadelphia Eagles and Pittsburgh Steelers, dubbed the Phil-Pitt "Steagles." Phil-Pitt's co-coach, Greasy Neale, "knew a one-handed Don Hutson was still more dangerous than most two-handed receivers in the league," Algeo wrote.[13] With a splint on his index finger, Hutson one-handed a 24-yard touchdown pass from Irv Comp in the closing minutes to insure a 38–28 Green Bay victory. Hutson grabbed six passes for 56 yards and two TDs, plus kicked a field goal and five extra points—20 total to lead the league in scoring that year with 117 total points.

At the close of his career, Hutson totaled 488 receptions for 7,991 yards, and 99 TDs. That sort of scoring frequency is unheard of in any era of pro football: Every fifth time he caught a pass, he scored a touchdown. He led the NFL for five years straight in scoring, from 1940 through 1944, as he kicked PATs and field goals. He held 18 NFL records when he retired after the 1945 season, and was among the 17 members of the inaugural class of 1963 inducted into the newly constructed Pro Football Hall of Fame in Canton, Ohio. When Hutson's record of 17 TD catches in a year (tied in 1951 by Crazy Legs Hirsch) was broken after 42 years, by Miami's Mark Clayton in 1984, the Dolphins' quarterback, Dan Marino, completed more passes, 362, than the entire Packers' team attempted, 330, in 1942.

"[Hutson] was also a great defensive back, too," Buckets Goldenberg

Nine. The First Receiving Superstar: Don Hutson

remembered. "They never threw in his area. He was a sure, tough tackler."[14] Hutson led the NFL in interceptions in 1940 with six (tied with Ace Parker of Brooklyn and Kent Ryan of Detroit), and picked off seven in 1942 (one behind league leader Bulldog Turner of Chicago with eight), and eight in 1943 (three off Sammy Baugh's league-leading 11).

"The individual skills were not as refined as they are today," recalled Giants owner Wellington Mara in the modern era. "[But] some were, like those of Don Hutson. But still he had to play defense, even though his specialty was that of being a great pass receiver, probably as great as any receiver we have in that game today, who only has to concentrate on catching footballs. Hutson wasn't able to hang up the statistics the receivers have today, because he had to make tackles on defense as well."[15]

"I kept announcing that I was going to retire from football and devote my entire time to my business interests," Hutson said. "But I kept coming back, until 1945 anyway. It was damn near impossible for me to quit football in Green Bay. You know what the Packers meant to the town and I'd been having some good years. I got the feeling they wanted me to play forever. But the time had come. Before the 1945 season, I told Curly I'd play that year only if he promised not to ask me to play again the next year. He said all right, and he was good to his word. And that was it."[16]

For years after that, the Alabama Antelope contented himself with family life and a car dealership in Racine, Wisconsin. He retired to Rancho Mirage, California, and died in 1997 at the age of 84.

Chapter Ten

Monsters of the Midway

Chicago Bears owner George Halas led the campaign to open up pro football's aerial game in the early 1930s by successfully advocating the lifting of restrictions on passing, even if that meant supplying possibilities for end Don Hutson of the Bears' archrival Green Bay Packers to flourish as an innovator against him. Hutson's great pass-catching abilities changed ideas about the effectiveness of aerial strikes on a unique and spectacular scale.

Green Bay and the league in general warmed to the pass, but still from the single wing. After the Bears proved that the T formation was as effective for quick running plays as it was for pass plays, the league transformation to the T followed. During the Bears' NFL-wide dominance of four championships in the 1940s, the T became fully recognized as the best all-around formation for offensive football, period.

As it was refined in the Bears' camp by Halas and coaches Ralph Jones in the early 1930s and Clark Shaughnessy later that decade, the T formation relied on speed, timing, quickness, deception, and top athletes. It was much less reliant on the brawn of the earlier eras, which had emphasized power running as the manifest basis of the game itself. The T in the hands of Bears quarterback Sid Luckman and an array of talented receivers—Ken Kavanaugh, George Wilson, Ray McLean, George McAfee, and Harry Clarke among them—secured the four titles via men in motion, backfield shifts, and slashing runs off play-action fakes.

The Bears clearly were pro football's marquee franchise up to and through the 1940s. Iconic owner and on-again-off-again head coach Halas established the team's winning tradition in the NFL's formative roaring twenties, strengthening the club with top players through the Great Depression and into the World War II era. The NFL itself, still a minor operation compared to Major League Baseball, scrambled for success and a bigger fan base, even as its star players required offseason jobs to compensate for their low football salaries.

The tenacious Halas did all he could to enhance the team—on the field, financially, and with the fans. The club capitalized on the moniker "Monsters of the Midway" during the war. This was actually the appropriation of the local college team's notoriety. The University of Chicago Maroons had been known as the "Monsters of the Midway" way before the Bears glommed onto the nickname. "Midway" actually references the Midway Plaisance, a lawn bordering the southern end of the University of Chicago campus on the city's South Side between 59th and 60th Streets—or 12 miles from the Bears' home turf of Wrigley Field.

The fact that the great World War II air-sea Battle of Midway coincided with the Bears' dominance in the early 1940s also was referenced by the media (and led to Chicago Municipal Airport being renamed Midway International Airport). Midway, in Chicago terms, never had anything to do with the city's Midwestern geographical situation as the stopover point between coasts. Never one to give up an advantage, Halas borrowed more from the university than the fearsome label. He also took away head coach Clark Shaughnessy along with the coach's innovative T formation playbook, and even co-opted the red "C" on the sides of the Maroons' helmets when the college decided to give up football after the 1939 season.

The Bears won NFL Championships in 1940, 1941, 1943, and 1946—before, during, and after the United States intervened in World War II (1941–1945). The Bears posted a record of 81–28–3 in the decade and made it to the championship game five times. Even as Halas spent a stint in the Navy and many key stars were lost to wartime service, the Bears didn't lose their winning ways. In discussions of dynasties that usually fixate on the Super Bowl era, the Bears of the 1940s often get short shrift. Moreover, this rough and physically overpowering team rarely receives recognition as the great innovative offensive team that it became.

More than any dynasty before or since, the Bears of the 1940s transformed the game of football itself. They did this by installing and refining the age-old T formation and launching a passing attack from it that became the basic blueprint for offenses from the war years up until today. Concurrently, in the more popular college game, Clark Shaughnessy, the same innovator who conspired with Halas to run the T in

Chicago, overhauled the hapless Stanford Indians into an undefeated and Rose Bowl-winning 1940 season by installing the T. By 1943, Frank Leahy had moved from coaching Boston College to his alma mater, Notre Dame, and committed the blasphemy of phasing out the formation named for the South Bend institution, the Notre Dame Box, then wrote a book in 1949 entitled *Notre Dame Football—The T Formation*.[1] Green Bay installed the T the year after Hutson retired, and Greasy Neale's Philadelphia Eagles adapted to it, winning NFL titles in 1948 and 1949 with a superbly balanced offense. *Football Digest* estimated that, by the early 1950s, 250 of the major 350 college teams in the nation used the T. The last pro team to adopt the T, the Pittsburgh Steelers, did so for the 1953 season.[2]

As a league founder and one of its more influential rules committee members whose ideas helped evolve the sport into the modern game that we know, George Halas, quite literally, personified the old guard in pro sports. He turned 44 in 1939, and by then had spent nearly half of his life not only in the league, but nurturing, advancing, and literally personifying the league. He had played end for the Bears until 1928, and not only was schooled in the responsibilities and potentialities of that position, but he evolved the curriculum, too, on the fields of Canton, Akron, Pottsville, Frankford, Providence, and elsewhere.

After the Chicago Bears retooled the T formation, all levels of football followed. When Frank Leahy became coach of Notre Dame in the 1940s, he installed the T formation as the basis of his offense and posted six undefeated seasons and five national championships in 11 years (Collegiate Collection, courtesy Charles G. Lamb).

Ten. Monsters of the Midway

As both a sporting gentleman dedicated to the game and as a shrewd businessman, Halas had always been on the lookout for ways to improve the professional game and make it more exciting. Also, like the other coaches in the NFL, Halas had been at a loss twice a year as to how to contain the mercurial Hutson of Green Bay. The Bears' secondary was consistently being beat by the archrival Packers, no matter who won the game, most of the time by Hutson. So, Halas perceived that there might be a way of exploiting the aerial attack more. Two men helped convince him that this was the case: Clark Shaughnessy and Sid Luckman.

Shaughnessy refined the old T formation playbook as coach of the cross-town University of Chicago. Shaughnessy and Halas resumed Ralph Jones' investigation of the T as early as 1935, and the college coach went on the Bears payroll as an assistant. Shaughnessy brought his college quarterback, Solly Sherman, with him. Sherman had run the T for the university, and he became Shaughnessy's on-field eyes and ears as the Bears' backup QB to the second man to influence Halas to install the T—the one hand-picked to command it on the field: Luckman.

"With Sid we created a new type of football player—the T quarterback," Halas said. "Newspapers switched their attention from the star runner to the quarterback. Colleges used Luckman as their model in molding quarterbacks. In Sid's 12 years with the Bears, football completely revolutionized."[3]

If any one player can be seen as the link between the leather-helmeted, grind-it-out days of pro football's formative years and the postwar era of facemasks and athletic new stars, it would be Luckman. Sammy Baugh threw a prettier spiral. Don Hutson became the archetype of the precision receiver. Steve Van Buren, Marion Motley, and Joe "The Jet" Perry were the power rushers who transcended the three-yards-and-a-cloud-of-dust tradition into the era of offensive specialists and televised sports.

But more than any player, Luckman personified success. As the leader of the 1940s Chicago Bears, he was the archetype of the dynasty quarterback, the antecedent of Otto Graham, Bart Starr, Terry Bradshaw, and Joe Montana. He fronted for Halas' well-stocked arsenal, and used it judiciously and dominantly, establishing the basic offense that all levels of football would use through to the present generation.

The Bears sought to bring Luckman to Chicago even before his Ivy League exploits. Halas was aware of Luckman's stardom at Erasmus High School in Brooklyn. At Columbia, Luckman completed 180 of 367 passes for 2,413 yards and 20 touchdowns. He was an Associated Press backup All American in 1937 and 1938, and finished third in the latter campaign's Heisman Trophy voting behind quarterback Davey O'Brien of Texas Christian University and halfback Marshall Goldberg of Pittsburgh. Luckman had starred as a single-wing tailback for the Lions, and was a versatile and shifty runner who also passed, kicked, punted, and played defensive back.

Halas and Shaughnessy correctly envisioned Luckman as just the athlete to run their T formation. To safeguard against Luckman going somewhere else, Halas conspired with Art Rooney, owner of the Pittsburgh football Pirates, to make sure that Luckman ended up a Bear. Halas sent end Edgar "Eggs" Manske, a Northwestern product from Nekoosa, Wisconsin, to the Pirates (which were renamed the Steelers two years later) in exchange for the second pick overall in the first round of the NFL draft, specifically with the intention of selecting Luckman. On the first round, the Chicago Cardinals chose center Ki Aldrich of Texas Christian University, leaving Luckman for the Bears.

Halas and Rooney's back-room wheeling and dealing determined Luckman's fate. Both owners were horse traders of note, Rooney literally. He came to own several racetracks and dealt in gaming and thoroughbreds. He was also a political back-scratcher from Pittsburgh's Northside. Rooney felt it best to be on a chummy basis with his fellow owners and to bolster the league's fortunes, a mission that was also unflagging in Halas' dealings. Rooney did this even at the expense of his own mediocre team. His son, Dan Rooney, later ran the Steelers on a businesslike and less cavalier basis.

Halas' debt to Rooney was paid up front, during 1938, or before the draft for the following season, held on December 9, 1938, the week after the regular season ended. Manske started four of the six games he played in for Pittsburgh and caught nine balls for 113 yards and a TD. He then returned back to the Midwest, where he hauled in 10 passes in six games for Chicago for 197 yards and TD. His 19 total receptions for 310 yards were good for sixth place in the NFL in both categories. The payback was Sid Luckman.

Ten. Monsters of the Midway

"Better yet to Halas' way of thinking," wrote Jeff Davis, "Manske was only on loan to Rooney, who returned him to Chicago once the season was underway so nobody would complain that Halas had rigged the draft."[4] The pawn was no insignificant figure. Eggs Manske led the Philadelphia Eagles in scoring in 1935, and was one of the several players to occasionally be cited as the last to play without a helmet (in the 73–0 championship game in 1940). He went on to coach at Holy Cross, Boston University, and Maryland before being inducted into the College Football Hall of Fame for his three stellar years as a player at Northwestern. Eggs even made it onto a Wheaties box in 1936 in a seeming contradiction in breakfast philosophy for cereal giant General Mills. But in retrospect, Eggs Manske's enduring significance may be in his half-season of odd-man-out status in the arming of the first great passing offense of modern football.

Luckman didn't intend to play pro ball. This was in the era when NFL players earned salaries commensurate with, or less than, the average working man. But he was intrigued by the T formation. His plans to work for his wife Estelle's family's trucking company evaporated after Halas arranged to have dinner with Sid and Estelle in their New York apartment. After the meal, the coach turned on the Papa Bear charm, which was supplemented by a $5,500 contract for the 1939 season. Luckman signed on the spot, bringing superior athletic skills, intelligence, quiet authority, alacrity for the game, and his namesake luck to the Windy City, where he became a mainstay for nearly a generation. Halas previously had wooed Red Grange into a nationally famous barnstorming tour with the Bears in 1928 that earned the great University of Illinois All American halfback more than $100,000 through the shrewdness of his agent, C.C. "Cash & Carry" Pyle.

With the contract, Halas dispensed a glop of honey remembered by both gentlemen. "You and Jesus Christ are the only two people I would ever pay this to," Halas told Sid, a Jewish descendent. Aware of the coach's overextended moxey, Luckman replied, "Thank you, coach. You put me in great company."[5]

Luckman's initiation into the T had its experimental phase in his rookie season of 1939. He initially had trouble with quick handoffs, forcing Halas to abandon the T for a few games, and reinstalling the single wing with Bernie Masterson at the helm and Luckman at tailback. But on November 5, with the Bears at 4–3—on the verge of a so-so season—and deep into the fourth quarter of a characteristic slugfest with Green Bay, Halas put Luckman back in at QB to run the T formation. Sid threw the winning touchdown pass in a 30–27 victory, and Chicago went on to win its final four games.

"It didn't take long to realize that the whole T formation system was based on split-second timing," Luckman wrote at the end of his career. "When it failed, you saw a mob of puzzled athletes running harem-scarum. That's why this system demanded closer concentration than any other."[6]

With Luckman back at the helm, Chicago posted a strong 8–3 season, but lost the West Division title to the Packers, who went 9–2, splitting their Chicago encounters. Nevertheless, the Bears became the first pro team to pile up more than 4,000 yards in total offense. Experimental year or not, whether he started at quarterback in the T or tailback in the single wing, Luckman gave the Bears a fresh edge. Nearly half of those 4,008 yards in total offense, 1,965, came through the air as Halas deployed an interchangeable group of receivers.

End Dick Plasman led the Bears with 19 grabs for 403 yards and tied teammates Bob MacLeod, a halfback, and left end Les McDonald with three receiving TDs. The 5-foot-11, 190-pound Luckman threw nearly a quarter of the team's passes. He completed 24 of 51 attempts for five touchdowns and four interceptions.

The following year brought confirmation and the payoff for all of those years of experimentation with the T formation—in terms of total offense, running and passing the football. In 1940 the Bears jumped out to a 7–1 West Division lead, sustained back-to-back loses to the Detroit Lions and Washington Redskins, and finished 8–3. That was good enough to win the division as Green Bay fell to 6–4–1. Luckman started most of the season, completing 49 of 105 passes for four TDs. The Bears completed the second-fewest number of passes in the league, 68, but were spearheaded by the best running offense in pro football. In 1940, the Bears led the NFL in rushing (1,818 yards), carries (494), and rushing touchdowns (16), deploying a six-man committee in Halas' platoon T-formation backfield. Halfbacks Ray Nolting and Joe Maniaci averaged 4.8 and 4.4 yards per carry, respectively.

In 1940, the Bears used the T to spread defenses across the field and send fleet runners into the holes between linemen. The line's job became not necessarily creating holes in this scheme, but detaining their defensive opponents long enough for the quick ball carriers to slide past them. And with the run working as strongly as it did, the need for the pass was reduced. The pass still was not viewed as an interchangeable offensive asset with the run, and considered a resort. If the run was clicking, there was no need to put the ball in the air and risk an interception. Ken Kavanaugh led the Bears with 12 catches for 276 yards and three touchdowns.

The 1940 NFL championship game is legendary in football lore, and was all the more notable for being the first title game heard coast-to-coast on network radio as the Mutual Broadcasting System carried it to 120 stations via the voice of Red Barber, bringing the dominant Monsters of the Midway into living rooms across America. The Bears rampaged through the most lopsided title game in NFL history and in pro sports history when they whipped the 9–2 East Conference champion Redskins, 73–0. The Bears owned the field from the get-go, as fullback Bill Osmanski ripped off a 68-yard run for a TD on the second play from scrimmage. By halftime, the Bears led 28–0.

The Bears' defense was helped by the fact that Washington was forced to play hurry-up to catch up. With Baugh, the Redskins were certainly equipped for a quick turnaround. However, the Bears scored three TDs on interception returns of Baugh passes—all in the third quarter. Baugh threw a championship-game-record eight interceptions. Three Bears TDs were tacked on in the fourth quarter, two on runs by Harry Clarke. A scribe asked Baugh if a dropped pass in the end zone by one of his receivers very early in the game was crucial to the outcome. Baugh stared a moment. "Hell, yes," he said, "the score would've been 73–6."[7]

"The Bears did not score all their points with plays from the T," wrote Stanley Woodward, the esteemed sports editor of the *New York Herald-Tribune* and one of the premiere gridiron analysts of the day. "In fact, so wholeheartedly did the men of George Halas convert Washington passes into touchdowns that there was some question whether they were more dangerous when they had the ball or when Washington had it. But the T formation rolled up more points than are customary in big league football, and the conclusion that must be drawn is that hundreds, perhaps thousands, of football teams will be using it next fall. They will substitute quick openings, speed, head feints, and indirect handling for the ponderous and generally slow-moving line-interference plays which have been popular in the last twenty years."

"The great Halas has been fooling around with the T formation for years, but he never has given such a vivid demonstration of the virulence which may be forthcoming from it as he did today.... He is a second-growth pioneer into realms which other football men have abandoned as fruitless, and he apparently is on the verge of starting a stampede back to first principles," Woodward wrote.[8]

To Woodward's first principles were added speed and more speed, and an aerial attack. The following year, for the first time in NFL history, a team threw for more than 2,000 yards—2,002 to be exact, by, of course, the Bears. The installation of the T by Chicago and its spreading of oppositions' defenses opened up the Bears' potent running and passing games in 1941. What became known as a balanced attack—as much yardage produced by passing as running—was established as the Bears broke their own total offense record by rolling up 4,158 yards. With Luckman in firm grasp of the offense, the Bears cruised to a 10–1 season, winning by large margins and losing only a 16–14 midseason grudge match to Green Bay. As he had with his running backs, Halas platooned a variety of receivers, and four of them collected between 11 and 14 receptions: ends Dick Plasman, Bob Nowaskey, and Ken Kavanaugh, and rookie halfback Duke Gallarneau.

It rained TDs in the Windy City. Future Pro Football Hall of Famer George McAfee, a second-year halfback out of Duke, led the NFL in touchdowns with 12 (tying Don Hutson of the Packers), scoring five on runs, three on receptions, and one each on returns of a kickoff, punt, interception, and blocked punt. Very few players would ever again show that sort of ball-hawking versatility in one season. Placing second on the league's TD list was Gallarneau with 11. His eight rushing TDs led the NFL. Kavanaugh placed second in the league to Hutson in receiving TDs with six. He defied the odds by scoring on most of his 11 receptions (for 28.5 yards per catch). Luckman started all 11 games for the first time, and completed 57.1 percent of his throws.

The Bears and Curly Lambeau's Packers both closed the year at 10–1, each having lost their only games to the other, necessitating the first pre-championship playoff game in NFL history. The battle of the Midwestern titans in Chicago didn't live up to its billing as the Bears dominated the contest, leading at halftime, 30–7. They cruised to a 33–14 victory. Green Bay's future Pro Football Hall of Fame fullback Clarke Hinkle initiated the scoring on a one-yard plunge in the first quarter, but the Bears settled down with a ball-control offense, fronted by their two rookie backfield mates from Stanford: The shifty Gallarneau scored on an 81-yard punt return, and fullback Norm Standlee scored on runs of three and two yards in the second quarter.

The victory set up the NFL championship game with the East Division winner, the 8–3 New York Giants, who were determined not to provide the Bears with an anticlimactic finish to a dominant season.

Running out of the single wing, the Steve Owen-coached Giants relied on tailback Alphonse "Tuffy" Leemans to both run and throw. But after putting up a strong front for a field goal-trading half in which Chicago led, 9–6, the Giants gave ground. Standlee powered into the end zone twice in the third quarter, from two and then seven yards out. McAfee ran five yards for a fourth-quarter TD and Kavanaugh added another by picking up a fumble and racing 42 yards for the tally. The final score was 37–9. Luckman completed nine of 12 passes for 160 yards, including several big gainers: a 48-yarder to Dick Plasman, one of 42 to McAfee, 34 to Standlee, and 26 to John Seigal.

In 1942, the Bears posted their second undefeated regular season, going 11–0. The team scored more than 40 points five times, and its closest games were 21–7 victories over the Cleveland Rams and the crosstown Chicago Cardinals. The Bears again led the league in rushing with 1,881 yards, and they placed second to the Packers in passing yards. Green Bay gained 2,407 yards through the air—more than half of it (1,211) by throwing to Don Hutson—compared to the Bears' 1,974. While Green Bay didn't switch to the T until 1947, after Hutson retired, the greatest receiver of his time enjoyed his greatest year, catching 74 balls for an unheard-of 17 touchdowns. Because most of the Bears' games were foregone conclusions, and Luckman wasn't needed for the durations, the Bears' backup QB in Halas' platoon system, Charlie O'Rourke, threw for almost as many yards (951) as Luckman (1,024).

If anyone could be called Luckman's main downfield target in his early years, it was Ray McLean, who placed second in the league in 1942 in five statistical categories to Hutson. In an era when individual statistics had less meaning than they do today, "Scooter Ray" McLean's minor fortune was to have had such an outstanding year during Luckman's ascendency to greatness, and the speedy receiver's minor misfortune to have been so outstanding during the most astronomical season of Hutson's illustrious career—actually one of the greatest single seasons of any player at his position in NFL history (see the Hutson chapter). McLean in 1942 was second in the league in receiving yards (571), receiving yards per game (51.9), receiving TDs (eight), total TDs (nine), and scoring (54 points).

A deep threat who had played at Saint Anselm College in New Hampshire, McLean amassed 2,232 yards on 103 career receptions for 21 touchdowns (and 30 TDs in all) from 1940 to 1947, including the longest pass play of 1944, an 86-yarder against the Boston Yanks. At 5-foot-10 and 168 pounds and nicknamed both "Rabbit" and "Scooter Ray," McLean was ultra-light, even for that era, and relied on speed and deception to get open. McLean returned punts for touchdowns in each of his first three years in Chicago, and later became a trivia answer as the Packers head coach who vacated Green Bay in 1958 to make way for Vince Lombardi.

As fate would have it, the Bears' second perfect regular season was spoiled by a 14–6 loss in the championship game to the avenging Redskins. Washington did not switch to the T until the training camp prior to the 1945 season, when the Redskins hired former Halas assistant and then University of Pittsburgh head coach Clark Shaughnessy to initiate Sammy Baugh in the intricacies of the formation. Baugh was yet a tailback out of the single wing, but his and Washington's offense that day was enough to outscore the vaunted Bears. He threw a 38-yard TD strike to Wilbur Moore in the second quarter, and Andy Farkas ran for the other Redskin tally in the third stanza. But both clubs' staunch defense was the story beyond the upset, as Washington intercepted three passes, one by Baugh, to Chicago's two picks. The Bears' only score was a 50-yard fumble return by tackle Lee Artoe (the kick failed). The Bears' minor bright spot was a four-reception day by McLean. Luckman completed five passes for two yards and was dropped twice behind the line of scrimmage.

Luckman experienced one of his worst Sunday afternoons in one of the Bears' biggest games. Yet, he and the team and offensive football

Ten. Monsters of the Midway

were on the verge of bigger and better things. As if in consonance with the war effort, which was beginning to be waged around the globe with new armaments in bold style on a spectacular scale, the Bears and the T went on to greater glories.

CHAPTER ELEVEN

The Pivotal 1943 Season and After

The turning point in terms of spectacular results for the T formation for the Bears and for football offenses in general occurred in 1943, when Sid Luckman became the first quarterback to throw as many as 28 touchdown passes in a season, and the first to throw seven TD passes in one game. This occurred against the Giants, and is a mark that was matched five times and surpassed only by Peyton Manning in 2013. Chicago's aerial attack out of the T in 1943—when many NFL stars and starters were lost to the armed forces—led to an 8-1-1 Bears regular season and another showdown with NFL East winner Washington (6-3-1).

"That season did it," sportswriter Peter King assessed from 1999 perspective. "After 20 years of domination by the run, the name of the game was passing, and the quarterback was the main man. From the 1940s onward, in the pros and in college ... the T formation held sway, and it befuddled defenses. Defenders couldn't load up against the run anymore. They had to respect the pass. And so was born the modern chess match of offensive coordinator-versus-defensive coordinator that we see every week in the NFL."[1]

While the Bears broke pro records, the college world also gradually adopted the T beyond the impressive 1940 seasons mounted by Stanford and Minnesota. The entire football world shifted, so to speak. In 1943, Notre Dame went 9-1, with Angelo Bertelli at quarterback in the T formation, a role inherited on the Fighting Irish through the mid-1940s by future Bears QB Johnny Lujack, after Bertelli enlisted in the Marine Corps. But while teams at all levels were adapting to the T, the Bears perfected it.[2]

The Bears' transformation into a passing team with Luckman at the T's helm was hastened by the war, which claimed the services of many star players across the league, but which especially decimated Chicago's backfield. Fullbacks Bill Osmanski and Norm Standlee, and halfbacks George McAfee and Harry Clarke, each one of whom had ended at least one season as one of the NFL's top five rushers, were all gone for three seasons. This reduction of backfield players was a factor in Bronko Nagurski's return to fullback in 1943. Halas himself rejoined the Navy (he had been the Most Valuable Player in the 1919 Rose Bowl as the star on the Great Lakes Naval Training Center team, which beat coach Hugo Bezdek's Mare Island Marine Corps team, 17–0).

Filling in as co-head coaches of the Bears from 1942 through 1945 were two former Chicago players, Luke Johnsos and Hunk Anderson. Johnsos had been an end who led the NFL in receiving touchdowns (three) in 1933, and Anderson was a lineman in the 1920s. But even as Johnsos and Anderson were upgraded, Papa Bear was a phone call away, stationed in Norman, Oklahoma, but occasionally returning to the Great Lakes Naval Training Center on Lake Michigan at North Chicago, Illinois.

Halas' pioneering tradition of spelling his starters, keeping them fresh, accounted for the wide number of skill-position players to excel on the Bears. His team and players put up big numbers for the era, especially in 1943, and racked up touchdowns. Luckman sprayed the ball in all directions, short and long, to ends and backs. "No passer will deny that without a set of able receivers his efforts will be in vain—passes can fall short of the mark or sail futilely over someone's head," Luckman wrote. "Outside of Hutson of Green Bay, few receivers have won any sort of rightful acclaim in this business. Newspapers have made a tin god of the passer for years. The T formation on this score hasn't helped matters much. It is built on many parts, many receivers, many styles. It is really less spectacular than others, as a passing medium, because of all this deception mixed in with a single maneuver. The T doesn't let a lone receiver stand out, as Green Bay's attack did for Hutson."[3]

When Luckman piled up the 28 TD throws, nine receivers scored and seven of them logged at least two touchdowns. George Wilson and Hampton Pool caught five TD passes apiece, and Scooter Ray McLean caught 18 balls for 435 yards and two TDs. But Harry Clarke turned out to be the go-to receiver.

That year, Clarke, a 186-pound halfback out of West Virginia, made his last season on the Bears his career year, becoming the first back in pro history to rush for more than 500 yards and catch passes for more than 500 yards in a single season—23 passes for 535 yards and seven TDs. The NFL's second-leading scorer with 10 touchdowns, he was also its third-leading rusher (556 yards on 120 carries) and third-leading receiver in terms of yardage gained. Clarke posted a league-leading 1,091 yards from scrimmage and was a first-team Associated Press and United Press All-Pro selection. Clarke entered the service after the season for the duration of the war. He returned to football as a spot starter for three years in the All America Football Conference, playing for the Los Angeles Dons and Chicago Rockets.

Despite the fact that the 1943 season was reduced because of the war, from 11 games to 10, Luckman averaged nearly three TD passes a game. He threw three TDs in each victory over Detroit. He tossed three in the win over the season's wartime combination of the Philadelphia Eagles and Pittsburgh Steelers—the Phil-Pitt "Steagles." Luckman threw six against the Chicago Cardinals in two victories (two in the first crosstown contest and four in the season finale), two versus the Brooklyn Dodgers, and two in each game against Green Bay.

"The T system did not begin and end with the forward pass," Luckman wrote in his 1949 autobiography, "but things sure were leaning that way around 1943, when ground battles became so scarce that, as one coach quipped, 'We'll soon let our plunging fullbacks carry the water buckets.'"[4]

As sharp as he was all year in 1943, Luckman's best game also was the worst defeat ever suffered by the New York Giants. In a 56–7 shellacking of coach Steve Owen's club on November 14, 1943, at the Polo Grounds, Luckman set six NFL records. As if paying appropriate homage to the fans who turned out to celebrate the former Columbia University star's return to New York on "Sid Luckman Day," the namesake of those 24 hours turned it into an all-time quarterbacking day. The former All American completed 23 of 30 passes for 453 yards (breaking Cecil Isabel's record by 33 yards), and a record seven touchdowns (breaking Sammy Baugh's mark of six).

(The seven TDs established a record that was tied by Adrian Burk of the Philadelphia Eagles in 1954, George Blanda of the Houston Oilers

Eleven. The Pivotal 1943 Season and After

in 1961, Y.A. Tittle of the Giants in 1962, and Joe Kapp of the Minnesota Vikings in 1969. Peyton Manning's record-breaking eight TD passes in 2013 was for the Denver Broncos.)

Luckman was even-handed about spreading the ball around against the Giants, tossing no more than two scoring strikes in any one quarter or to any one receiver. Luckman hurled TD passes of 40 and 27 yards to Hampton Pool, 15 and four yards to Jim Benton, 62 yards to Harry Clarke, 31 yards to Connie Mack Berry, and three yards to George Wilson.

After his fifth TD throw, Luckman was pulled from the game in third quarter. But the Sid Luckman Day crowd chanted, "We want Luckman! We want Luckman!" and an informed soul pulled coach Luke Johnsos aside and told him that one more scoring toss by Luckman would tie Sammy Baugh's record. The Redskins' thrower set the mark two weeks previously against the Brooklyn Dodgers. Johnsos conferred with his co-coach, Hunk Anderson, and they put Luckman back in the contest on the next offensive series. The Bears proceeded down the field like clockwork and the drive ended with the short TD toss to Wilson. The crowd gave Luckman a standing ovation, then cheered when he returned for the next series, which was capped when Hampton Pool leaped between defenders to snare a 40-yard Luckman bomb in the end zone. Pool stood amid the ovation for Luckman, which lasted several minutes, then placed the ball gently on the ground.

"As a Columbia undergraduate and since he joined the Bears to make them what they seem today—one of the greatest if not the greatest aggregation in football history—Sid has had many a field day, but none to compare with yesterday," assessed *The New York Times*. "His was passing artistry of a kind probably never before witnessed on any gridiron, and although his wizardry sent the Giants down to depths they never had explored, the fans gave the black-haired star a tremendous ovation when he trotted from the field after chucking his final toss to Hampton Pool a trifle more than five minutes before the game ended."[5] In the *New York Post*, Leonard Cohen wrote that the game was "one of the highlights of our twenty-five years of attendance at football contests."[6] Luckman owned the Polo Grounds that day. "It just happened to be one of those days that come to a player once in a lifetime," the QB said.[7]

The Bears had one more bit of business to attend to in 1943. They had finished the season 8–1–1 and won the West Division outright while the Redskins and the Giants topped the East with identical 6–3–1 records, necessitating a playoff. The Redskins blanked New York, 28–0, as Andy Farkas scored three touchdowns on short runs, and Baugh lived up to his billing as one of the most versatile athletes of his time, completing 16 of 21 passes for 199 yards and a touchdown, intercepting two Giants aerials, and averaging more than 40 yards a punt.

Luckman and Baugh suffered comparisons to one another as the predominant passers of their era. They were often compared in a manner similar to 1960s quarterbacks Johnny Unitas and Bart Starr: The Colts' Unitas was the superior talent, but the Packers' Starr was usually the champion. Baugh was used to leading more than the Redskins. This great all-around talent led the NFL in 1943 in passing percentage (55.6), completions (133), passes (239), interceptions as a defender (11), punts (50), and punting yards (2,295). In the record books, the bolded numbers of Baugh's individual league-leading exploits across 16 seasons jump at the reader the way the those of Babe Ruth and Walter Johnson do from the baseball record.

Luckman, however, led the league in passing yards (2,194) in 1943 as well as TDs. But his crowning achievement was avenging the 14–6 loss sustained at the hands of the Redskins in the previous year's championship. It's as if the two great quarterbacks switched awful afternoons: Luckman's bad 1942 luck was visited upon Baugh on December 16, 1943, at Wrigley Field. Baugh suffered a concussion early in the first quarter trying to tackle, of all people, Luckman. "Slingin' Sammy" was replaced by George Carfego, while the Bears built a three-TD lead by the third quarter. Luckman had hit Harry Clarke with a screen pass that was good for a 31-yard score, and connected on TD strikes of 36 and 66 yards to Dante Magnani. Bronko Nagurski rumbled in from the three for another tally.

Baugh returned for the second half, but the damage had been done. Jim Benton and Clarke caught Luckman TD passes in the fourth quarter to seal the deal. The Bears racked up their third NFL championship in four years, 41–21. Luckman's dominance of the contest extended to a defensive role that rivaled Baugh's signature style: Luckman intercepted three passes. He completed 15 of 26 passes for 286 yards and a playoff-record five TDs. He also ran eight times for 64 yards to lead all rushers

Eleven. The Pivotal 1943 Season and After

on the day. He considered the game his farewell to football as he joined the Merchant Marine in January 1944 for the war effort, never considering that he had a gridiron game left in him—let alone seven more seasons with the Bears.

Serving aboard an oil tanker in the North Atlantic for nearly two years, Luckman received allowances to play in seven Bears games in 1944 and all but one in the autumn after the August 1945 treaty with Japan ended the Second World War. He led the NFL in passing yardage and touchdown tosses in both 1945 (1,727 yards and 14 TDs) and 1946 (1,826 and 17), the year in which he also led Chicago to their fourth and final NFL title in the1940s.

In 1946, the Bears went 8-2-1 in the West Division, earning the right to face one of the two teams they lost to all year, the 7-3-1 East Division-winning Giants, in the NFL championship game. That year, Chicago's receivers slightly out-gained their rushers, 1,950 yards through the air to 1,719 on the ground. In true Halas-team fashion, seven receivers caught passes numbering in the teens, led by Ken Kavanaugh with 18 catches for 337 yards and five TDs. Ray McLean caught 17 for 348 yards and two TDs; rookie Jim Keane had 14, 331 yards, and three TDs; Dante Magnani, 14, 156 yards, and a TD, and Duke Gallerneau, 12, 185 yards, and a TD.

Controversy surrounded the 1946 title game as Giants fullback Merle Hapes was bribed by gamblers to throw the game. Knowledge of the bribe was shared by quarterback Frankie Filchock. Neither player reported the unseemly approach to the NFL, a violation of league rules. Hapes was suspended for the game, but Filchock was allowed to play. The Bears got off to a quick start as Luckman threw touchdown passes in the first quarter of 21 yards to end Ken Kavanaugh and 19 yards to Dante Magnani, and Chicago dominated the rest of the game, winning, 24-14.

The NFL added a game to the regular season in 1947, and that 12th contest helped the Bears to become the first team in pro history to roll up 5,000 yards from scrimmage, 5,052 to be exact. Most of that, 3,093 yards, was through the air. That also established a new league record. However, Chicago's 8-4 record was only good for also-ran status. Just as the most dominant run team of pro football history, the 8-4 Detroit Lions of 1936, didn't win the division, so, too, the most dominant passing team, the 8–4 Bears of 1947, didn't win the division. That won-lost record was one off the other Chicago team's 9–3 mark. The Cardinals came into their own in 1947, and won their lone NFL title. The Bears lost their first two games, won eight in a row, and lost the final two. The season-closer pitted both 8–3 Chicago teams against each other for bragging rights and the chance to play in the NFL championship game.

That particular contest was anticlimactic for Midwestern football fans. The fact that the two squads with the biggest shoulders in the City with Big Shoulders were clashing for the NFL West title was a singular fascination. After all, the Cards had been the "other" pro team in Chicago, the continual also-rans, the Second City's second-class citizens, football-wise. The Cards had only won one NFL championship to that point, the still controversial 11–2–1 season of 1925 (when the 10–2 Pottsville Maroons beat them in the final game, claiming the NFL title). The notion that coach Jimmy Conzelman's Cards might knock Halas' great Bears—the greatest pro team of all time—off their perch, held immense drama for any season's final game. The Cardinals marquee players formed the "Dream Backfield" of quarterback Paul Christman and interchangeable backs Marshall Goldberg, Charley Trippi, and Pat Harder, supplemented by Elmer Angsman, who replaced the injured Goldberg (who returned that year on defense only).

In the first quarter, it was bombs-away. Cardinals quarterback Paul Christman hit halfback Babe Dimancheff with an 80-yard TD bomb in the first quarter, reciprocated by Sid Luckman's 81-yard hurl to Ken Kavanaugh for a TD. The Bears, however, turned the ball over too many times, throwing four interceptions and losing two fumbles with the Cards' one interception thrown and one fumble lost. The Cards continually had great field position, and Angsman ran for two TDs while deep threat Mal Kutner gathered in a 33-yard Christman pass for another.

The Cards led, 27–7, at halftime. Luckman's backup, Nick Sacrinty, threw two 44-yard TD passes to Jim Keane in the fourth quarter, but it was too little too late as the Cardinals prevailed, 30–21. Keane's admirable work—seven receptions for 161 yards and two TDs—went for naught. The Cards won not only the West Division, but defeated coach Greasy Neale's Philadelphia Eagles, 28–21, for the NFL Championship.

Luckman enjoyed his personal best year in 1947, in which he threw nearly 100 more passes than he had in any other season, 323, and completed 176 for a 54.5 completion percentage, 2,712 yards, and 24 TDs. He was bested in each category by the mercurial Baugh, but both watched as Christman led the Cardinals to the NFL Championship. Luckman's two main receivers all year long were Jim Keane, who led the league in receptions with 64, and the durable Ken Kavanuagh, who led the league with 13 TD catches. Keane gained 916 yards on those 64 grabs, and scored 10 touchdowns. Keane and Kavanaugh were the only two receivers in the NFL in 1947 with TDs in double figures. In Luckman's last year as the starter, almost all of his 24 TD flings went to these two tall targets.

A 6-foot-4, 217-pound 18th-round draft choice out of Northwestern, Keane had arrived for the 1946 championship and played for the Bears through 1951 before ending his career in Green Bay in 1952. He was a classic overachiever who played mostly as a spot starter, and yet he led the league. He amassed 224 career catches for 3,222 yards and 24 TDs in seven seasons.

Kavanaugh and George Wilson were the two longest-serving members of the Luckman era's receiving corps. Kavanaugh's career was split by the war, and he played on the 1940, 1941, and 1946 title teams, scoring a TD in each championship game. Kavanaugh enjoyed his best years after he won the Distinguished Flying Cross as a heavy-bomber pilot during the war, leading the NFL in touchdown receptions in 1947 and 1949 with nine (tied with Hugh Taylor of Washington and Tom Fears of the Rams). At 6-foot-3 and 207 pounds, Kavanaugh was one of the first tall targets of the increased-passing era of the 1940s, and was a favorite go-to receiver for both Luckman and Lujack—although not enough for the subject himself. He complained then and later that Luckman never threw enough to him. His 13 TDs in 1947 came on only 32 catches (for 818 yards and 25.6 yards a catch). Of course, he was playing on the Bears, a team that platooned players more than any other in the era, based on Halas' philosophy of resting stars during games.

Drafted by Halas out of Louisiana State on the third round in 1940 on the recommendation of Clark Shaughnessy, All American end Kavanaugh wasn't considering pro football for the future as he fulfilled his childhood dream growing up in Little Rock, Arkansas, to play professional baseball. He played first base for the St. Louis Cardinals' farm club in Houston in the East Texas League. Signed by Branch Rickey to a $300-a-month contract, Kavanaugh ignored Halas' calls, then told the Bears coach he required $300 a game to play football.

After starting with a $50-a-game offer, the frugal Halas eventually agreed to the demand. Kavanugh went to Chicago, and came back, too, after the war, setting records. He retired as Chicago's all-time leading receiver with 162 receptions for 3,626 yards and 50 touchdowns. The most remarkable thing about these numbers is that nearly a third of his catches resulted in TDs. His 22.4 yards per catch for many years was second on the all-time career list to the Oakland Raiders' Warren Wells' 23.1.

The baseball-loving boy stayed in football the rest of his life. He coached the Bears receivers, then those at Boston College and Villanova. In 1955 he joined the staff of New York Giants coach Jim Lee Howell—a group that included Vince Lombardi and player-coach Tom Landry. With these coaches in charge, Howell once said, all he did was pump air into the balls—even though the Giants won the NFL title in 1956. After 15 years as a Giants coach, Kavanaugh became a scout and was influential in securing the services of several important receivers, including Mark Bavaro. Kavanaugh died in Sarasota, Florida, in 2007 at age 90.

Wilson was the most consistent receiver through the Bears' dynasty. He played for Halas from 1937 through 1946 and caught 111 career passes for 1,342 yards, and 15 TDs. A native Chicagoan who had been a fullback at Northwestern, Wilson was the player who most exemplified Halas' own style of play at end during the coach's rough-and-tumble 1920s. A powerful blocker at 6-foot-1 and 199 pounds, Wilson unwittingly was the precursor of the tight end in the T formation. In the 73–0 game, the first score came on the second play from scrimmage, a 68-yard run around left end by Bill Osmanski. Faced with both Redskins safeties as he entered the secondary, Osmanski was surprised when they were wiped out like bowling pins, one kicking out the other. Wilson had circled around from his right end position and cleared the way, creating a moment that has been memorialized in that corner of the universe where great blocking is savored. Halas, who had witnessed perhaps more football than anyone, said, "That was the greatest, most vicious block I ever saw."[8]

Wilson continued his winning ways as a rookie head coach. When Buddy Parker resigned in a huff as head coach of the Detroit Lions before

Eleven. The Pivotal 1943 Season and After

the 1957 regular season, his assistant, Wilson, stepped in to lead the team to the NFL title via an 8–4 season and a 59–14 whipping of the Cleveland Browns in the championship game. His leading receiver that year was the tough Jim Doran, a very George Wilson–like end, who pulled in 33 passes for 624 yards and five TDs. Wilson also was the first head coach of the first expansion team in the American Football League, building the 1966 Miami Dolphins from castoffs and draft choices. Wilson's coaching record was 68–84–8. He died in Chicago in 1978.

Luckman started at quarterback from 1939 through 1948, and was first-team All Pro in 1941, 1942, 1943, 1944, and 1947. He led the league three times in passing yards and three times in passing TDs in a decade when quarterbacks on other teams were also adopting the T formation and passing more and more, including Sammy Baugh in Washington, Cecil Isabel in Green Bay, Bob Waterfield for the Cleveland Rams, and Frankie Filchock for the Giants. Halas felt the need to keep his T formation offense hot, so he stockpiled QBs toward the end of Luckman's career. By the time Luckman retired after the 1950 season, he had been replaced as the starter by Johnny Lujack, who had won the 1947 Heisman Trophy at Notre Dame, and was joined on the Bears sidelines by two future Pro Football Hall of Famers: Bobby Layne out of Texas in 1948, and George Blanda from Kentucky in 1949.

By the time the 1940s Bears had played out their run, pass blocking was only beginning to be perfected. "Pass-blocking wasn't organized," Luckman said. "You didn't have a guy in the press box phoning down adjustments. You were expected to dodge one or two guys rushing you."[9] There weren't any "pocket" diagrams until Paul Brown took his professorial coaching style into the All American Football Conference after World War II and created blocking schemes for pass patterns. Pass blocking until Brown's scientific approach in the late 1940s amounted to not letting the guy in front of you get past you. This had been enough—practical and sound information for any lineman or blocking back. These players were to buy time for the quarterback to get off the pass that had been called.

The real Monsters of the Midway were not just exceptional blockers. Five of them are on the short list of greatest linemen to ever play professional football. Without them, of course, the T would not have been so successful. The future Pro Football Hall of Fame inductees on

Chicago's offensive line in the 1940s were led by center Clyde "Bulldog" Turner, and included 270-pound guard George Musso, and tackles Danny Fortmann, Joe Stydahar, and George Connor. Guard Ray Bray played throughout the run and tackles Lee Artoe and Fred Davis were multiple-years starters.

The other NFL teams watched as Luckman and the Bears used the T formation to pass to championship success. Each team integrated the T and phased out the single wing with the exception of the Steelers, who were the very last single-wing offense to make the playoffs, in 1947. (The Steelers and Eagles tied for the East crown with 8-4 records and the Eagles won the playoff game, 21-0.) Quarterbacks emerged molded in the Luckman tradition, throwing out of the T formation, bootlegging, rolling out, throwing on the run, becoming the cereal-box figures of the 1950s—Norm Van Brocklin in Los Angeles, Bobby Layne in Detroit, Otto Graham in Cleveland, Y.A. Tittle in San Francisco, Charlie Conerly in New York, and eventually Johnny Unitas in Baltimore.

By 1945, two teams using the newly installed T formation other than the Bears would play for the NFL championship as the Cleveland Rams edged the Washington Redskins, 15-14. By the end of the decade, Earle "Greasy" Neale had installed the T in Philadelphia and his Eagles won back-to-back championships in 1948 and 1949, led by the completion combo of Tommy Thompson to Pete Pihos, complementing the rugged rushing of Steve Van Buren and Bosh Pritchard.

"I had seen George Halas beat the Washington Redskins 73-0 with the T in the title playoff in 1940," Neale once recalled. "I decided that I would scrap the single and double wing I had used in my collegiate and professional coaching if I could just get the full details of how Halas was using the T." As recounted in a 1964 *Sports Illustrated* story by Gerald Holland, Neale said he bumped into a Fox Movietone cameraman at the Parisien Restaurant in New York City. "I said, 'I marvel at the way you fellows seem to catch the outstanding plays of every game in the few minutes you show on the screen. How are you able to do that?' The fellow said, 'Oh, we film the entire game and select the important plays from the complete footage.' I almost choked on my rye whiskey—this was before I swore off—and I said after a minute, 'Would you by any chance have the entire footage of that Bears-Redskins game?' The fellow said, yes certainly he did."

Eleven. The Pivotal 1943 Season and After

He went on: "I said, 'Could I buy it?' I was beginning to shake all over. You must remember this was before the days when teams began exchanging the game films. Well, to cut it short, I bought that film for $156, and I believe I ran it three, four, five hours a day for three months in the apartment of Lex Thompson, the Eagles' owner, until I had it down pat. I made some alterations, of course, gave it some outside running strength. It was the T, adapted to our horses, that won us three divisional titles and our two NFL championships."[10]

One development that helped receivers in spacing their routes and using the sideline to their advantage was the decision for the 1945 season to move the hash marks five yards further toward the middle of the field on each side. That might not seem like a big difference. But for precision route runners operating in the seams, it was a boon. Against defenses that weren't as sophisticated as they became even five years later, the larger operating space against the sidelines gave shifty and enterprising receivers an edge.[11]

It helped the Cleveland Rams' Jim Benton perform in the greatest game in terms of yardage by one receiver up to that time. In a crucial, late-season contest against the Detroit Lions at Briggs Stadium, Benton caught 10 passes from Bob Waterfield for 303 yards, including a 70-yard TD catch in the second quarter. The win propelled the Rams to a 28–21 victory and the West Division title.

At 6-foot-3 and 200 pounds, Benton was one of the more underrated receivers of the era, playing as he did—and they all did—in the shadow of Don Hutson. Benton led the NFL in receiving yards in both Cleveland's championship year of 1945 with 1,067, and in Los Angeles in 1946 with 981. In the 1945 championship game, Benton caught nine passes for 125 yards and a TD. His 63 catches in 1946 was also the league high. Benton retired after the 1947 season with 288 career receptions for 4,801 yards, and 48 touchdowns.

Because of the war, the Cleveland Rams suspended operations in 1943 and many of the players went with one of the eight competing NFL clubs. That was the year Pittsburgh and Philadelphia combined forces as a wartime measure into the Phil-Pitt "Steagles." Benton was selected by the eventual NFL Champion Chicago Bears. It was the only season in which he wasn't a Ram. That year, he contributed 13 catches for 235 yards and three TDs in the Halas platoon system. Benton extolled former

Bears end and co-head coach Luke Johnsos' coaching moxey. "Luke was a really smart offensive coach and he was responsible for a lot of our success that year," Benton said.[12] After that single season, Benton was back in Cleveland and back as an NFL champion in two years.

Benton preferred to praise his quarterback when asked about his uncanny pass-catching talents against the sidelines. "Bob [Waterfield] can put them anywhere with handles on them," Benton once said. "Whatever I did to get open at the last second, when I do, there comes the ball right when I need it."[13]

Benton's single-game yardage mark stood until 1985, when Stephone Paige of the Kansas City Chiefs caught eight passes for 309 yards and two TDs versus the San Diego Chargers. The only other receiver in NFL history to gain more than 300 yards in a game was Flipper Anderson of the Los Angeles Rams, who caught 15 balls for 336 yards and a TD in a 1989 game against the New Orleans Saints.

Quarterbacks such as Luckman, Waterfield, and Van Brocklin were changing the game. The position's ball-handling and field-general status made them into natural leaders, spokesmen, and team stars. But the receivers, too, were significant in the strategy and the glory. Because of Halas' platoon system on the Bears, and his tendency to stockpile skill-position players, no one receiver emerged as an all-time star in the 1940s, even though Ken Kavanaugh made a significant impact. And Kavanaugh never would have been the player that he became if it wasn't for Clark Shaughnessy, who urged Halas to draft and sign him.

CHAPTER TWELVE

Clark Shaughnessy and Offensive Firepower

Clark Shaughnessy might be called the prototype professorial football coach, a forerunner to Paul Brown, Bud Wilkinson, Don Coryell, Chuck Noll, Bill Walsh, Mike Martz, and others whose gridiron command came with a distinctly intellectual approach. His playbook was sacrosanct. And George Halas guarded it as much as anyone. Despite Shaughnessy's miserable records as coach of the University of Chicago Maroons in the 1930s, cross-town counterpart Halas held him in high esteem.

Football analysts occasionally point to various assistant coaches through the years as worthy of the Pro Football Hall of Fame solely for their outstanding performances in their supporting roles—no matter what else they did as a player or head coach. Defensive coordinators Buddy Ryan with Mike Ditka's 1980s Bears and Dick LeBeau of later Pittsburgh Steelers teams have often been cited (and LeBeau was enshrined in the hall as a player in 2010—he snared 62 interceptions during a 14-year career with the Detroit Lions). But Shaughnessy begs comparison to no one. After his years as the guru of the T formation, he spent his last and longest-lasting job in pro ball, as defensive coordinator of the Bears from 1951 to 1962, designing ways to thwart the offense that he strove to perfect.

Born in St. Cloud, Minnesota, in 1892, Shaughnessy preceded Bronko Nagurski by a little more than a decade as fullback (as well as tackle and end) for the University of Minnesota. He assisted coach Henry L. Williams there for a year and moved to Tulane as head coach, posting a 57–28–7 record over 11 seasons. During seven seasons at Loyola of the South, Shaughnessy compiled a 48–18–5 record. After accepting the daunting task of replacing college coaching legend Amos Alonzo Stagg at the University of Chicago, Shaughnessy posted a subpar record there of 18–33–4.

Shaughnessy was an eccentric Mr. Clean, a nondrinking Irishman who detested imbibers and a nonsmoker who hated tobacco users. He sometimes retired before sundown and rose at 3 a.m. Longtime University of Illinois coach Bob Zuppke once cracked, "The world lost the greatest undertaker when Clark Shaughnessy decided on football coaching."[1] Richie Petitbon, who was coached in the Bears' defensive backfield by Shaughnessy in the 1960s, gave the coach latitude for his imperious reputation. "He could be sharp-tongued, abrupt, and impatient," Petitbon told Len Pasquarelli. "But I feel like a lot of people who think on a higher level in any [endeavor] are like that."[2]

Shaughnessy's play calls were occasionally extremely complex. "From these formulas," wrote historian Michael MacCambridge about one of his defensive package calls, "came a blinding array of blitz, pass rush, and secondary coverage calls that could be as simple As 'Green Tornado,' or as complicated as 'Brown Stash Mutt Purple Jack Shuffle Right Wheel Left.'"[3] But his abrasiveness was repellent to some. Independent, thorny, and authoritative, Shaughnessy had a way of clashing with other figures of authority, including, not unexpectedly, George Halas. But whereas Halas coexisted with him to get the best out of him—to the point where he re-hired Shaughnessy in the 1950s to devise defenses to thwart the T—others in command came to loggerheads with him, including the administrations of colleges where he coached—at Tulane, Chicago, and Pittsburgh.

When his 1925 Tulane team went 9–0–1 and received an invitation to the Rose Bowl, the university administration turned the offer down. Two reasons have traveled through history for the declinature: the bowl game would take students away from their studies, and Tulane's players were too small. Disgusted by Tulane's declination of football's then greatest honor, a Rose Bowl bid, Shaughnessy coached the Green Wave one more year and moved on to Loyola of the South in New Orleans, then to Chicago.

Inheriting the University of Chicago team in 1933 from Stagg, Shaughnessy provided very mixed results. He coached the versatile halfback Jay Berwanger to the very first Heisman Trophy win, in 1935. But developing a winning attitude or even a few wins at Chicago proved to be difficult. For someone dubbed an offensive genius, Shaughnessy had a deceptive way of demonstrating that. His miserable teams in the late 1930s made it easy for the university president, Dr. Robert Maynard Hutchins, the esteemed educational theorist who had been dean of the Yale Law School, to act decisively. "I did not de-emphasize football at the University of Chicago," Hutchins said. "I abolished it."[4]

Shaughnessy's 1937 squad scored in three games. His final team before football was killed off at the university for good, the 1939 edition, had beaten Wabash and Oberlin, but lost to Michigan, Ohio State, Illinois, Virginia, Harvard, and Beloit, a small Wisconsin college near the Illinois state line, by a combined score of 306–0. This sort of showing in any level of organized sports has sent coaches into complete oblivion. Hutchins mercilessly pulled the plug on football at the university, but Halas stayed with Shaughnessy on the Bears, using him to groom Sid Luckman into the T system that same year. Halas referred to Shaughnessy as "The greatest play designer in the game."[5]

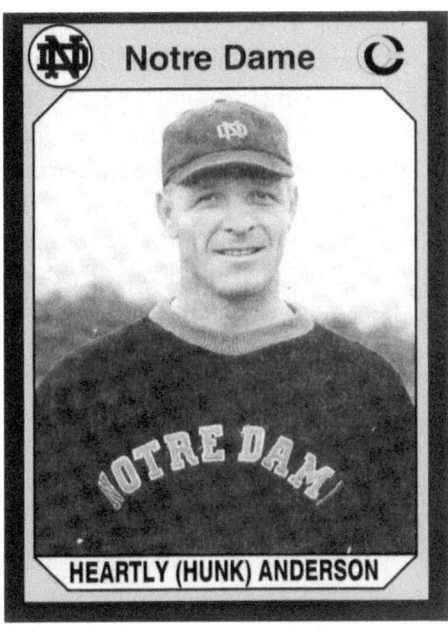

Not everyone was pleased with Shaughnessy or Halas' opinion of him. Heartley "Hunk" Anderson, a Notre Dame alumnus who played guard on the Halas-coached Bears of the 1920s, and became a longtime Bears coaching assistant, treated Shaughnessy as a glorified hanger-on. "Shaughnessy had a plagiaristic streak," Anderson wrote in his 1976 autobiography. "Plays that Luke [Johnsos] or Paddy [Driscoll] came up with, or something on which I had changed some blocking, would come back to us diagrammed and credited as Shaughnessy's creation."[6]

Heartley "Hunk" Anderson, a lineman from Notre Dame who played for the Chicago Bears and Cleveland Bulldogs, also co-coached the Bears from 1942 to 1945. He was among the football cognoscenti who didn't share Bears owner George Halas's high opinion of Clark Shaughnessy (Collegiate Collection, courtesy Charles G. Lamb).

Even as Shaughnessy kept in touch with Halas and Luckman through the 1940s, he moved on become one of the great phoenix-like stories in American coaching annals. Few college head football coaches have risen as quickly from the abject ash pile as triumphantly as did Clark Shaughnessy. The year after he embarrassed the University of Chicago completely out of the football business, Shaughnessy was hired as head coach at Stanford. Based on his most recent showing with the Maroons, the sagacity, slide rules, and common sense at Palo Alto suddenly seemed on hiatus.

"The hiring of Clark Shaughnessy as football coach at Stanford for the 1940 season struck most alumni, fans and critics at large as an act of folly comparable to employing an arsonist as fire chief," wrote Ron Fimrite in *Sports Illustrated* in 1977.[7] Instead, Shaughnessy installed the T formation, and a Stanford team that had won one game in 1939, went 10–0 during the regular season and defeated Nebraska, 21–13, in the Rose Bowl. Even though the Associated Press poll placed Stanford at No. 2 behind Minnesota, the Indians were No. 1 to their fans and poll critics. They were quarterbacked by Frankie Albert, an irrepressible rover on and off the field and a dexterous pivot-man not unlike Luckman, who could play-action fake with the best of them. Albert and the Indians became immortalized on the college football landscape as the "Wow Boys." While Albert would later play quarterback for the San Francisco 49ers in both the All American Conference and the NFL, half the Stanford backfield was transferred over to Halas and Luckman on Shaughnessy's advice.

Norm Standlee, one of the biggest fullbacks of his day at 6-foot-2 and 238 pounds, was drafted out of Stanford on the second round in 1941 by Chicago. He immediately became one of the NFL's top ground gainers with 414 yards on 81 carries for a 5.1 average and five touchdowns. Joining Standlee and Luckman in the Bears' backfield for the 1941 championship campaign was Standlee's Indians running-mate, halfback Hugh "Duke" Gallarneau, who was selected by Halas two rounds after Standlee. Gallarneau became a Bears mainstay and also contributed immediately to the 1941 champs with an NFL-high eight rushing TDs.

Shaughnessy left Stanford after two years, because the university announced that it was discontinuing football because of the war. He became head coach at the University of Maryland in 1942, when the Ter-

Twelve. Clark Shaughnessy and Offensive Firepower

rapins went 7–2, and in 1946, when they were 3–6. These seasons were split by three losing years (10–17 overall) at the University of Pittsburgh. The committee on athletics at Pitt intended to rehire Shaughnessy for the 1946 season if he relinquished his relationship with the Washington Redskins. George Preston Marshall had hired him to coach Sammy Baugh in the intricacies of the T formation, and Shaughnessy had split his time between Pittsburgh and Washington. The coach wouldn't agree to the condition and walked away. An Associated Press writer joked that the man who refined the man in motion had become "football's man in motion" himself, never landing anywhere long enough to build a team.[8]

The result of Shaughnessy's commuter relationship with Baugh was phenomenal. For the first time in NFL history, a starting quarterback completed more than 70 percent of his passes. In 1945, Baugh, fully adapted to Shaughnessy's T, completed 70.3 percent of his throws in leading coach Dudley DeGroot's 8-2 Redskins to the East Division crown. The Redskins lost a 15–14 heartbreaker in the title game to the 10-1 West Division-winning Cleveland Rams. Baugh also led NFL passers in completions (128), completions per game (16), yards per game (208.6), interception percentage (2.2), and passer rating (109.9). Six receivers for "Slingin' Sammy" caught more than 10 passes, but his go-to guy was Notre Dame alumnus and halfback Steve Bagarus, who caught 34 passes for 617 yards and five touchdowns.

"I switched from a single wing tailback to a T formation quarterback in 1944 and that was the most difficult thing that I had to do in my football career," Baugh told historian Richard Whittingham. "It was tough for the whole team. No one had ever played it before. Mr. Marshall got Clark Shaughnessy to put it in for us. He'd put it in for a lot of ballclubs: the Bears, who were the first to use it, and I think he also got Green Bay ... to using it. Well, we just had no experience at all with it and everybody was confused. After about a year or so we got it down pretty good. The hardest parts were the simple things, like just taking the ball from the center, turning and faking to one man, and then giving it to another. You had to have such precision working out of the T. You had to learn different steps, fakes, moves. Hell, I remember talking to Sid Luckman one time and he told me when he switched over to the T with the Bears he darn near cried it was so damn frustrating. But he sure learned it, and, of course, became one of the great ones at it."

"Actually, the T was good for me," Baugh said. "I'd played about ten or eleven years of single wing ball, counting college, and I figured I only could go maybe another year or two as a tailback. Hell, I was getting beat up and hurt all the time, and my shoulders and knees were getting beat up pretty bad by that time. Never had a broken bone, but I was hurt a lot. But with the T formation, I didn't take such a beating and that enabled me to play another seven or eight years."[9]

After his last Maryland season, Shaughnessy coached the Los Angeles Rams for two extremely significant years, launching the most potent offense that the NFL had yet seen. His Rams went 6–5–1 for a third-place finish in 1948. In 1949, the Rams posted an 8–2–2 record and won the West Division by exploiting a loaded passing offense with two future Hall of Fame quarterbacks in Bob Waterfield and rookie Norm Van Brocklin and a pair of future Hall of Fame receivers in Elroy "Crazy Legs" Hirsch and Tom Fears. The latter set an NFL record that year with 77 receptions.

Shaughnessy exploited the talents of his two gifted throwers in a premeditated and prototype example of the modern quarterback controversy. Waterfield had been the NFL's Most Valuable Player in his rookie year, 1945, leading the Cleveland Rams to the NFL championship, and had led league passers in five statistical categories in various years as the avowed team leader after it arrived on the West Coast.

But Shaughnessy was never fazed by the human issues, and his appreciation of his stars had nothing to do with the joys of winning. "I used Waterfield to test the defenses and set things up for the big play," he said. "Then I'd put the kid [Van Brocklin] in and with that great arm he'd throw the bomb and get all that applause. But Bob was a real pro. He didn't care for the situation, but he helped make it work. He was a real pro. He didn't depend on cheers for his satisfaction."[10]

Coaches are not often fired after such success, but Shaughnessy, being Shaughnessy, developed a personality clash with Rams owner Dan Reeves. Offensive genius or no offensive genius, Shaugnessy was replaced for the new decade by Joe Stydahar, an assistant coach and former outstanding Bears tackle who was eventually destined for the Pro Football Hall of Fame.

As a parting shot, Shaughnessy allowed that he could coach any high school team for a year and stack it against a Stydahar team. While

Twelve. Clark Shaughnessy and Offensive Firepower

Shaughnessy momentarily was out of football, Stydahar's Rams made it to the NFL championship game without tripping over a schoolboy squad. The Rams lost the ultimate struggle, 30–28, to the 10–2 Eastern Conference-champion Cleveland Browns in the Browns' maiden NFL year. The loss was particularly heartbreaking, coming as it did on a 16-yard field goal by Lou "The Toe" Groza with 28 seconds left in the game after quarterback Otto Graham had engineered a classic come-from-behind drive in the final two minutes.

The 1950 Rams and Bears had tied at 9–3 at the top of the NFL's Western Conference, necessitating a playoff game. L.A. won that playoff, 24–14, for the privilege of meeting the Browns, relying on TD receptions of 43, 68, and 27 yards by the dominant Fears, who amassed 198 receiving yards. Along the way that year, Stydahar found nothing really broken, and true to the rule, fixed nothing. He ran the version of the T that Shaughnessy had installed. Stydahar did, however, make one crucial adjustment. He put Hirsch at flanker full-time.

The Rams set 22 offensive records, including 38.8 points per game, a mark that still stands—466 points in a 12-game season. The all-time bests up to that time also include 3,709 yards through the air as Van Brocklin led the league in passing. Fears broke his own reception record with 84 balls, good for 1,116 yards and seven TDs. Both Hirsch and back Glenn Davis, the 1946 Heisman Trophy winner while at Army, caught 42 passes apiece. Van Brocklin's 54.5 completion percentage was only bested in the NFL by his backup, Bob Waterfield, with 57.3. Fullback Bob Hoerner scored 10 TDs, one less than Johnny Lujack's league-leading 11 for the Bears.

The following year, the Rams were 8–4 under Stydahar, captured the Western Conference, and finally won their championship, a 24–17 victory over the 11–1 Eastern Conference-champion Browns. L.A.'s winning touchdown came on a 73-yard, fourth-quarter bomb from Van Brocklin to Fears in the first pro football game to be televised coast-to-coast, on the DuMont Network. Despite superbly talented teams in later years, the Rams never brought another championship home to Los Angeles. It wasn't until after the team moved to St. Louis that the Rams again won it all, defeating the Tennessee Titans, 23–14, in Super Bowl XXXIV.

Of all the receivers to have flourished under Shaughnessy, Fears and, by extension, Hirsch have remained the most notable, Hall of Famers who built their reputations out of the master's T, carrying on as league stars long after the coach returned to Chicago. Fears and Hirsch were the stars of what the press deemed the "Three End Offense," referring to the fact that one halfback, usually Hirsch, was more often than not split wide as a flanker. The third receiver in the Rams' postwar troika was Bob Shaw in 1949, and Verda "Vitamin" Smith and/or Bob Boyd in the early and mid-1950s. In 1953, Boyd's 22.8 yards per catch led the NFL. His career year was 1954 as he caught 53 passes for a league-leading 1,212 yards and six TDs.

Fears, quite literally, was invented as an NFL star by Shaughnessy. As a defensive back in the first game of 1948, his rookie year, Fears intercepted two passes and returned one for a TD in a 44–7 rout of the Detroit Lions. Shaughnessy understood that the 6-foot-2, 215-pound Fears wasn't the fastest of players, but he had tenacity and a nose for the ball. The coach's intuition was nudged by Fears' ball-hawking ability, and he switched the defender to offensive left end for the very next game. Shaughnessy had Fears line up a distance from the left tackle, and the player became the first consistently "split" end, nomenclature that came into the NFL language to describe him and copycats. Fears instantaneously became the league's second great receiving star—after Don Hutson. Along with counterpart Hirsch, and their prickly delivery boy, "The Dutchman," as the driven and vocal Van Brocklin was known, Fears reigned as a major NFL figure during the postwar boom in American sports.

Red Hickey, one of Shaughnessy's assistants on the Rams who had played end with the Steelers and Rams and later coached the 49ers, once said that Fears was "as quick as a cat despite his size, and he has a great pair of hands," but also allowed that there was something else that made him great. "It's his insane desire to win,"[11] Hickey said. Fears, like Hutson, ran precise routes. Without great speed, he was often well covered by defensive backs, but Van Brocklin and Waterfield knew that Fears would usually outfight defenders for the ball. Fears became known for wresting balls away that appeared to be sure interceptions or at least batted-away incompletions. A defensive specialist through college, Fears played split end with the sensibility and physicality of a ball-hawking linebacker.

Born in Guadalajara, Mexico, to an American mining engineer and

Twelve. Clark Shaughnessy and Offensive Firepower

his Mexican wife, Fears attended Manual Arts High School in Los Angeles, playing football there before attending Santa Clara University. He spent the war years in the service and belatedly became an Air Force pilot, specifically with the intent to fight in the Pacific Theater after his father was captured by the Japanese. Instead, the Air Force kept him at Colorado Springs, playing ball in a wartime service league. Fears was drafted on the 11th round by the 1945 NFL Champion Cleveland Rams on the eve of their move to Los Angeles for the 1946 season.

Fears decided to stay in school and transferred to UCLA, where he played two more seasons, earning honors as an All American end before joining the cross-town pros as a 25-year-old rookie. He enjoyed the Bruins' perks, and was cleared with teammates in a potential sugar-daddy scandal over their work in advertisements for a Los Angeles clothing store. Fears joked that when he did sign with Rams for $6,000 a year and a $500 bonus, he was taking a pay cut.

When Shaughnessy put Fears on offense, he was trying to plug the hole left by Rams longtime star Jim Benton, who had played end from 1938 through 1947 (except for 1943). As fine a receiver as Benton was in the years in which the NFL was adjusting to the T formation, Fears became the first postwar poster boy of the receiving business. He led the league in receptions in 1948 (51), 1949 (77), and 1950 (84), and in receiving TDs in 1949 (nine) and yards in 1950 (1,116).

In a 51–14 victory over Green Bay in December 1950, Fears caught 18 passes, a record that stood for half a century (or until Terrell Owens caught 20 in a 2000 game for the 49ers against the Bears). Fears played through the 1956 season and retired as the league's all-time leading receiver with an even 400 catches. He also amassed 5,397 yards and 39 TDs in his nine seasons, all with the Rams.

Fears became an assistant coach under Vince Lombardi in Green Bay in 1959 and from 1962 to 1965. He was also on the coaching staffs of the Rams and Atlanta Falcons before his appointment as the first head coach of the expansion New Orleans Saints in 1967, a post he stayed in until 1970, when he was fired. The Saints' most outstanding player during the Fears era was wide receiver Danny Abramowicz, who led the league in receptions in 1969 with 73. Fears also was offensive coordinator of the Philadelphia Eagles in 1971 and 1972, head coach of the Southern California Sun of the World Football League in 1974 and 1975, and an executive for the Los Angeles Express of the United States Football League from 1983 to 1985. One of the first Mexican American athletes to become a star of national stature, Fears was inducted into the Pro Football Hall of Fame in 1970, and the College Football Hall of Fame in 1976.

Teammates Fears and Hirsch brought out the best in each other and were essential members of the greatest offense the NFL had yet seen. The Rams' 1951 edition rolled up even more yards than the previous year's team—5,506 in total offense, setting a new NFL mark. The offense became more balanced as the so-called "Bull Elephant" backfield battered defenses for a remarkable 5.2 yards a carry. This outsized group for its day consisted of 6-foot-3, 225-pound Paul "Tank" Younger, the first NFL player out of Grambling, along with 6-foot-2, 225-pound "Deacon Dan" Towler from Washington & Jefferson College in Pennsylvania, and veteran fullback Bob Hoerner, a 6-foot-4, 220-pound workhorse. The team accumulated 2,210 yards rushing, with Towler gaining 894 yards on 156 carries for six TDs. His 6.8 average per carry was second only to Green Bay quarterback Tobin Rote's 6.9.

This rushing game plus the presence of the irrepressible Fears on the other side of the line enabled Hirsch to have one of the greatest single seasons in NFL history. As defenses started to become more sophisticated to face the challenges presented by T formation offenses, Fears drew double-coverage. This freed up Hirsch to go one-on-one against a defender or other minimal coverage, and the result was a feast year. Hirsch caught 66 passes for a record 1,495 yards and 17 touchdowns in a 12-game season. The 17 TDs tied Don Hutson's 1942 record (in an 11-game season), which had been presumed unassailable.

During his record-shattering 1951 season, Hirsch caught the longest pass of the NFL year, a 91-yarder against the Bears, and caught six passes of 70 yards or more and eight passes of 50 yards or more—all for touchdowns. He scored three TDs in the season opener against the New York Yanks, and blazed through secondaries all year-long, with TD catches of 81 and 72 yards against the Packers, and 79 and 76 yards in back-to-back contests versus the 49ers, followed on the next November Sunday afternoon by 53 and 54 yarders for TDs against the Chicago Cardinals.

Born in Wausau, Wisconsin, in 1923, Hirsch was nicknamed "Crazy Legs" after his first season with the University of Wisconsin. *Chicago*

Twelve. Clark Shaughnessy and Offensive Firepower

Daily News sportswriter Francis Powers saw him play against the Great Lakes Naval Training Station in 1942, and wrote, "Hirsch ran like a demented duck. His crazy legs were gyrating in six different directions, all at the same time during a 61-yard touchdown run that solidified the win."[12]

The 6-foot-2, 190-pound Hirsch was a shifty specter. His ability to change direction as a runner, feinting and faking with his legs, made him unusually conspicuous. The moniker "Crazy Legs" helped carry Hirsch's notoriety outside the sporting world, as did his exposure in movie roles, including the starring role in his own story, *Crazylegs* (1953). Hirsch starred in his own radio and television shows in the Los Angeles market.

Hirsch's participation in the V-12 U.S. Navy Training Program required him to transfer from Wisconsin to the University of Michigan, where he became the only athlete to letter in four sports: football, track, basketball, and baseball. A halfback throughout his collegiate career, he chose to play for the Chicago Rockets of the All American Football Conference even though the Cleveland Rams selected him as their first-round draft choice in 1945 (the same draft in which Fears was chosen 11th by the Rams). Hirsch played three years with the Rockets, suffering several injuries, including torn ligaments in his left knee and a fractured skull above his right ear. When he joined the Rams as damaged goods for the 1949 season, Shaughnessy outfitted him with a molded plastic helmet, which was sanctioned that

Elroy "Crazy Legs" Hirsch, the great Los Angeles Rams star, became the first back to consistently play flanker in the NFL. He led the NFL in 1951 in receptions (66), yards (1,495, a new seasonal record), and TDs (17, tying Don Hutson's 1942 record) (Topps® Bowman® courtesy The Topps Company, Inc.).

year by the league, largely through the advocacy of George Halas and the Bears. Hirsch became one of the first players to wear the plastic headgear that soon became a league standard.

"The first year I was with the Rams, they had a lot of good backs, and Shaughnessy thought I was brittle," Hirsch told historian Stuart Leuthner. "Red Hickey, one of the assistant coaches, felt I would make an end, but Shaughnessy didn't think so.... The next year, Joe Stydahar replaced Shaughnessy, and he decided that Hickey had a good idea. I wasn't sure it was such a good idea at first.... I started getting better.... I was the first of the flankers, and on most pass plays I would be split outside ... four to 10 yards from the right tackle."[13]

Stydahar deployed Hirsch on the opposite side of the field from Fears. In effect, Hirsch became the first player to consistently play flanker in the NFL. Previously, halfbacks had occasionally or even often been split wide on passing plays or as decoys as part of the halfback's duties in any offence. But none had been split on such a consistent basis as was Hirsch in Shaughnessy's T offense. After Stydahar and Hickey's conversion of Hirsch from one of the T formation halfbacks into a regular flanker, many teams began using their swifter and more sure-handed halfbacks as flankers.

By 1960, the flanker became codified as a regular position. Many players who entered the NFL as backs in the 1950s eventually became flankers. Because of their split-receiver status on many or most plays, flankers occasionally were misidentified as split ends, and the term "wide receiver" came into the NFL language in the 1970s to identify both the very similar positions of flanker in the backfield, and split end on the line. Among the notable pro halfbacks who played flanker consistently after Hirsch established the position as a singular post in the T formation offense were Ray Renfro and then Bobby Mitchell for the Cleveland Browns, Ollie Matson for the Chicago Cardinals, Pete Retzlaff and then Tommy McDonald for the Philadelphia Eagles, Frank Gifford for the New York Giants, Lenny Moore for the Baltimore Colts, Ray Mathews and then Jimmy Orr for the Pittsburgh Steelers, and R.C. Owens for the San Francisco 49ers. Their identity as flankers can be traced to Crazy Legs Hirsch.

Hirsch played nine seasons for the Rams, from 1949 to 1957. He led the league twice in yards per catch with 22.7 in 1951 and 23.6 in 1952. In

Twelve. Clark Shaughnessy and Offensive Firepower

1953 he enjoyed his second-best all-around season with 61 receptions for 941 yards and four TDs. Consistency was Hirsch's hallmark as he grabbed 32 passes for 477 yards and six TDs in his final season. He retired with 387 catches for 7,029 yards and 60 touchdowns. Hirsch succeeded Pete Rozelle as general manager of the Rams, after Rozelle became commissioner of the NFL in 1960. Hirsch ran the Rams organization from 1960 to 1969, posting strong winning seasons from 1966 through 1969 (a cumulative 40-13-3) with George Allen as the head coach with a receiving corps that included Jack Snow, Bernie Casey, and Billy Truax. Hirsch was inducted into the Pro Football Hall of Fame in 1968, and was athletic director at the University of Wisconsin–Madison from 1969 to 1987. He died of natural causes in 2004.

Converting players such as Fears and Hirsch into all-time great receiving specialists was only one of the residual successes of the Shaughnessy approach to the T formation. Shaughnessy had ushered the T away from consideration as an oddball alignment for an occasional surprise play. By its very nature, the spread T formation enhanced running plays even as it facilitated passing plays. Quick-hitting handoffs to slashing backs into wider holes between linemen than the single wing offered allowed such ball carriers as Chicago's George McAfee, Hugh Gallarneau, and Harry Clarke, as well as the Rams' "Bull Elephants"—Dan Towler, Tank Younger, and Bob Hoerner—deeper penetrations into opposing secondaries.

The Chicago Bears offense as envisioned by Shaughnessy and implement by Halas and Luckman in the 1940s was the archetypal scheme from which the Los Angeles Rams' offense evolved. Shaughnessy's and, later, Stydahar's Rams represented the pinnacle of the T's exploitation with the "three end" offense using Tom Fears, Crazy Legs Hirsch, and Bob Boyd running under passes from Norm Van Brocklin and Bob Waterfield. The Rams' success represented the culmination of Clark Shaughnessy's knowledge and intuition.

These quarterbacks and the others to come—all of them—were beneficiaries of Clark Shaughnessy's work with Sid Luckman in Chicago, Frankie Albert at Stanford, and Sammy Baugh in Washington. Particularly with Luckman and the Bears, and having learned with Halas from the experimentation of Ralph Jones using Red Grange as the man in motion, Shaughnessy perfected the T and the positions on either end of the forward pass. He further defined the split end and flanker positions, and the quarterback post.

"By positioning the quarterback directly behind the center for a hand-to-hand exchange, and by making the position the undeniable focus of an offense instead of merely a glorified blocker in the single wing, Shaughnessy forever altered the game," wrote Len Pasquarelli in 2009. "He conjured up the man in motion, misdirection, the counter play, and the three-wide receiver formation. Shaughnessy prioritized deft ball-handling and intelligent decision-making by quarterbacks, and made the ground game more viable and modern by drawing up quick hitters and eliminating much of the backfield traffic that slowed the run and previously rendered the game a ponderous exercise in physical superiority."[14]

The QB's value as a specialist and leader was enhanced, and teams worked to exploit as well as "protect" their most important offensive player. Rules were instituted in later years to also protect the QB's vulnerability. The sophistication of the position increased dramatically after the war. In 1946, the Bears final championship year during their 1940s run and the first full postwar season, Luckman found himself calling audibles on as much as 25 percent of the plays.

Twenty-five percent would seem like nothing in the era of Peyton Manning's bellowing and traffic-cop pantomimes. But, in fact, audibles had been in use for years before Luckman's adoption of them as an integral part of the quarterback's responsibilities. Luckman's "read" of defensive alignments and other tip-offs caused him to change plays—which he had called in the huddle—at the line of scrimmage, often with "Red!" to signal the cancellation of a play, then to trick the defense into believing it meant cancellation.

After he retired from the Bears in 1962, Shaughnessy coached one more college season, leading the 1965 University of Hawaii squad to a 1-8-1 record. His uneven overall record as a long-serving if vagabond collegiate head coach is an honorable 149–116–17. Shaughnessy's reputation as a football genius has endured, not only through his analytic work for Halas, but also through his shining years at Stanford and for the Rams. However, his later-career defensive work for the Bears can't be overrated, as he devised plans to stop the T he unleashed. An advocate of man-to-man coverage, he devised "combo" zone schemes to run with "man" coverages as early as the 1950s.

Twelve. Clark Shaughnessy and Offensive Firepower

Five years after his retirement, and two years after being inducted into the College Football Hall of Fame, Shaugnessy, suffering hypertension, died in 1970 in Santa Monica, California, at the age of 78. *Chicago Herald American* and later *Washington Post* sportswriter Roger Treat, who compiled the first NFL bible, *The Official NFL Football Encyclopedia* (1952), thought the game too rough for the man. "I always looked upon Clark Shaughnessy as a conscientious idealist who might better have followed the trail of Father Flanagan of Boys Town," Treat wrote. "He may never be entirely happy in the jovial thuggery of pro football, where every man has a little assassin in him."[15]

Chapter Thirteen

Paul Brown in the AAFC and NFL

Chicago Tribune sports editor Arch Ward invented the Major League Baseball All Star Game and football's annual College All Star Game. Ward also conceived of a postwar alternative to the National Football League. With the flood of servicemen back home from the Second World War, and increased leisure time in an era of prosperity, a boom occurred in American sports.

But when Ward and his associates devised the All American Football Conference, they didn't count on the superior force and utter domination of the Cleveland Browns. The team won the AAFC title in all four years of the league's existence, compiling a 47–4–3 record from 1946 through 1949. The Browns won the Western Division in each of the league's first three years and posted the best record of the seven remaining undivided teams in its last year. Cleveland won every AAFC playoff game in which it played.

The only thing besides abject failure that could have killed such a league was that kind of monster success. In 1948, the Browns were undefeated, and overpowered the Buffalo Bills in the AAFC championship game, 49–7. Coach Paul Brown's namesake team dominated the AAFC so thoroughly that its games were foregone conclusions. That situation doomed the conference. The Browns decimated all comers with a bruising ground game and a superb aerial attack that transformed all of pro football once the team joined the NFL.

The Browns became one of three AAFC teams—along with the Baltimore Colts and the San Francisco 49ers—to merge into the NFL, ceasing Arch Ward's valiant if money-draining conference. The other AAFC teams folded. At the time, NFL traditionalists and general naysayers looked upon the Browns as a fluke.

Thirteen. Paul Brown in the AAFC and NFL

To welcome the Browns into the NFL, the league scheduled the first 1950 game as a Saturday showcase featuring the Ohio power against coach Greasy Neale's Philadelphia Eagles, reigning NFL champions for the second straight year. On the face of it, the game was a battle royal of league champions. But undertones in the NFL establishment portended a roughhouse "pro"-style indoctrination for the Browns. The Eagles moved the game from their usual venue, Shibe Park, to accommodate the more than 71,000 fans that filled Philadelphia Municipal Stadium on Saturday, September 16, 1950, for the ceremonial thrashing of the Ohioans. However, the Browns sliced and diced through Philadelphia's secondary with effective short and medium-range passes.

The indoctrination, in the long view, proved to be a case of Cleveland showing the NFL the way into a new era of professional football. The Browns won, 35–10. Quarterback Otto Graham completed 21 of 38 passes for 346 yards and three touchdowns—one each to his key receivers, ends Dante Lavelli and Mac Speedie, and halfback Dub Jones. Speedie caught seven balls for 109 yards.

"We just never played against a team that threw to a spot as well as Cleveland," said Eagles defensive back Russ Craft. "We would be on top of their receivers but they caught the ball anyway because it was so well timed. It was like trying to cover three Don Hutsons ... impossible ... impossible."[1]

Along with hyperbole was some kicking and screaming about Philadelphia not expecting a "basketball game," or, if an interpretation might be pardoned, the Midwesterners might want to play manly football next time.[2] Not that Paul Brown wanted to emphasize his team's strength in all phases of the game or anything, but on December 3, when the Eagles faced Cleveland again that season, the Browns ran the ball 41 times for 69 yards, and Graham threw not a single pass. Defensive back Warren Lahr returned an interception 30 yards for a touchdown, and Lou Groza kicked a couple of field goals as the Browns prevailed, 13–7.

The Browns won the "big league" championship in that maiden season of 1950. They went 11–2, then avenged their two losses to the 10–3 New York Giants in the first playoff game, 8–3. The win was sealed by two Lou "The Toe" Groza field goals and Bill Willis' safety for tackling Giants QB Charlie Conerly in the end zone. The 30–28 victory over the

Los Angeles Rams in the NFL championship game at Municipal Stadium featured Graham throwing four TD passes, two to Lavelli, and one each to Dub Jones and Rex Bumgardner. The Browns' last-minute drive broke the Rams' hearts, capped by a 16-yard Groza field goal with 28 seconds remaining on the clock.

The Browns went to five straight NFL championship games from 1950 through 1955 and six in seven years, counting 1957—and won three of them. Certainly, Paul Brown's innovative coaching as well as Otto Graham's accuracy out of the T formation were keys to this unparalleled NFL success. Graham had led the AAFC in passing yards three times in the short-lived league's four years, commanding the top offense in professional football. The overarching reason for the team's superior play was a new way of thinking about football. That fresh approach saw the forward pass as not just another tool in the box, but a primary tool.

"It was like nothing pro football had ever seen before," historian Andy Piascik wrote for the Pro Football Hall of Fame's *Coffin Corner*.[3] While NFL teams such as Chicago and Green Bay realized the importance and power of balanced running and passing attacks, the Browns refined that mix to an extraordinary degree. The Browns, according to Dan Rooney, who inherited the Pittsburgh Steelers from his father, Art Rooney, "had pioneered a new pass offense, one that confounded opponents and wowed fans. The Browns broke the game wide open with their aerial attack, which by itself could win games."[4]

The Browns' passing attack was innovative on several levels. "Paul, Otto Graham, Mac Speedie and I developed several passing options that were new to football and later would be copied by other teams," Lavelli remembered. "The most famous of these was 'the come back toward the passer' option. After it appeared that a pass pattern was not going to be successful, the end would break his pass pattern and turn back toward his passer. It would take another second or so for Otto to hold the ball before passing it, but it proved a valuable addition for our offense."[5] Another of the Browns innovations was the down-and-out sideline pass, often completed just before the receiver stepped out of bounds.

Eventual Pro Football Hall of Famer Lavelli and Mac Speedie, the ends, were not only the best receivers on the Browns, they also were the best receivers in the AAFC. Some might go so far as tagging them the best receivers in pro ball at the time. They transferred their stardom wholesale into the NFL.

"The Graham-Lavelli-Speedie triumvirate was the fulcrum of the attack, but the Browns regular use of their backs in the passing game was also an innovation not seen before," Piascik wrote. "It was an attack of deadly efficiency that got even better when flanker Dub Jones joined the team in 1948."[6] As a complete offensive package, the Browns also had the power game clicking. Workhorse fullback Marion Motley ran behind the best line in football.

Everything to do with Cleveland's success came right from the top. Paul Brown took a sweeping, ultra-serious, and cerebral approach to governing, developing, and especially teaching his players. He evolved his coaching style through his own stepping stones in each level of organized football, from high school on up. Brown was born in Norwalk, Ohio, in 1908, two years after the forward pass was legalized in college. The coach-to-be developed his own sophisticated coaching regimen after boyhood fandom for Glenn "Pop" Warner's national championship University of Pittsburgh teams in 1915 and 1916. Brown followed 1917 Pitt All-American guard Jock Sutherland's exploits on the Massillon Tigers of the pre–NFL semipro Ohio League in 1919, and especially his coaching techniques as he succeeded Warner to lead the Panthers to four Rose Bowl berths from 1924 to 1938.

The Washington High School Tigers in Massillon were 80–8–2 in Brown's nine years as their coach. Brown's Ohio State Buckeyes were 18–8–1 in three seasons, 1941 through 1943, claiming the national championship in 1942, despite the talent drain of World War II. His service teams at the Great Lakes Naval Training Station in North Chicago, Illinois, went 15–5–2 in 1944 and 1945. Brown became known as "Precision Paul," for his exactitude and business-like approach to the sport.

When Brown accepted the post with Cleveland's AAFC team, he institutionalized some things that had been occasionally used by other coaches. George Halas of the Chicago Bears and other coaches had used game films to scout opponents, but Brown intensified game-film studies into essential preparation. He brought a systemic approach to shrewdly selecting college draftees. Brown also literally invented aspects of the game that became football rituals. Brown exercised complete offensive control by calling plays for his quarterback using messenger guards, swapped in and out of the game on each play.

Brown required players to pass written examinations on the team's playbook, and take IQ and personality tests. Brown's practice drills were regimented by the first year-round pro coaching staff. He devised faceguards for helmets, and invented the "taxi squad," a pool of replacement and practice players who made ends meet by driving cabs for Browns owner Arthur B. "Mickey" McBride.

The only one of Brown's football innovations to supersede his increased use of the forward pass as a singular advance for the sport, enriching offensive football to an unprecedented degree, was his cultural and humanitarian foresight in breaking the color barrier in pro football. This sporting-world advance has been completely overshadowed by the same act in the more popular 1940s sport of baseball. But Brown signed African American players in 1946 and fielded them as integral teammates the year before the Brooklyn Dodgers' general manager, Branch Rickey, famously did so with Jackie Robinson in 1947 big-league baseball.

Brown signed black players Bill Willis, a guard, and Marion Motley, one of the great fullbacks of all time. Brown had coached Willis at Ohio State and Motley at Great Lakes. On September 6, 1946, both debuted as pros in a 44–0 trouncing of the Miami Seahawks at Cleveland Municipal Stadium. (This was three weeks before the Los Angeles Rams broke the color barrier in the NFL on September 29, 1946, playing Kenny Washington and Woody Strode, who had been Jackie Robinson's collegiate football teammates at UCLA, in a 25–14 loss to Philadelphia at Los Angeles Memorial Coliseum.)

Motley and Willis were franchise players before the phrase came into the sporting lexicon, and both have been enshrined in the Pro Football Hall of Fame. They were the first African American players allowed in pro football since 1933, when Ray Kemp played tackle during the maiden season of the Pittsburgh Pirates (before they were the Steelers) and Joe Lillard was a tailback on the Chicago Cardinals. Blacks were quietly banished from pro football for 13 years, or until Motley and Willis. The abuse these two men faced from oppositional racists tested their mettle more than their brawn, even as it was plainly evident that they were among the greatest players to ever perform at their positions.

Unlike Robinson, they felt the literal blows of racism. The powerfully built Motley was a punishing runner, adept receiver, and superb blocker. With the ball, he became a bull's-eye for cheap-shot artists who piled on, stomped hands, and kicked heads. In a story often retold by Joe Horrigan of the Pro Football Hall of Fame's staff, Motley had such a vivid recollection of the first official, Tommy Hughitt, to penalize defensive thugs for beating on him, that the big fullback never forgot the moment or Hughitt's name.[7]

At 6-foot-1 and 232 pounds, Motley possessed surprising speed for a wide-body load as well as a don't-quit determination that made sharp impressions on all defenders. "I never will forget a game in 1952 in Cleveland when I had my first chance to tackle Marion Motley," Rams defensive back Dick "Night Train" Lane remembered. "He looked like a big tank rolling down on me. But you got to take him on. I hit him with my head in his knees, and he came down. I saw a few stars, but I felt good because I tackled Marion Motley."[8]

Motley was essential to Cleveland's unprecedented success in the AAFC and the NFL. The premiere postwar power back, he also was a run-smothering linebacker on defense. Brown has said that Motley would have been a Hall of Fame choice as a defender if he had never played a down on offense. The career AAFC rushing leader with 3,024 yards, Motley led the NFL with 810 yards and a 5.8 average per carry in his first "big-league" season when Cleveland was admitted to the NFL after the AAFC folded. Motley was a particularly vigilant and enthusiastic blocker for the quarterback as part of the passing "pocket" devised by Brown to protect Graham in the backfield, looking for receivers. The "pocket" was a semi-circle of pass blocking created by back-peddling offensive line.

Motley also occasionally slipped out of the pocket for a screen pass or other short pass or was a decoy in the would-be passing game. The Leesburg, Georgia, native, who had played at South Carolina State, then Nevada-Reno, before joining Brown at Great Lakes, became the first draw-play fullback. As such, Motley was the central figure in another Brown innovation. He hesitated as if readying to pass-block in the backfield after the snap—as Graham retreated from center toward him with the ball—convincing defenders that a pass play was developing. But Graham then quickly stuffed the ball into Motley's grasp. The fullback charged across the line of scrimmage into the "underneath," which had been vacated by linebackers dropping into coverage. Brown designed the draw play—the inverse of the play-action pass—to exploit Motley's size and speed as the archetype of defender-shedding athletic big men who powered the rock in the 1950s: Deacon Dan Towler, Tank Younger, John Henry Johnson, Joe Perry, et al. The draw play's consistent success was one reason Motley averaged 6.2 yards per carry during his AAFC years, and 5.0 during his NFL tenure.

In one way, Motley enhanced the Browns' passing game without touching the ball, not only as a blocking back in the pocket protection for Graham, but also as a decoy. He was one of those great players whose mere presence added to every aspect of his team's proficiency. "With the great Motley running the ball, the Browns did not have to throw the ball all over the place," Piascik wrote. "What they did instead was use the pass and run to complement each other, throwing more than most teams of the era, and utilize the long pass much more than was common."[9]

Motley averaged about a catch a game during his starting years, but also, in retrospect, caught one touchdown of significance that wasn't considered consequential at the time. The breaking of pro football's color barrier and Brown's increased use of the forward pass combined on September 22, 1946, when Motley became the first African American pro football player in 24 years to score a touchdown via the air. Motley caught a 33-yard score from Graham in the first period of a 28–0 victory over the Buffalo Bison (soon to be Bills) at War Memorial Stadium. According to the incomplete statistics of the NFL's fledgling years, the only other black players known to have caught TD passes were possibly Paul Robeson of the Milwaukee Badgers in 1922 (according to *Total Football*) and at least Fritz Pollard of the Akron Pros in 1921 (according to *Total Football* and www.NFL-Reference.com). Robeson, a transcendent cultural figure who had played end at Rutgers University and had earned a law degree at Columbia University, would later gain Broadway stardom in the Eugene O'Neill plays *The Emperor Jones* and *All God's Chillun Got Wings* and the hit musical *Show Boat*.

Cleveland's use of the forward pass for a significant portion of the offensive plays for as many years as their dynasty reigned in either league was the result of great offensive proficiency and Brown's play variations, but also a collection of exceptional talents. Otto Graham was a tailback out of Northwestern who Brown acquired with the express purpose of turning him into a T-formation quarterback. Graham's success as a QB was beyond anyone's expectations as he led the Browns to an unequalled 10 straight AAFC or NFL championship games, winning seven of them. As a thrower, runner, and field general, Graham coalesced into the greatest player of the postwar decade. In half of his 10 seasons, Graham led his league in passing yards, four times in completion percentage and passer rating, and three times in TD passes. From the get-go and for all four AAFC years, and after, Graham, Motley, and Willis were the best players at their offensive positions in pro ball.

Tackles Lou Rymkus and Lou "The Toe" Groza, who doubled as the kicker, anchored the offensive line. Each of Graham's centers was voted all-league: Mo Scarry, Lou Saban, Tony Adamle, and, in the NFL years, eventual Pro Football Hall of Famer Frank "Gunner" Gatski. Wide boy Abe Gibron, a 5-foot-11, 243-pound lineman out of Purdue, who had played a season with the Buffalo Bills, joined Willis at guard and became a perennial All-Pro. Gibron later was head coach of the Chicago Bears, and was joined in the 1950s by messenger guard Chuck Noll, later head coach of the Pittsburgh Steelers. While this group opened the holes for Motley, it also pioneered the passing "pocket."

One multifaceted Jones at halfback, Edgar "Special Delivery" Jones, a college star out of Pittsburgh, supplemented Motley's running during the AAFC years. Brown remembered Special Delivery from their collegiate days when the Pitt back charged through the coach's Ohio State line. Special Delivery was nicknamed after "his lightning-fast running style in getting off the mark and through the line of scrimmage," according to sportswriter Jack Clary.[10] Meanwhile, William "Dub" Jones, a Tulane alumnus who had played with Miami and Brooklyn in the AAFC, overlapped halfback duties with Special Delivery, and had an intensified role as a receiver during the team's NFL years. With Motley the chief runner, the Joneses kept up with each other by running, blocking, receiving—and scoring.

In 1948, Special Delivery Jones rushed for 400 yards to Motley's 964. But while Motley scored seven TDs that year, Special Delivery racked up 10—five of those on receptions. Dub Jones became even more of an end zone magnet. He led the team with 11 TDs in 1950 and 12 in 1951. Each year, five of those scores were on passes. In fact, Dub Jones tied Ernie Nevers' 1929 record of six touchdowns in a game on November

25, 1951, against the Bears (the record was equaled another time, by Gale Sayers in 1965). Jones rushed for 116 yards, and scored on four of his nine carries, on runs of two, 12, 27, and 43 yards.

Jones also scored on passes of 34 and 43 yards from Graham. He scored on the last five times he touched the ball. The players were aware that Jones had a chance to tie the record after his fifth TD, and Graham admitted that he defied Paul Brown for one of the few times in his career. In the third quarter, Brown sent in a running play, and Graham called it off and told Jones to run a deep route. Jones says that he looked up at the last second on the route's terminus, noticed the ball, and snagged it in the end zone. In a 10-year career, Dub Jones scored 50 touchdowns, 19 of them on passes.

On a team of all stars, the two most exciting players were also the two best receivers in the league: Dante Lavelli and Mac Speedie—the two leading receivers in terms of yardage in AAFC history. One or the other led the conference in receptions in each of its four seasons. The appropriately named Mac Speedie amassed 3,554 yards in those four seasons on 211 catches and scored 24 touchdowns.

Speedie was the only career AAFC receiver to average more than 50 catches a season, and the only one to attain 1,000 yards in receptions. He passed the 1,000-yard mark twice, catching 67 passes for 1,146 yards and six touchdowns in 1947, and grabbing 62 balls for 1,028 yards and seven TDs in 1949. He led the league in receptions both years as well as well as in 1948, when he caught 58 passes for 816 yards and four TDs.

"'Mac' became a great 'move' man," Brown told Jack Clary. "His track experience taught him a wonderful sense of how to run, how to change speed and no one knew quite how to play against him. Because of this, Lavelli was the fast one, and Speedie was fast, too, but he made so much use of his slow-fast-slow technique that no one realized just how much speed he really had.... Speedie was perhaps a more instinctive receiver and more deceptive [than Lavelli]. He was so tall that when running at top speed, he seemed to be gliding easily. That's why so many defensive backs were fooled by his running style."

"If I played against him, I might have considered guarding him with three men in some combination. Everything he did was instinctive, whereas Lavelli made a great study of his opponents and planned his moves and his fakes," Brown said.[11]

Thirteen. Paul Brown in the AAFC and NFL

Speedie's level of determination came from a childhood in which he suffered from Perthes Disease, a lack of blood-flow into the ball and socket of his left hip. He was bedridden, then presented with crutches to lessen the pain in his hip. His left leg was two inches in diameter smaller than the right and an inch shorter.

"He refused to use [the crutches] or an artificial brace an orthopedist had subscribed to help him walk with more comfort," Brown remembered. "Instead, he went out and climbed trees, jumped off roofs and did everything his pals did, just to prove to them he was not a cripple."[12] Speedie's condition eventually stabilized, and he became a multi-sport star in high school at Salt Lake City and at the University of Utah. His achievements as a pro athlete are all the more remarkable for having overcome such a physical limitation.

He ended his AAFC/NFL career with 349 receptions for 5,602 yards and 33 TDs. He left the Browns on top, after the 1952 season, when he led the NFL with 62 receptions for 911 yards and four TDs. In seven seasons, he led the AAFC or the NFL in receptions on four occasions, was All Conference or All Pro six times, and played on five league-championship teams and in the championship game every year.

His departure was the lure of big money, double the $11,000 that Paul Brown was willing to pay him. Speedie signed with the Saskatchewan Roughriders of the Western Interprovincial Football Union, a forerunner of the Canadian Football League. He played three seasons in Canada, leading the league with seven TDs in 1953. He became an assistant coach with the AFL's Houston Oilers and then posted a record of 6-19-1 as the head coach of the Denver Broncos, for whom he worked as a scout after resigning during the 1966 season. Speedie died in Laguna Hills, California, in 1993.

Speedie was a finalist for enshrinement in the Pro Football Hall of Fame in 1970 and 1972. He never received the necessary votes to get in. Brown blamed Speedie before the 1953 season for not honoring his contract, and this rift is cited for the receiver not making the Hall of Fame. Speedie actually said that the Brown told him that he would "get even" with the receiver. A potential reconciliation at a college all-star game in 1977 was curtailed abruptly by Brown, whose reported recognition of Speedie was "You're the one who went to Canada."[13] The denigration through the years of both the AAFC and the CFL is also blamed for keeping Speedie from enshrinement. But in 1991, Otto Graham said, "Paul wasn't the type of guy you crossed. He would never forget it."[14]

Speedie's instinctive playing style was countered by Lavelli's absolute precision. For Graham, it was like having the best of both worlds. On Lavelli's short and medium routes, Graham would have the ball in flight before or during the cut, before Lavelli looked. Johnny Unitas and Raymond Berry of the Colts would become famous for this predetermined throw before the receiver glanced back. Weeb Ewbank coached the Colts in that era. "Weeb, of course, had learned it while coaching with us at Cleveland," Brown said.[15] With Lavelli and Speedie, the Browns perfected the square-out or sideline pass, often completed right at the out-of-bounds line. "We developed the timed sideline attack," Graham said in 1998.[16]

Lavelli, who was born in Hudson, Ohio, had played for Brown at Ohio State and fought with the 28th Infantry Divison at the Battle of Bulge before returning to the states. A highly valued all-around athlete, he turned down contracts with baseball's Detroit Tigers and the Cleveland Rebels of the newly formed National Basketball Association to sign with the Browns. Lavelli accumulated 2,580 yards on 142 receptions and scored 29 TDs in the AAFC portion of his career. Lavelli's 40 receptions and 843 yards led the league in 1946, and he was second in both categories (49 catches for

Pro Football Hall of Fame end Dante Lavelli ended every one of his 11 seasons in the playoffs. In the Cleveland Browns's first NFL year, 1950, they defeated the Los Angeles Rams, 30–28, in the title game, in which Lavelli caught 11 passes for 128 yards and two TDs (Topps® Bowman® courtesy of The Topps Company, Inc.).

799 yards) in 1947 to teammate Speedie. Lavelli was all-AAFC each of the four years and All Pro twice in seven NFL seasons. In 11 pro years, he caught 386 passes for 6,488 yards and 62 TDs.

A 215-pounder in an era when many linemen were that size, Lavelli lined up as much at tight end as split end. He caught the winning TD pass, a 16-yarder, from Graham in the 1946 AAFC title game, a 14–9 victory over the New York Yankees. In the 1950 NFL championship game, he caught a remarkable 11 passes for 128 yards and two TDs in the 30–28 nail-biter over the Los Angeles Rams. All but 20 of the passes he caught in his 11 years were thrown by Graham. Possessed of a high-pitched voice, he was known to scream, "Otto! Otto! Otto!" to alert Graham when he was open.[17]

"Lavelli had one of the strongest pairs of hands I've ever seen," Brown said. "When he went up for a pass with a defender you could almost always count on him coming back down with the ball. Nobody could take it away from him once he had it in his hands."[18] A Pittsburgh Steelers scouting report labeled Lavelli "Mr. Clutch."[19] The nickname that stuck was "Glue Fingers." "The reason was his great concentration on the ball and the best pair of hands I've ever seen on any receiver," Brown said. "They had an almost liquid softness, which seemed to almost slurp the ball into them. He always seemed to catch every ball that was thrown near him and he took many away from defensive backs who thought he was beaten."[20]

Lavelli's and Speedie's importance to the Cleveland offense in the postwar era was as integral to the club's success as Hutson was by himself to the Green Bay Packers before and during the Second World War. Cleveland's overpowering offense and the proficiency and superb skills of Speedie and Lavelli were such that when the Browns joined the NFL, these two never missed a beat and immediately became two of the "big" league's best receivers. Lavelli was especially consistent. In 1953 he caught 45 passes for 783 yards and six TDs and the next season grabbed 47 balls for 802 yards and seven TDs as Cleveland continued its winning ways with three NFL championships in the 1950s. Lavelli was inducted into the Pro Football Hall of Fame in 1975.

The legacy of Lavelli and Speedie on the Browns often dwarfed most other aspects of AAFC receiving. However, five other AAFC players caught 100 or more passes in the league's four seasons: Alyn Beals (177) of the 49ers, Lamar Davis (147) of the Seahawks and Colts, Al Baldwin (132) of the Buffalo Bills, Fay King (115) of the Bills and Chicago Rockets/Hornets, and Billy Hillenbrand (110) of the Rockets and Colts. Although Beals and Baldwin made some impact in the playoff games in which their teams played, the AAFC Playoffs were mere preambles to Cleveland's eventual championships. The New York Yankees won the 1946 and 1947 Eastern Division titles with 10-3-1 and 11-2-1 records, respectively, but the Browns' high-powered offense was always too much for the Yankees.

The hardest-luck team in the AAFC was the 49ers. Over the history of the league, San Francisco posted a record of 38-14-2, but rated as a perennial also-ran to the Browns in the Western Division. Coach Buck Shaw's 49ers team boasted such outstanding offensive talents as quarterback Frankie Albert, who had guided Stanford to its 10-0 1940 season using coach Clark Shaughnessy's T-formation offense, as well as future NFL star fullback Joe "The Jet" Perry and brilliant receiver Alyn Beals.

The 49ers went 12-2 in 1948, but were forced to sit out the championship game in the year that the Browns went undefeated. San Francisco's only losses in 1948 were to the Browns. In overall head-to-head competition, the 49ers could claim that they handed Cleveland half of its AAFC losses, since they were 2-7 against them. In the final year of the AAFC, the divisional races were discontinued and a two-tier playoff system was instituted as a chance for more winning teams to vie for the title. The 49ers went 9-3-0 that season, beat the New York Yankees, 17-7, in the first playoff round, but then lost 21-7 to the Browns in the championship game.

While the fortunes and notoriety of Speedie and Lavelli rose with those of the Browns, Beals' achievements are rarely, if at all, recalled. But Beals is the all-time leading scorer in AAFC history with 285 points. Beals also was the first professional player to achieve double figures in touchdowns for four consecutive seasons. Even the prolific Don Hutson, the NFL's all-time leader in touchdown receptions with 99 when he retired in 1945, had only logged three straight seasons (1941 through 1943) with 10 or more TDs. Not until fullback Jim Brown entered the league and racked up seven back-to-back seasons (1957 through 1963) with 10 or more touchdowns—most of them, of course, by rushing—was Beals' record broken.

Lance Alworth and Art Powell were the first receivers to equal Beals' mark, both in the American Football League over the same four-year stretch (1963 through 1966). Bob Hayes was the first NFL receiver to tie the mark (1965 through 1968). Eventually, receiving star Jerry Rice took the issue to an astronomical level when he logged 10 consecutive seasons with 10 or more TDs (1986 through 1995).

"Beals was my main receiver," said Frankie Albert, who threw 29 TD passes in 1948, 14 of them to Beals. "Boy, did he have some great moves! He was a good faker. I can remember several times setting up to pass and watching the defensive back fall down after Alyn put a fake on him. The back would trip over his own feet. I'd look at the defensive man lying on his butt while Alyn was wide open."[21]

Thoroughly knowing his home turf might have made a difference. Beals never played a home game outside San Francisco's Kezar Stadium. Both of his alma maters, San Francisco Polytechnic High School—which was across the street from Kezar—and Santa Clara University, played their home games in Kezar. The 49ers played their home contests in Kezar Stadium for 25 years, from 1946 through 1970.

The AAFC's records, players and stats still are not recognized by the NFL. However, the Pro Football Hall of Fame and such record keepers as *Total Football* and Pro-Football-Reference.com do recognize the AAFC's four years of existence. (The AFL's history and stats were automatically incorporated into NFL records after the 1970 merger.) The teams the AAFC brought into the NFL—Colts, 49ers, Browns—have since claimed great portions of the big league's history, and a great deal of receiving history.

Paul Brown's influence has been pervasive at all levels of football, and especially in the province of the forward pass. Teams throughout the NFL adopted his techniques and plays, which had a trickle-down effect on the collegiate and high school ranks. The great NFL dynasties that followed the Browns borrowed wholesale from Paul Brown's football worldview. Each great dynasty that followed the postwar Cleveland Browns either learned very directly from the master, or adopted his policy and tactics.

- In Green Bay, notes Brown biographer George Cantor, Vince Lombardi closely studied Brown's techniques and applied them to the Packers, winning five NFL titles (including the first two Super Bowls) in the 1960s.[22] Lombardi evolved the tight end position with Ron Kramer while his split receivers benefited wholesale from his regimented offense: Boyd Dowler, Carroll Dale, and Max McGee.

- Weeb Ewbank, who won two NFL Championships with Baltimore and the Joe Namath-"guaranteed" Super Bowl III with the New York Jets, had been an assistant to Brown for five years. Ewbank established many key practices on the Colts that were modeled after Browns traditions. The sideline pass was only one of those. Ewbank's trust in Johnny Unitas led directly to the success of Raymond Berry, Jim Mutscheller, and Lenny Moore. Namath's gifts brought greater glory to Don Maynard and George Sauer.
- Blanton Collier coached the Browns to their only Jim Brown-era championship, in 1964, and won five conference or divisional championships in eight years as Cleveland's head coach. Collier had been Paul Brown's top assistant coach for nine years. Paul Warfield and Gary Collins became Collier's go-to receivers in the 1960s.
- Don Shula, who received his indoctrination into pro ball in 1951 as a defensive back, drafted by Brown out of John Carroll University, used his experience to win an NFL championship in Baltimore and five AFC Championships and two Super Bowls for the Miami Dolphins, through it all becoming the winningest pro coach of all time with a record of 328–156–6—a .676 winning percentage. In Baltimore, his receivers included John Mackey. At Miami, he traded for Warfield and developed receivers to gather Dan Marino's passes: Nat Moore and the "Marks brothers," Mark Duper and Mark Jackson.
- Chuck Noll, who was drafted by Brown in 1953 out of the University of Dayton and played linebacker and messenger guard in Cleveland, shuttling plays to Otto Graham, built the most formidable NFL champion of them all as coach of the Pittsburgh Steelers, winning an unprecedented four Super Bowls in six years. In the most legendary one-time draft, 1974, the Steelers selected four future Hall of Famers, including wide receivers Lynn Swann and John Stallworth (along with Jack Lambert and Mike Webster).
- Bill Walsh, who established the "West Coast Offense" in San Francisco, learned much of it on the north shores of the Ohio River in Paul Brown Stadium as an assistant coach for eight seasons under Brown

with the Cincinnati Bengals. Walsh won three Super Bowls as coach of the 49ers, and the team he built won two more titles after he left the game. His greatest receiver was the incomparable Jerry Rice.

- Other head coaches who either played or coached under Paul Brown, and spread the gospel of his football sense, with or without attribution, included Lou Saban, Otto Graham, Abe Gibron, Lou Rymkus, Mike McCormack, Walt Michaels, John Sandusky, Ara Parseghian, Bill Johnson, Sam Wyche, Bruce Coslet, et al.

Of course, the coaching trees that spread the seeds of the Brown influence under Lombardi (to Tom Fears, Forrest Gregg, Dick Jauron, et al.), Ewbank (to Charley Winner, Walt Michaels, Buddy Ryan, et al.), Shula (to Dom Capers, Bill Arnsparger, David Shula, et al.), Noll (to Bud Carson, Tony Dungy, John Fox, et al.), and Walsh (to George Seifert, Dennis Green, Brian Billick, et al.) are too numerous to mention.

CHAPTER FOURTEEN

Between the AAFC and AFL: More Deep Threats Emerge

When the All American Football Conference folded after the 1949 season, the Cleveland Browns, San Francisco 49ers, and Baltimore Colts joined the NFL and prospered. The Browns won three NFL championships in the 1950s, due in no small measure to premiere receivers Dante Lavelli and Mac Speedie, both of whom thrived as NFL stars. The 49ers developed the brilliant Billy Wilson, who led the league in receptions three times. And Baltimore reached great heights with Raymond Berry, who was a big factor in the Colts championships of 1958 and 1959, leading the league in receptions both years.

The two teams that won the most championships in the decade, the Browns and the Detroit Lions—with three titles apiece—waged some of the 1950s' most bitter battles. In Detroit, coach Buddy Parker's club went 9–3 in 1952 and 10–2 in 1953 with quarterback Bobby Layne running the offense, defeating the Browns in the NFL championship game both years, 17–7 and 17–16, respectively. Like Otto Graham in Cleveland, Layne and every other quarterback in pro ball ran his offense out of the T formation. Discussions of the T faded as a prescient subject when it became completely incorporated by every team. Offensive football from the 1950s onward implied T-formation football.

The Lions' leading receiver, yardage gainer, and scorer in 1952 was, by far, left end Cloyce Box, who caught 42 passes for 924 yards and 15 touchdowns. In the succeeding championship year, Box was overmatched by defensive attention, grabbing 16 balls for 403 yards and two TDs. That year the 1948 Heisman Trophy-winner, Doak Walker of Southern Methodist University, became Detroit's go-to guy both as a

Fourteen. Between the AAFC and AFL

runner (337 yards) and receiver (30 catches for 503 and three TDs). His running mate, fullback Bob "Hunchie" Hoernschmeyer, scored nine touchdowns.

To the Lions' credit, their 1957 championship, which came via a surprising 59–14 whipping of the Browns, was without Parker, who resigned before the season began after a flap with management and boosters. He moved on to coach the Pittsburgh Steelers. Former Bears end George Wilson took over the Lions and the cast of characters had changed, too. Bobby Layne's leg was broken late in the season, and backup QB Tobin Rote led the team to the championship. The offense relied on the running of John Henry Johnson, acquired from the 49ers, along with Howard "Hopalong" Cassidy; Doak Walker had retired (after six pro seasons). Jim Doran led the team in receiving with 33 grabs for 624 yards and five TDs.

Walker was a case of national celebrity in the postwar era, when sports culture began to deepen in America and the NFL gained a larger and more respectable profile than it had in previous decades, even as the college game was still the more attended level of football. Walker's college fame and his gentleman's reputation in a sport that tended not to tolerate niceties followed him all the way to the Pro Football Hall of Fame, where he was enshrined in 1986. He had been Layne's high school teammate in Dallas. Even though he was

Doak Walker helped lead the Detroit Lions to NFL championships in 1952 and 1953. As a halfback, he gained more yards (2,539) and scored more TDs (21) receiving than he did rushing (1,520 and 12). Despite playing only six seasons, he was elected to the Hall of Fame in 1986 (Topps® Bowman® courtesy of The Topps Company, Inc.).

All Pro five times and a member of two NFL championship clubs, Walker might be called the most overrated skill-position player in the Hall of Fame.

Billy Wilson might be considered just the opposite. Wilson was one of the best all-around athletes playing end in the NFL decade of Lavelli and Speedie, Crazy Legs Hirsch and Tom Fears in Los Angeles, and Pete Pihos and Pete Retzlaff in Philadelphia. Wilson led the NFL in receptions three times, all after 1953, when he led the league in receiving TDs with 10. He caught an NFL-leading 60 passes for 830 yards and five TDs in 1954, 60 for 889 yards and five TDs in 1956, and 52 for 757 yards and six TDs in 1957. In his 10 years, 1950 to 1959, all with the 49ers, Wilson caught 407 passes for 5,902 yards and 49 TDs.

A Dust Bowl son from Oklahoma, Wilson moved with his parents to the West Coast and attended San Jose State. He was a 22nd-round draft choice in 1950 by the 49ers, and more than just earned a roster spot. When asked to name the toughest receiver he ever faced, the great defensive back Emlen Tunnell said, "Billy Wilson of the 49ers." He qualified the remark: "He's probably the greatest end I ever saw. He gave me more trouble than anybody. Anybody who ever covered him would probably say the same thing."[1]

Billy Wilson of the San Francisco 49ers was the great unsung receiver of the 1950s. He led the NFL in receiving TDs (10) in 1953, and in receptions in 1954 (60), 1956 (60) and 1957 (52). He shone in his only playoff game, a 1957 loss to Detroit, with nine catches for 107 yards and a TD (Topps® Bowman® courtesy of The Topps Company, Inc.).

Fourteen. Between the AAFC and AFL

Wilson's reputation for agility is comparable to such later receiving stars as Lance Alworth and Lynn Swann. His ability as a blocker while playing outside receiver was known league-wide—a George Wilson or Hines Ward of his day at an increasingly specialized position. Billy Wilson also possessed exceptional speed, and, like Fears and Lavelli, was known to wrestle the ball away from would-be interceptors.

"I remember a play Billy made when he caught a pass, leaped straight up into the air over myself and two other defenders and ran it in for a touchdown," said Don Shula, a former Browns defensive back. "It was a great play and he truly was a great receiver. He is one of the few players of another era that would excel today."[2]

Wilson played on 49ers teams known for their runners, particularly the "Million Dollar Backfield" club of 1954, meaning quarterback Y.A. Tittle and running backs Joe Perry, John Henry Johnson, and Hugh McElhenny—all four future Hall of Famers. But Tittle certainly appreciated Wilson's toughness and skill. "He was one of the fiercest competitors I ever played with," Tittle said. "He was our No. 1 receiver. Whenever we needed a big catch, I went to him, because I knew he would make the play."[3]

Former 49ers coach Bill Walsh was a great Wilson proponent for Hall of Fame enshrinement. Wilson worked for him and the 49ers as an assistant coach and scout for three decades after his playing career ended. But as the years have gone by, Wilson's greatness has been obscured by the excellent 49ers receivers who have played after him: Gene Washington, Dwight Clark, Terrell Owens, and Jerry Rice.

Unlike Wilson, Raymond Berry's reputation remains intact over decades, particularly as the most precise route runner of his time. Not possessed of great speed, he ran his patterns and made his cuts exactly as he had practiced them with Johnny Unitas. The Colts' quarterback often threw the ball on slants or down-and-out routes before Berry had looked or even cut. He and Unitas were in total synch. "There is no higher standard of excellence in the art of pass receiving than this intricate knowledge of timing, knowledge of the workings of someone else's body as well as those of your own," Paul Zimmermann wrote. "There have been many great passers and many fine receivers, and quite a few good combinations of both. But the Unitas-Berry combination was the greatest of all."[4]

Pass Receiving in Early Pro Football

Paul Brown's Cleveland teams are credited with inventing the precision throw, with the ball in the air before the receiver looked for it, with Otto Graham in the late 1940s throwing to Speedie and Lavelli. Brown coaching minion Weeb Ewbank took the quick-throw technique to Baltimore when he became head coach of the Colts, who were guided by a particularly gutsy and motivated precision thrower in Unitas and top talents in the receiving corps, with ends Berry and Jim Mutscheller and flanker Lenny Moore. The Colts took full advantage of this type of passing play and ingrained the precision route into football culture.

"If as Carlyle said, genius is an infinite capacity for taking pains, then Berry's qualifications are of the highest order," Red Smith wrote. "A rather bony individual out of Southern Methodist with 185 pounds on a chassis measuring six feet two inches, he regarded improvisation as a mortal sin. 'No,' he would say flatly if somebody tried to make up a play in the huddle. 'I haven't practiced it. I'm not prepared.' He was Johnny Unitas' favorite target on passes because he ran his patterns with scrupulous precision and the quarterback always knew where he would be on a given play. He had no great speed, and his patterns were designed like a Swiss watch, the product of endless hours of studying films."[5]

Born in Corpus Christie in 1933, Berry was a 20th-round draft choice by the Colts in 1954. He became a starter in his second season

RAYMOND BERRY
END • BALTIMORE COLTS

Raymond Berry led the NFL in receptions in 1958 (56), 1959 (66), and 1960 (74) for the Baltimore Colts, which won league championships in '58 and '59. When he retired after the 1967 season, Berry held the then all-time reception record of 631. He was inducted into the Hall of Fame in 1973 (Fleer Corporation, courtesy Tootsie Roll Industries).

and came into his own when Unitas joined the team for the 1956 season after being cut by the Steelers. Receiver and QB saw in the other kinship as relentless perfectionists. The pair became famous in Colts lore for staying after practice to further perfect passing routes.

Berry led the NFL in receiving three years in a row with 56 catches in 1958, 66 in 1959, and 74 in 1960. He led in receiving yardage in as many seasons, with 800 in 1957, 959 in 1959 and 1,298 in 1960. He led the NFL in receiving TDs in both championship years with nine in 1958 and 14 in 1959. In the so-called "greatest game ever played," the 1958 NFL Championship, in which the Colts beat the Giants, 23–17, in overtime, Berry caught an NFL playoff record 12 passes for 178 yards and a TD. He caught crucial balls of 25, 15, and 22 yards on the drive late in the fourth quarter that led to the game-tying field goal by Steve Myhra, and two passes for 33 yards on the drive that won it in OT.

Berry's remarkable consistency was a direct byproduct of his absolute dedication to the game and the job of pass receiving. For instance, after he had been in the league for 10 seasons, his numbers were 58 catches for 739 yards and seven TDs in 1965, and 56 catches for 786 yards and seven TDs in 1966. Berry ended his NFL career as the all-time leader in passes caught, with 631, and pass receiving yardage, with 9,275 yards. He scored 68 touchdowns. A six-time Pro Bowler and three-time All-NFL first team, Berry was inducted into the Pro Football Hall of Fame in 1973. He later coached the wide receivers for five teams, coached the quarterbacks for two others, and was head coach of the New England Patriots from 1984 to 1989.

Berry was the most notable receiver on the NFL champion at the close of the 1950s, and deservedly garnered much attention for his precision and importance on the best football club in the land. A lot of other guys were making strides in receiving outside the championship spotlight in the postwar era. Bob Mann, who broke Big 10 receiving records with the Michigan Wolverines, became the first African American player on both the Detroit Lions, in 1948, and Green Bay Packers, in 1950, and led the NFL in receiving yardage in 1949 with 1,014. Billy Howton was one of Green Bay's few bright spots in the 1950s, twice leading the league in receiving yards, with 53 grabs for 1,231 yards and 13 TDs in 1952, and 55 for 1,188 and 12 TDs in 1956. Harlon Hill of the Bears posted two seasons of league-leading yards-per-catch, with 25.0

in 1954 (45 catches for 1,124 yards and 12 TDs) and 24.0 in 1956 (47 catches for 1,128 yards and 11 TDs). Jimmy Orr, a 25th-round draft choice of the Rams, caught on with the Steelers in 1958 and grabbed 33 passes for 910 yards and seven TDs for one of the highest per-catch averages of all time, 27.6. There were others—Mal Kutner and Don Stonesifer of the Cardinals, Gordie Soltau of the 49ers—whose deep-threat abilities for two or three years presaged the advent of the bombs-away AFL in 1960.

Sid Gillman, who coached the Los Angeles Rams during the waning seasons of Crazy Legs Hirsch and Tom Fears (1955 to 1959), used a Paul Brown–like cerebral approach to the aerial game with the newly minted Los Angeles Chargers in the AFL in 1960. Gillman had learned wide-open-style football as an all-Big Ten end at Ohio State, playing for the high-scoring, trick-play master, coach Francis "Close the Gates of Mercy" Schmidt, in the Depression Era, before Paul Brown's reign with the Buckeyes.

Gillman's Chargers lost the AFL championship game four times in the league's 10-year history, in 1960 to the Houston Oilers, and, after the club moved down the coast to San Diego, to Houston again in 1961, and to the Buffalo Bills in 1964 and 1965. Still, Gillman's Chargers stood out as a big-play club in a pass-happy league, and he began a tenure that led to his notoriety as the "Father of Modern Passing."

Harlon Hill played eight seasons for the Chicago Bears, posting nearly duplicate numbers in 1954 (45 catches for 1,124 yards and an NFL-leading 12 TDs) and 1956 (47 grabs for 1,128 yards and 11 TDs). The year in between, 1955, he also led the league in TD receptions with nine (Topps® Bowman® courtesy of The Topps Company, Inc.).

Fourteen. Between the AAFC and AFL

Gillman unleashed a bold offense that was worthy of the team's lightning-bolt uniform stripes as one of football's most electric. With flanker Lance Alworth, drafted out of Arkansas in 1963, and quarterback John Hadl stepping up in 1964 at quarterback, this long-bomb combo became Gillman's centerpiece connection while tight end Willie Frazier and split end Gary Garrison became constant threats, often on the other side of the line from the virtually consistently double-teamed Alworth. Chargers running backs Paul Lowe, Keith Lincoln, and Dickie Post provided other receiving dramatics.

Gillman's coaching influence was pervasive, and his importance to later football generations was transferred to such assistant coaches as Chuck Noll, Al Davis, Don Coryell, Bum Phillips, and Jack Faulkner. Of these, Coryell developed a potent and winning passing game as head coach of the St. Louis Cardinals from 1973 to 1977, and transferred that success back to San Diego for the 1980s when his famous "Air Coryell" attack included the sterling receiving unit of Kellen Winslow, John Jefferson, and Charlie Joiner.

The subject of potent West Coast offenses prior to the vaunted "West Coast Offense" of the San Francisco 49ers' Bill Walsh era brings up a couple of relatively time-obscured innovations by the 49ers in the late 1950s. They became standard practices in later decades by most NFL clubs: the Alley-Oop pass and the shotgun formation.

In 1957, San Francisco's rookie receiver R.C. Owens, a 6-foot-3, 197-pound former basketball player from the College of Idaho, conspired with quarterback Y.A. Tittle on what became known as the "Alley-Oop." Tittle would fling a high-arching pass to a spot, often in the end zone, and Owens, an agile rebounder, would outleap the always shorter defenders for touchdowns. The play was named after a comic-strip character that swung in the treetops. V.T. Hamlin created "Alley Oop," which was syndicated for four decades by the Newspaper Enterprise Association. Tall receivers in the 1990s and 21st century adept at premeditated plays designed on their superior height and ability to outleap defenders have included Randy Moss, Terrell Owens, Plaxico Burress, Calvin Johnson, and A.J. Green.

The shotgun essentially uses a long hike from center to the quarterback, standing five to seven yards deep in the backfield. It was used to quickly initiate the QB's "check-down" of possible receivers without him having to back-peddle from the center's snap while the offensive line formed his passing pocket. The shotgun usually tipped off a passing play, but not always. In the 1940s, Greasy Neale dabbled with the formation, which had been used in the Canadian Football League. Neale's Philadelphia Eagles facilitated some of QB Tommy Thompson's throws to Pete Pihos and Jack Ferrante with the shotgun.

San Francisco coach Red Hickey is usually credited for evolving the formation in the modern era, with Tittle or John Brodie throwing to Owens and others. The first time Hickey used the formation was specifically to neutralize the fierce pass rush of the Baltimore Colts on November 27, 1960. It worked in that the 49ers won the game, a 30–22 upset, and several subsequent games via the shotgun. But it failed in its essential purpose. With Tittle sidelined by an injury, Brodie started the game, but was knocked out of action when the Colts' Big Daddy Lipscomb stormed into the backfield for a vicious sack, and third-string QB Bob Waters had to finish the contest. The 49ers won several games to begin 1961 with the shotgun and three rotating quarterbacks: Brodie, Waters, and Billy Kilmer (Tittle had been traded to the New York Giants). But Hickey gave up on the formation after the Chicago Bears spent as much time in his backfield as his QB trio in a 31–0 loss.

The shotgun was used by Weeb Ewbank in the late 1960s on the New York Jets in the AFL to better protect the light-bulb knees of injury-prone Joe Namath, throwing to Don Maynard and George Sauer. Coach Tom Landry used the shotgun rather famously in the 1970s on the Dallas Cowboys to better protect Roger Staubach, throwing to Drew Pearson, Preston Pearson, and Billy Joe Dupree. As usual with an old standard that proved "new" again, the shotgun was pegged as a revelation and a great Landry invention. However, Pop Warner actually used a similar formation, called the Double Wing B formation, at Stanford University in the late 1920s. That same formation had been used effectively by Sammy Baugh in the 1930s at Texas Christian University. While the long snap to the QB hadn't until then been used by teams that generally operated out of the T formation, as Neale's Eagles and Hickey's 49ers did, the Double Wing B had the same effect—start the play, whether it was a throw or not, more quickly in the backfield. Today, the shotgun is situationally used by practically every team at every level of organized football, often on third down and especially third-and-long.

Chapter Fifteen

Tight End: Biography of a Position

On November 24, 1963, the Sunday after President John F. Kennedy was assassinated in Dallas, Texas, the Chicago Bears slugged it out with the Steelers at Forbes Field in Pittsburgh. The NFL had decided to play the games as usual in the assassination's aftermath. The government decided that normalcy was the best course for healing the nation. Once the Bears took the field, the gloomy national mood for tight end Mike Ditka had evaporated into another windy, 35-degree, autumn afternoon.

"I couldn't control what happened to President Kennedy or what was happening in our country at that time," Ditka said in an interview years later. "I had to go out there and line up against a bunch of guys called the Pittsburgh Steelers."[1]

It was Ditka's first return as a player to the Steel City since he was an All American at the University of Pittsburgh, drafted by the Bears as their first-round pick in 1961. He was deployed all day against the Steelers and had grabbed six passes by the waning stages of the fourth quarter. It had been a grueling game as coach Buddy Parker's 6–3 Steelers scrambled (unsuccessfully, it turned out) for a playoff berth, relying on the rugged running of John Henry Johnson and Dick Hoak to hold onto a tenuous lead, 17–14. Coach George Halas' Bears, 9–1 after defeating their archrivals, the 8–2 Green Bay Packers, the previous week, needed at least a tie to stay on top in the West Division.

The Bears were deep in their own territory. Quarterback Billy Wade called for Ditka to go long. "I was tired," Ditka later remembered. "I said, 'Bill, I can't go deep. You throw something to me short. I'll go down about 14 yards and hook. Then I'll try to run with it.' I told him we didn't have to go all the way anyway. All he had to do was make a couple of first downs and kick a field goal."[2]

149

Wade faked a toss toward the left flat, then fired a strike to Ditka, who had hooked over the left middle. Ditka caught the pass, and the first Steeler to hit him was safety Clendon Thomas. Ditka turned, shook him off, and chugged across midfield, hit by six more guys, although the number has occasionally fluctuated upward depending on who told the story. Three Steelers collided in a round-robin cancellation of each other as Ditka kept going. Another Steeler latched on for a rodeo-ride facsimile. By the time Ditka crumpled, 63 yards later, the persistent Thomas succeeded in his second tackle attempt on the same play.

What transpired between Thomas hits was one of the great exhibitions of a gridiron gladiator remaining upright and moving forward against seemingly impossible odds. In a television era more than a generation before ESPN's all-highlights all the time, this rumble became a show-stopping extra, a TV news feature in a carnival sort of way, showing that will and determination as much as size and strength can lead to success. The Bears were in chip-shot field goal range, and Roger LeClerc kicked an 18-yarder. The Bears avoided a loss with the 17–17 standoff.

The tie was crucial to Chicago's season. The eventual 11–1–2 Bears edged out the 11–2–1 Packers to win the NFL's West Division, then defeated the New York Giants, 14–10, for the NFL Championship. Ditka caught three passes for 38 yards in the title win. It was the last Bears championship prior to the Ditka-coached 1985 Super Bowl winners. Ditka's gutsy effort in Pittsburgh was the play of Chicago's year and went a long way in defining his "Iron Mike" reputation.

He collected seven passes from Wade that day for 146 yards. That third season might have been Ditka's roughest—after being named Rookie of the Year in 1961, when he became the first bona fide tight end in modern football to gain 1,000 yards through the air, and another stellar sophomore season in 1962. After he got to his feet in Forbes Field, he played three more regular-season games and closed out 1963 with 59 receptions for 794 yards and eight touchdowns. Although he would make his third Pro Bowl, Ditka was named consensus All Pro for the first time by the news agencies and sportswriters who made such annual choices.

George Allen, later head coach of the Los Angeles Rams and Washington Redskins, also was on the Chicago staff. "It was the greatest run

Fifteen. Tight End: Biography of a Position

I've ever seen," Allen said. "It wasn't speed that got him down the field. It wasn't his moves. It was just sheer determination. He literally carried defensive players on his back."[3]

If an NFL position can have a defining moment, this was it for the tight end, effort-wise and timing-wise. The tight end wasn't but a few years old and only in its second year of recognition from the league itself and from the sports writers and sportscasters who portrayed the game for the public. The specter of Ditka, loping unrelenting against the resistance of Steelers' manpower—for most of the length of a football field—helped ingrain the tight end position into the national consciousness of a growing sport.

Prior recognition was brought on by events in the previous two seasons. The modern tight end in pro ball came of age in 1961. That year, circumstances in Chicago and Green Bay highlighted the tight end as a receiver's position rather than as a blocking position, which it was and remains most of the time. Ditka's Rookie of the Year honors with the 8–6 Bears came for catching 56 passes for 1,076 yards and 12 touchdowns in the most outstanding receiving season for a tight end up to that time. The same year, Ron Kramer caught 35 passes for 559 yards and four touchdowns for the 11–3 Packers. Kramer became an integral part of the Packers' offense, which defeated the New York Giants, 37–0, in the NFL Championship. Kramer scored TDs in the title game on passes of 13 and 14 yards from quarterback Bart Starr.

Ditka's season and Kramer's postseason provided surges in performance at the position, were highlights of the NFL year, and underscored the development of the tight end in proficient pro football. But Ditka's spectacular success in 1961 illustrated the possibilities for the position. With the 6-foot-3, 228-pound Ditka's capabilities—following in the footsteps of previous NFL ends Bob Shaw, Pete Pihos, and Elbie Nickel—the position on the Bears became a role for a go-to receiver rather than a safety-valve or broken-play last resort.

Ditka played six seasons with the Bears, enjoying his best year in 1964 when he caught 75 passes for 897 yards and five TDs, ranking second in the NFL in receptions behind his teammate, flanker Johnny Morris, with 93 catches. Ditka signed a lucrative contract with the Houston Oilers in the rival American Football League in 1966, when the frugal Halas wouldn't pay nearly as much. But soon after Ditka's AFL signing, such contracts were ruled premature when both leagues entered negotiations that year to merge. In a move that was viewed by NFL aficionados and Ditka as banishment, Halas then traded his tight end to the Philadelphia Eagles. During his two years in Philadelphia and four more with the Dallas Cowboys, Ditka was used mostly in a reserve role.

Ditka finished his 12-year career with 427 receptions for 5,812 yards and 43 TDs. He played in five Pro Bowls. He stayed in the game as an assistant coach to the Cowboys' Tom Landry. After making it known to the Halas family that he wanted to coach the Bears, fences were mended, and Ditka was hired back. Under the microscope of the head coach's post, Ditka's pugnacious demeanor began to be nearly a weekly TV episode. The postgame television cameras were always sure to catch his brash commentary. His defense-oriented Bears won the 1985 Super Bowl, and the ex-tight end became a transcendent sports personality—a snarling, hard-headed ham, beloved by fans of "da Bears." He compiled a 121–95 record as coach of the Bears, then the New Orleans Saints, over 14 seasons. He moved to network-TV sports analyst, and was elected in 1988 to the Pro Football Hall of Fame.

The television era was kind to Kramer as well. When Vince Lombardi turned the Packers around and coached the 8–4 team to the 1960 NFL West Division title, Kramer caught four passes as a backup. But in 1961, on their way to a dynasty-making five league titles in the 1960s, the Packers replaced Gary Knafelc with Kramer at starting tight end while championship limelight descended on the team. At 6-foot-3 and 240 pounds, Kramer had the dimensions of a guard of the era. He wasn't the first pass catcher of bulky size; he just happened to be very visible on the Green Bay Packers. His exploits were on national TV more Sundays than those of other ends. For four straight years he provided remarkable consistency, catching between 32 and 37 passes for about 550 yards each year, with a TD high of seven in 1962.

Kramer's notoriety has waned a bit with time, and was not helped when Lombardi traded him to the Detroit Lions for the 1965 season. But he was integral to the success of the Packers in more ways than one. He had the most important blocking role in the most famous offensive play of all time—during the heyday of that play. The Green Bay power sweep, the pride of Lombardi's chalkboard, was a handoff right or left, usually to Jim Taylor or Paul Hornung, who was led parallel to the line

Fifteen. Tight End: Biography of a Position

and around end by the other setback and pulling guards Jerry Kramer and Fuzzy Thurston. Immortalized on film, the sweep is explained in the often repeated footage of Lombardi, barking near a blackboard, emphasizing the blocking that sealed off of a path for Taylor to take after he turns the corner and runs "*in the alley!*"

"The tight end, the key blocker in the sweep, moved out wider from the right tackle, exactly nine feet to the tackle's right," David Maraniss wrote. "Lombardi could sense immediately if it was eight feet or ten feet, and it had to be exactly nine feet. The block of the tight end, Gary Knafelc or Ron Kramer, determined the entire shape of the play. Lombardi instructed the tight end not to leave his feet or smash into his opponent, but rather to calculate, in the split second after the snap, which direction the left outside linebacker could be pushed. If the linebacker was moving inside, the tight end has to stop him from penetrating the line of scrimmage and bump him toward the middle. If the linebacker was moving outside, the tight end's mission was to get in his way and keep bumping him farther outside, passively allowing the linebacker to beat on him during their contact. The point, said Lombardi, was to block the linebacker: 'Whichever direction he takes, drive him in that direction.'"[4] And Kramer did just that.

Ron Kramer helped define the tight end post, contributing to Vince Lombardi's 1960s Green Bay Packers dynasty as both the key blocker on the coach's vaunted power sweep and a reliable receiver. After eight years in Green Bay, he played three more seasons for the Detroit Lions (Philadelphia Gum Company, courtesy of Tootsie Roll Industries).

"He was the reason that the Lombardi sweep was successful," Hornung told *The New York Times* when Kramer died in 2010 at age 75. "He was the main blocker."[5] Forrest Gregg, the Pro Football Hall of Fame tackle who played on the same Green Bay line, claimed that Kramer was the best tight end he ever saw. "He didn't have a real long career, but, man! he was awesome when he was in his heyday," Gregg claimed. "I don't think there was anybody any better."[6]

Kramer enjoyed extra-sports status as one of the trio of playboy roommates on the Packers profiled on a CBS special along with Heisman Trophy-winning Notre Dame "Golden Boy" Hornung and the veteran split end Max McGee. Kramer retired after three years with the Lions. In 10 years, Kramer caught 229 passes for 3,272 yards and 16 TDs. After football, he operated a specialty advertising business, Ron Kramer Industries, in Fenton, Michigan, near Ann Arbor.

Both Ditka and Kramer handled the linemen's aspects of tight end duties on most plays by run blocking and pass blocking as well as the guards and tackles. In fact, both had reputations as devastating blockers, who often drove their opponents to the turf. They represented the upsizing of the position as players in general came into the league larger and larger through the 1960s. "Other abilities being equal, size not only adds to the tight end's blocking effectiveness in the running game, but helps him in going over the middle where they are likely to be hit by two or more people after catching the ball," wrote former San Diego Chargers and New York Jets guard Sam DeLuca in 1978, reasoning, "The bigger the tight end, the better the chance of his outfighting the defender for the ball."[7]

Along with size, tight ends in the 1970s and after, more often than not, had the speed to get deep. Still, they were mostly deployed on short routes, often after chip-blocking an outside linebacker or defensive end.

"There may be enough time for him to run deep routes," DeLuca described the position in the 1970s, "but the chance of his being detained on the line of scrimmage by the corner linebacker makes the shorter pass more attractive to the normally conservative NFL coach. The reason the tight end is used more against the zone is the difficulty of throwing deep to anyone when the defense is in zone coverage. Most teams use the wide receivers to spread the zone (since they can get off the line faster), and then try to hit their tight ends and set backs on short and medium passes between the defenders in the dead spots."[8]

Because of the increased use of zone defense in pro football, the tight end became a key offensive receiver for many teams, including the

Fifteen. Tight End: Biography of a Position

Dallas Cowboys and the Oakland Raiders. The Cowboys kept the position well-stocked for several generations: Pettis Norman (1962–1973), Mike Ditka (1969–1972), Billy Joe Dupree (1973–1983), Doug Cosbie (1979–1988), Jay Novacek (1990–1995), and Jason Witten (2003–2015). Zone defenses were the main reason that the Cowboys and other teams began throwing more consistently to both tight ends and running backs. Tight ends such as Dave Casper on the Raiders as well as Riley Odoms of the Denver Broncos, and Bob Tucker on the New York Giants became essential weapons in their respective offensive arsenals.

While the tight end came of age during the early tenures of Ditka and Kramer, the position was born a little more than a decade earlier, out of Clark Shaughnessy's ongoing, postwar tinkering with the T formation. As head coach of the Los Angeles Rams in 1948 and 1949, Shaughnessy established a basic scheme with his receivers that has remained in place with most teams at all levels of play into the 21st century. The general label first applied to this spread offense was the "three-end" offense. Of course, this moniker wasn't exactly correct, since the flanker remained a step back from the line in the backfield, and, logically speaking, any line has but two ends. But the phrase caught on as a way to explain Shaughnessy's strategy.

Prior to 1949 and largely for a decade after that on most other teams, the T formation was run, according to the rules, with the backfield four—quarterback, fullback and two halfbacks—behind the seven linemen. Shifts and counters and stacks were parts of most offensive packages, with either one or two ends occasionally split wide, and perhaps one halfback lined up as the flanker, occasionally after going in motion. But generally, both offensive ends lined up on either side of the line beside the tackles. With the Rams, Shaughnessy made the wide end and the widely split flanker mainstays of his offense. This occurred after he converted Tom Fears from a linebacker to left end, and the coach's successor, Joe Stydahar, took the advice of assistant coach Red Hickey and converted halfback Elroy "Crazy Legs" Hirsch into primarily a full-time flanker.

The idea was to get two or three talented receivers running deep and semi-deep routes, creating what in later decades would be described as the vertical passing game, and using them to decoy the defensive backs on running plays. Not only did Shaughnessy find gold in Fears

155

and Hirsch, but his alternating quarterbacks were veteran Bob Waterfield and rookie sensation Norm Van Brocklin. Helped along by the explosive "three-end" strategy as well as later offensive innovations by other coaches, both quarterbacks and both receivers would eventually end up enshrined in the Pro Football Hall of Fame. Long after Shaughnessy left, fired after the 1949 season for his intractability with Rams management, the same players, with a few adjustments, won an NFL championship for Los Angeles in 1951.

The one of the "three" ends in 1949 who still lined up in the old-fashioned manner, next to right tackle, was Bob Shaw. A 6-foot-4, 226-pound Ohio State product who had been drafted by the old Cleveland Rams on the eighth round in 1944, and had been in and out of football, Shaw caught 29 passes that year for 535 yards and six touchdowns as a very integral part of Shaughnessy's offense. When Shaughnessy went, so did Shaw, to the Chicago Cardinals, where he had a great season, catching 48 passes for 971 yards and an NFL-leading 12 TDs. On October 2, 1950, Shaw became the first receiver to catch five touchdown passes in one game, against the Baltimore Colts. He hauled in eight total passes that day from Cards QB Jim Hardy for 165 yards. Shaw quit playing at the top of his game. He became an assistant coach with the Colts, then the San Francisco 49ers. After a three-year stint as head coach of New Mexico Military Institute, he coached in the Canadian Football League.

Shaw was the regular right end in the first offense that used widely split receivers. He might be called the first tight end, but the position was not yet known as that. He was merely playing offensive end the way it had always been played, playing the same position that he had been playing—that most ends played in the 1940s and early 1950s. He lined up next to the tackle, blocked on running plays and occasionally deployed as a receiver. To apply the term "tight end" to his career might seem accurate from a modern perspective. But for him and the NFL in general, it was status quo—playing offensive end, generally, as George Halas played it in the 1920s, Bill Hewitt played it in the 1930s, and George Wilson played it in the 1940s.

The two other guys in the vaunted "three-end" offense—Fears and Hirsch—were playing conspicuously different roles than any receivers had in the past, and performing brilliantly as two of the most outstanding players in the game. Through them, Shaughnessy redefined the look,

Fifteen. Tight End: Biography of a Position

use, and scoring capabilities of the receiving corps, and both players became national names.

The two former Chicago Bears who took over the Rams offense upon Shaughnessy's and Shaw's departures, head coach Joe Stydahar and backfield coach Hampton Pool, threw out the close-set end altogether. Fears and Hirsch continued on as spectacular deep threats (and their exploits are covered elsewhere in this story), the latter now playing right split end to Fears' left split end. Pint-sized rotating flankers were instituted into this reassigned receiving corps, including Glenn Davis, Tommy Kalmanir, and return specialist Vitamin Smith. This offense continued devastating the NFL through 1951, when they defeated the Cleveland Browns, 24–17, for the NFL Championship.

Stydahar threw a change-up at the league again the next year as he unleashed the "Bull Elephant Backfield," a full house of fullbacks—225-pound bruisers each: Deacon Dan Towler, Tank Younger, and Bob Hoerner. Fears and Hirsch alternated with Bobby Boyd, another split receiver, and continued grabbing Van Brocklin's passes downfield. With the big backs blocking as well as carrying the ball, the team was still absent the end who usually stayed on the line and blocked.

"It was an explosive and devastating attack that produced total offense and passing and scoring records that lasted," Paul Zimmerman wrote in 1984. "It gave the Rams a divisional championship and an NFL title, but it wasn't the offense of today. It had no tight end. When the defense countered with an overload of defensive backs (San Francisco used six of them in one game in 1951), Stydahar came back with his 'Bull Elephant' backfield."[9] Only when Fears returned to a position closer to the left tackle in his later years did the Rams once again begin looking like a modern offense. However, his blocking responsibilities were never comparable to true modern tight ends.

Pete Pihos became the first player who largely handled tight end duties to become a bona fide NFL star—before the phrase "tight end" was established in the sporting lexicon. A 6-foot-1 and 210-pound All American end at the University of Indiana, Pihos was drafted on the fifth round by coach Greasy Neale's Philadelphia Eagles in 1945. He played right end on offense and defense for the Eagles from 1947 to 1955, including on the NFL championship teams of 1948 and 1949, which were spearheaded by fullback Steve Van Buren running out of the T formation. Pihos scored one of the two touchdowns in the 1949 title game, a 14–0 defeat of the Rams, on a 31-yard TD pass from quarterback Tommy Thompson.

Coach Jim Trimble took over the Eagles from 1952 to 1955, and quarterback Adrian Burk began throwing more. And Pihos' role in the offense also dramatically increased. He became an outstanding short-situation receiver. In 1953, Pihos enjoyed a banner year, catching 63 passes for 1,049 yards, and 10 TDs—leading the league in all three categories. He also led the NFL in receptions in 1954 with 60, and in his final year, 1955, with 62. Pihos caught 373 career passes for 5,619 yards, and 61 touchdowns. Pihos was the only end ever to be named All Pro on both offense and defense, and went to six Pro Bowls. Pihos was inducted into the Pro Football Hall of Fame in 1970, the same year as Fears. They were the fifth and sixth receivers so honored, after Don Hutson, Guy Chamberlin, Wayne Millner, and Elroy Hirsch. Beefier than most receivers of his day and smaller than most of the linemen coming into the league during the 1950s, Pihos represented both the NFL in transition and a position in transition. He retired to his hometown of Orlando, Florida.

"Pete Pihos was the first great tight end," remem-

Pete Pihos was an integral member of coach Greasy Neale's 1948 and 1949 NFL champion Philadelphia Eagles at the beginning of his nine-year career, then added personal laurels in his final three seasons, leading the league in receptions in 1953 (63), 1954 (60), and 1955 (62) (Topps® Bowman® courtesy The Topps Company, Inc.).

Fifteen. Tight End: Biography of a Position

bered George Allen in 1982. "He didn't go deep very often, but he made the short catch, especially over the middle, very well, and he was a brilliant, brutal blocker. Pihos was a fine all-around athlete. He was one of the last to play both offense and defense. He was one of the last of the 60-minute players.... But he was a standout offensive end with sure hands who made more catches than anyone in his prime. He was no giant, but he was big enough. He was no sprinter, but he was fast enough. He was extremely tough and durable and determined, and he seemed to me an exceptionally smart player."[10]

Paralleling Pihos' career with similar high-level play without much notoriety was that of 6-foot-1, 196-pound Elbie Nickel for the Pittsburgh Steelers. Because the Steelers were the last pro team to adapt to the T formation, for the 1952 season, Nickel operated for the first five years of his 11-year career out of the single wing. Nickel had already demonstrated his deep-route capabilities by leading the NFL with a 24.3 yards-per-catch average in 1949 (26 catches for 633 yards and three TDs). But once the T was in place, the former 17th-round draft choice from the University of Cincinnati became a busy star on an otherwise run-oriented club, catching 55 passes for 884 yards and nine TDs in 1952, and 62 balls for 743 yards and four TDs in 1953. He totaled 329 receptions for 5,131 yards, and 37 TDs from 1947 to 1957.

"Elbie was a great player, a better player than people really know," Steelers Chairman Dan Rooney told Ed Bouchette of the *Pittsburgh Post-Gazette* when Nickel died in 2007. "In those days, there wasn't a position called tight end, but he really was a tight end. He could block, and he caught the tough passes over the middle."[11] Nickel's best work came in the final game of the 1952 season against the Los Angeles Rams when he caught 10 passes, scorching the legendary defensive back Dick "Night Train" Lane for 202 yards and a TD. After retiring, Nickel continued in the construction business in Ohio. Suffering from Alzheimer's disease in his later years, he died in Chillicothe at the age of 84.

Unwittingly, Bob Shaw, then Pihos and Nickel, pioneered the tight end post, which gradually took shape in the trenches with little notoriety. Coaches and historians with a long view back across the NFL wars, such as George Allen and Paul Zimmerman, recognize from a modern-era vantage point that Pihos and Nickel were performing tight end duties, even as that position hadn't yet become generally identified by the strategists. Described from a lineman's point of view, the position might rightly have been called the three-tackle concept rather than anything to do with three ends. Tight ends had to demonstrate versatility at a hybrid position, blocking and catching with equal dexterity.

Tight ends also took their licks. "Tight ends take the most punishment," wrote Paul Zimmerman, comparing roles in the receiving corps. "They're getting hit by bigger people, such as linebackers, and by more of them. A wide receiver often finds himself one-on-one with a cornerback, with a sideline next to him. The tight end works in traffic. One guy tees him up, another one finishes him off."[12]

There's an inherent schizophrenia in the position, part of its *modus operandi*, part of its singularity. "The receivers coach tells me to go with the linemen," said Russ Francis, who played tight end for the New England Patriots and San Francisco 49ers from 1975 to 1988. "The line coach says no, you go with the receivers. I'm in each group, and I'm not in them."[13]

Despite the lingering duality in the position by the time Francis was an All Pro, the tight end to the outside world two decades earlier was still a kind of mystery player. In the late 1950s, no distinctions in nomenclature were made between the speed merchants lining up at split end and the 235-pounders at tight end—positions that were even then as distinct as offensive tackle is from center and free safety is from outside linebacker. On the 1958 and 1959 World Champion Baltimore Colts, Johnny Unitas' receivers included Jim Mutscheller, the offensive end or "OE" on the opposite end of the line of scrimmage from star split end Raymond Berry. Mutscheller mostly lined up off the shoulder of the tackle, blocking on running plays and some passing plays, while Berry was split wide. Both players were designated "OE" or offensive end.

The pass-happy American Football League, which began play in 1960 in eight cities, helped establish more clearly the tight end's role. Top receivers in the first years of the new league included tight ends Dave Kocourek of the San Diego Chargers and Jim Whalen of the Boston Patriots. In 1961 in the NFL, Ditka arrived in Chicago, earning Rookie of the Year honors, coinciding with Kramer's notoriety with the rise of Lombardi's Packers. The following year, 1962, "tight end" or "TE" finally became codified in the All Pro and Pro Bowl selections.

The All-Pro selections prior to 1962 neglected tight ends altogether,

Fifteen. Tight End: Biography of a Position

and two of the leading speedsters at outside receiver often were selected as All Pro ends. For instance, in 1958, the first- and second-team pairs of ends selected for All Pro status by the four notable news-gathering organizations—*The Sporting News*, Associated Press, United Press International, and Newspaper Enterprise Association—all made their picks from a pool of split ends—Raymond Berry of the Colts, Woodley Lewis of the Cardinals, Jimmy Orr of the Steelers, Pete Retzlaff of the Eagles, Del Shofner of the Rams, and Billy Wilson of the 49ers.

But in 1962, offensive pass receivers were identified as more than just ends or "OE." The sporting press and pro football beat writers began recognizing "split end" or "SE" when the player lined up far away from either tackle, and "tight end" or "TE" when he lined up beside other linemen (*Street & Smith's Pro Football Yearbook* waited until 1967). The tight end became classified in sports consciousness as unique unto itself. A decade later, after the tight end's duties had become firmly established, the similarities of the split end and flanker would coalesce into their new identification as "WR" or "wide receivers."

In 1962, Ditka was the first-team tight end selection by the UPI and PE, and Kramer was on the second team. The players reversed spots on the AP list. *The Sporting News* selected all-star teams for each NFL division, with Ditka on the West and Preston Carpenter of the Steelers on the East. In the AFL, Dave Kocourek and Fred Arbanas were one-two on the All Star teams selected by the AP and UPI while Kocourek was the lone selection at the position by the league itself, which named its own All Star teams from its inception year of 1960 through 1966.

Bigger, faster tight ends started coming into the NFL after Kramer and Ditka established the viability and visibility of the position as a glory spot. John Mackey arrived from Syracuse as a second-round draft choice by the Baltimore Colts for the 1963 season. Johnny Unitas suddenly had a new weapon in the arsenal—a big, powerful lineman at 6-foot-2 and 224 pounds, who blocked with the best of them and also was a nimble pass catcher with the uncommon speed of an outside receiver. In fact, he caught Unitas' longest completion, 89 yards, against the Los Angeles Rams in 1966. Six of Mackey's nine TDs that year were longer than 50 yards. He averaged more than 20 yards a catch in his rookie year and in 1965. He caught 35 passes for 726 yards and seven TDs as a Pro Bowl rookie. A consensus All Pro from 1966 through 1968, Mackey eventually amassed 331 receptions for 5,236 yards and 38 TDs in 10 years, the final one with San Diego. He missed one game in that decade.

"He was such a powerful, explosive football player, both as a receiver and a blocker," maintained Don Shula, the Colts' head coach through Mackey's initial seven seasons. "He had great speed. After he caught the ball, he had great running ability. As a blocker, he would explode out of his stance and get into the linebacker's face, and just overwhelm him."[14] Mackey's speed gear gave him the edge over Ditka. Mackey could outrun linebackers and out-leap defensive backs.

"The tight end is Determination," explained Mackey in a sermon-like breakdown of the offensive positions ("The halfback is Hope.... The tackles are Strength..." etc.) in his autobiography, *Blazing Trails*. "[The tight end is] determined to get off the ball. He's determined to clear out the line. He's determined to catch the ball. He's determined to get the middle linebacker. The tight end is a little crazy, too, sort of like a middle linebacker. He has to be very aggressive. He's hit on every play. There is a linebacker on the other side who is taught not to let the tight end off the line of scrimmage.... If the tight end releases inside, there's a middle linebacker who wants to knock him on his behind. He knows he's going to get hit on every play. If he's not trying to catch the ball, he's trying to control someone else so that his

John Mackey was more agile and faster than other tight ends of the 1960s. A five-time Pro Bowler, he gave Baltimore Colts QB Johnny Unitas an extra edge. Mackey served as president of the NFL Players Association from 1970 to 1973. He was elected to the Hall of Fame in 1992 (Philadelphia Gum Company, courtesy Tootsie Roll Industries).

Fifteen. Tight End: Biography of a Position

teammates can get open—like I said, the tight end is Determination and a little bit crazy."[15]

Mackey was involved in one of the most memorable plays of the early Super Bowl era when, in Super Bowl V, he was the recipient of a 75-yard touchdown pass from Johnny Unitas in the second quarter of the Colts' 16–13 come-from-behind win over the Dallas Cowboys. The memorable margin of victory was Jim O'Brien's tie-breaking field goal with five seconds left. Unitas' medium-deep pass over the middle was intended for Eddie Hinton on a crossing pattern. Hinton only managed to deflect the pass, which then was slightly tipped by Cowboys' defensive back Mel Renfro, and landed nearly gift-wrapped in Mackey's hands. Mackey carried the ball into the end zone for a 75-yard TD, the longest up to that time in the Super Bowl. The Cowboys argued momentarily that Renfro never touched the ball, citing the then enforced rule that a reception is invalid if it's tipped directly from one offensive player to another. It has to have been touched in between by a defender, which this ball was (the rule was excised after the "Immaculate Reception" in Pittsburgh in 1972.).

Mackey was the second tight end inducted into the Pro Football Hall of Fame, in 1992, four years after Mike Ditka. In 1969, when the Pro Football Hall of Fame picked the 50th anniversary team, Mackey was selected as the sole tight end. In 1999 *The Sporting News* picked the 100 greatest players in pro history, and Mackey was No. 48—the highest-ranked TE. In 2010, the NFL Network's top 100 player rankings placed him at No. 42—also the highest-ranked TE, ahead of No. 45 Tony Gonzalez and No. 59 Ditka. In 2008 the NFL Network presented one of its informal, hour-long, top-10 specials specifically on tight ends, and ranked Mackey at No. 1.

Mackey was elected the president of the NFL Players Association in 1969 and presided through the merger with of the American Football League—and until 1973. In later years, he suffered from frontotemporal dementia. Mackey's paranoia caused his arrest at an airport screening facility in 2005, and, once, a glimpse of Marvin Harrison of the Indianapolis Colts, wearing Mackey's old jersey number, 88, enraged him. He resides at an assisted living facility. At first, the organization that he once guided, the NFLPA, refused to pay a disability income to him, because nothing proved that his condition had anything to do with having played pro football. The league and the NFLPA eventually created the "88 Plan," named for Mackey's old number (which has been retired at Syracuse) and for the fact that it provides $88,000 a year for nursing home care and up to $50,000 annually for adult day care.

For most football aficionados, Mackey remains the paragon of tight ends. On a team in which the stellar receivers included Pro Football Hall of Famers Raymond Berry and Lenny Moore as well as Jimmy Orr and Willie Richardson, and, later, Eddie Hinton and Roy Jefferson, the mighty John Mackey was often the go-to guy—and the *deep* go-to guy. He redefined the position's potential as a threat anywhere on the field, just as the NFL at large was recognizing tight end value.

Elsewhere in the league, finding long-term answers at the position were the St. Louis Cardinals by drafting Jackie Smith on the 10th round out of Northwestern Louisiana in 1963, the Washington Redskins by drafting Jerry Smith on the ninth round from Arizona State in 1965, and the Detroit Lions by selecting Charlie Sanders on the third round from Minnesota in 1968.

The 6-foot-4 and 235-pound Jackie Smith ended his career as the most productive tight end in terms of numbers in pro history. A former track and field star who ran the 100-yard dash in 9.8 seconds, Smith also was a first-rate blocker who, when he signed on for his final season with the 1978 Cowboys, had played more games, 198, than anyone in Cards history. He played 15 seasons with the Cards and one with Cowboys, catching 480 passes for 7,918 yards and 40 TDs. Smith's career year was 1967 when he caught 56 passes for 1,205 yards and nine TDs, coinciding with quarterback Jim Hart's first full year as the starting quarterback on coach Charley Winner's hard-luck Cardinals. Smith played during St. Louis' mostly fallow years and had the misfortune of dropping a crucial fourth-quarter pass from Roger Staubach that would have been a Dallas touchdown in Super Bowl XIII, won by the Pittsburgh Steelers, 35–31. Smith became the third tight end after Ditka and Mackey to be inducted into the Pro Football Hall of Fame, in 1994.

"The secret isn't in pure speed, but how you make your cut," Jackie Smith told Paul Zimmerman. "You've got to learn to make that cut, even if it's a 90-degree angle cut, without chopping your stride. The defensive back can read you once you start shortening your stride so the cut will be more comfortable to execute. That's where you separate the good

Fifteen. Tight End: Biography of a Position

JACKIE SMITH
ST. LOUIS CARDINALS   T. END-K

Jackie Smith played 14 years at tight end for the St. Louis Cardinals and a final one for the Dallas Cowboys. His best year was 1967 when he caught 56 balls for 1,205 yards and nine TDs. A five-time Pro Bowler, he was elected to the Hall of Fame in 1994 (Philadelphia Gum Company, courtesy Tootsie Roll Industries).

receivers from the ordinary ones, making that cut in full stride so the defensive back can't adjust. That's where you beat him. You also have to set him up—lure him away from the cut, so if he bumps you after you fake, it'll send you into the pattern, not out of it."[16]

Jerry Smith played all of his 13 seasons with the Redskins. His best year was 1967 when Washington quarterback Sonny Jurgenson heaved the ball everywhere and three of his receivers were among the NFL's top five in receptions. Smith, ranking second in the league behind teammate Charley Taylor (70), caught 67 balls for 849 yards and 12 TDs (the 'Skins' Bobby Mitchell was fourth with 60). A deep threat in the three-wide receiver tradition—the 6-foot-3 Smith was only 208-pounds—Smith played through the Jurgenson era and on coach George Allen's "Over the Hill Gang" era, retiring in 1977 with 421 career receptions for 5,496 yards, and 60 total TDs—the most scores by any tight end up to that time (despite Pihos' 61 TDs—before the tight end was defined in modern football). After football, Smith, co-owned the Boathouse, a gay bar in Austin, Texas. In a sad postscript, Smith became the first known former pro athlete to die of AIDS, in 1986 at the age of 43.

Roy Jefferson, the exceptional flanker for the Steelers, Colts, and Redskins, who played with Smith on the "over-the-hill" receiving corps, visited Smith before the end. "I was at his bedside three or four days before he died, and he told me, 'You know what?' We're taught all our lives that if you work hard enough, you can overcome anything. But there is nothing I can do now. If there was something I could do, I'd do it. But there's nothing I can do.' I was standing there crying," Jefferson told Thom Loverro. "If there was something he could have done, whatever it was, he would have done it if he could."[17]

Another Washington teammate, defensive back Mike Bass, said, "I measured Jerry by what he did on a football field. What he did outside was his business.... He was a football player, and I was very proud to be on the same field with him."[18]

Sanders was known for spectacular grabs—one-hand nabs, diving catches, and eventually secured circus bobbles. "Catching is psychological," Sanders told John Devaney. "When I have to make a difficult catch—one that I know is going to be difficult—I relax. My mind is relaxed, my body is at ease, because I know the people think there's no way I'm going to get it. And I'm thinking, they know I can't get it, so if I don't get it, it's no big deal. I usually come up with those because I'm relaxed."[19] Getting little national attention with the second-division Lions, Sanders was remarkably consistent, catching between 27 and 42 balls in nine of his 10 seasons, accumulating 336 career receptions for 4,817 yards, and 31 TDs. He was the seventh tight end to be inducted into the Pro Football Hall of Fame, in 2007, after Ditka, Mackey, Jackie Smith, Kellen Winslow, Ozzie Newsome, and Dave Casper.

Jerry Smith was one of the NFL's top tight ends in the 1960s. His best year was 1967 when he caught 67 passes for 849 yards and 11 TDs. He played all of his 13 seasons with the Washington Redskins. Smith was the first known former NFL player to die from AIDS (Philadelphia Gum Company, courtesy Tootsie Roll Industries).

Fifteen. Tight End: Biography of a Position

Sanders and the Smiths helped settle the post of tight end into a pro standard that every team sought to maintain. However, finding a fit for the position often meant adapting a specialist at something else— split end, sometimes fullback. As the fullback's role through the 1960s and 1970s developed into that of blocking back by the 1980s and 1990s, the fullback's skill set often mixed and matched with that of the tight end. Both blocked on halfback running plays and in pass protection for the quarterback. Of the players who split their careers between tight end and another position, the most outstanding was Pete Retzlaff.

Retzlaff played on the Eagles from 1956 to 1966. A fullback at South Dakota State College, he played halfback or flanker for Philadelphia from 1956 through 1958, and split end from 1959 into the 1962 season, when coach Nick Skorich asked him to play tight end after the starter there, Bobby Walston, was injured. Retzlaff remained a tight end for the rest of his career. Retzlaff led the NFL in receptions as a flanker in 1958 with 56 (for 766 yards and two TDs). However, he had his most productive years playing tight end, catching 57 passes for 895 yards and four TDs in 1963, 51 balls for 855 yards and eight TDs in 1964, and 66 for 1,190 yards and 10 TDs in 1965. He became the second tight end after Ditka to gain 1,000 yards in receptions (the third 1,000-yard TE was Jackie Smith in 1967).

"On the outside as a split end," Retzlaff told sports writer Dave Anderson, "I was primarily a receiver. I was concentrating 85 percent of the time on pass pat-

Pete Retzlaff played halfback, flanker, split end, and tight end in 11 seasons, all with the Philadelphia Eagles. He led the NFL in receptions with 56 as a halfback/flanker in 1958, but enjoyed his best year playing at tight end, in 1965, with 66 catches for 1,190 yards and 10 TDs (Philadelphia Gum Company, courtesy Tootsie Roll Industries).

terns. Playing the tight end, I'm a lineman, too. I have to throw blocks. I'm a factor in the running game. I no longer feel I'm a specialist. I'm more of a complete football player. At tight end I've got the linebacker standing over me, and I have to fight him for five or six yards to get free. Other times I have to block the defensive end or the linebacker. It would be senseless for me to try to overpower a 260-pound defensive end or a 230-pound linebacker. So I have to finesse them, and sometimes that's not easy. Sometimes I line up on the right side, sometimes on the left. This means I've got to study two defensive ends, two linebackers, and two safety men. When I was playing split end, I could go an entire half without knowing that I'd accomplished anything. As a tight end, I'm involved in every play. It's more rewarding."[20]

A 22nd-round choice by the Lions in the 1953 draft, Retzlaff didn't make the Detroit squad and went into the Army, returning to the Lions in 1956, when his contract was sold to the Eagles. At 6-foot-1 and 211 pounds, he never had the size of a tight end of the modern era, so the finesse he talked about and a mind for the game kept him in good stead. He ended his career with 452 receptions for 7,412 yards—Eagles records at the time—and 47 TDs. Like Mackey, Retzlaff served a stint as the president of the NFL Players Association. He eventually went into team management, serving as vice president and general manager of the Eagles from 1969 to 1972.

Retzlaff was among several tight ends in the 1960s and 1970s who were changed in or out of the position, either converted to tight end—like Dave Kocourek of the Chargers, Dave Parks of the San Francisco 49ers, and Gary Ballman of the Eagles—or from tight end to offensive tackle, in the cases of Paul Costa of the Buffalo Bills and Larry Brown of the Steelers.

Tight end Brown scored the insurance touchdown in Super Bowl IX on a four-yard pass from Terry Bradshaw in a 16–6 Pittsburgh win. Four seasons after skill-position glory was taken away from him by Chuck Noll in Brown's eighth year, the lineman finally made the Pro Bowl after the 1982 season, two years before his retirement.

Experimentation at tight end included the position's novel deployment in the American Football League by coach Hank Stram of the 1962 league-champion Dallas Texans. Stram devised a two-tight-end offense to thwart the rampaging blitzes of Boston Patriots linebackers Tom

Fifteen. Tight End: Biography of a Position

Addison and rookie Nick Buoniconti. Innovative in its time, the two-tight-end formation used rookies Tommy Brooker and Fred Arbanas to slow down the rush. The two-tight-end formation has been used by many teams since at all levels for power running plays, extra pass protection, and as a decoy. Washington Redskins coach Joe Gibbs learned the two-tight end offense as an assistant to coach Don Coryell with San Diego in the 1980s, when the Chargers used the set. With Washington in the 1980s and '90s, Gibbs facilitated his running game with Joe Washington and especially John Riggins by deploying tight ends Don Warren, Mike Williams, Doc Walker, and Clint Didier as interchangeable virtual third and fourth tackles.

Stram also put a huge twist on the tight end's duties after the Texans moved to Kansas City and became the Chiefs. He had drafted tailback Mike Garrett out of the University of Southern California for the 1966 season. Garrett had run out of Coach John McKay's I formation as the archetype tailback of the succession of runners—O.J. Simpson, Ricky Bell, Charles White, et al.—out of the Trojans' much vaunted tailback factory.

Stram included the I formation in his playbook to facilitate not only Garrett. Kansas City had drafted the mercurial Otis Taylor the year before out of Prairie View A&M, and Taylor became a revelation as the starting flanker with a breakout season in 1966. "Otis Taylor arrived to add a deep threat to the offense and the two-tight-end system gave way to one of the most dramatic innovations of the decade—the tight end in the I formation," wrote Tom Bennett in 1976.[21]

The Kansas City "I" was formed by a single-file backfield stemming from center E.J. Holub through quarterback Lenny Dawson and fullback Curtis McClinton (or Robert "The Tank" Holmes) to tailback Garrett. Used in college ball since the early 1950s, the I formation gave Stram new ideas. He designed plays in which the space behind Dawson and in front of the fullback became the odd, pre-snap starting point for Arbanas.

As Dawson called the signals, the tight end would shift to his appropriate position on the line—off the shoulder of either tackle. The key word here is "either." The significance of the delay before Arbanas would go into his three-point stance beside a tackle was that the defense wouldn't know which side was the strong side and which the weak until just before the snap, when Arbanas set at the line. This kept the defensive ends, outside linebackers and defensive backs in a state of suspense, throwing off their assignments until literally the last moment, when they scurried to facilitate coverage.

"When we reduce the other team's read-and-react time, we feel we have an edge," Stram said. "We also feel we will force them to play a normal defense. They can't overshift, because they don't know what the formation will be; they can't locate the tight end. We, in effect, freeze them—and pick up another edge."[22]

Since the rules stipulate that each play must start with seven men on the line and four in the backfield, one of the split receivers, usually Taylor but sometimes split end Chris Burford, would start the play on the line and take a step back into the backfield before the snap. The Chiefs went 11–2–1 in 1966 and won the AFL Championship, 31–7, over the Buffalo Bills before losing the Super Bowl's maiden run to the Green Bay Packers, 35–10. Both Taylor and Burford had terrific years, catching 58 passes apiece by slicing through secondaries that were not as prepared as they might have been had they not had to wait for Arbanas' cue.

Arbanas became one of the more visible and well known players in the AFL simply because his shifts from the I formation were seen and described on television so often. He was also one of the Chiefs' most integral offensive starters, protecting Dawson as well as gathering his throws, and was named the tight end on the all-time AFL team at the close of the 1960s. His best year was 1964 when he caught 34 passes for 686 yards and eight TDs. His most satisfying year was 1969 when the Chiefs defeated the New York Jets and archrival Oakland Raiders in the playoffs, and then beat the Minnesota Vikings, 23–7, in Super Bowl IV. Arbanas closed out his career in 1970 with 198 receptions for 3,101 yards and 34 TDs.

Arbanas was one of the more remarkable comeback stories in the AFL. While Christmas shopping in December 1964, the 6-foot-3, 240-pound Arbanas was assaulted, receiving a blow to his left eye. The Michigan State alumnus lost sight in the eye the following January. Any pro athlete with only one good eye is a liability, but a receiver with only one good eye would seem to have been an improbability. But Arbanas put in the extra time and effort—with the extracurricular help of his quarterback.

Fifteen. Tight End: Biography of a Position

"I wanted to keep on as a player," Arbanas said after he was back starting at tight end. "If you want something bad enough, you can do it. So I went out that spring with Lenny Dawson when the snow was still on the ground. I was wearing an eye patch. Lenny spent hours with me [throwing passes to me]."[23]

The AFL produced a few other exceptional tight ends, including Willie Frazier for the Houston Oilers and then San Diego, Alvin Reed with the Oilers, Pete Lammons with the Jets, and Bob Trumpy for the Cincinnati Bengals. Lammons was one of quarterback Joe Namath's main receivers during the last four years of the AFL, grabbing a career-high 45 passes for 515 yards and two TDs in 1967. Trumpy played 10 seasons, and caught 298 passes for 4,600 yards, and 35 TDs.

The one AFL club that experimented with the jack-of-all-trades position more than any other team—in the new league as well as later in the NFL—and fully exploited the position's possibilities, was the Oakland Raiders. In 1964, they acquired from the Oilers halfback Billy Cannon, the 1959 Heisman Trophy winner at Louisiana State and the AFL's leading rusher in 1961. The Raiders converted him in 1965 into a tight end. Conversely, the Raiders acquired tight end Hewitt "Hewie the Freight" Dixon from the Denver Broncos

Billy Cannon led the AFL in rushing in 1961 for the Houston Oilers with 948 yards and six TDs—*and* added nine TDs on receptions. Al Davis noticed and brought Cannon to the Oakland Raiders and switched him to tight end. In 1966, Cannon scored 10 TDs (on 32 catches) as a TE (Fleer Corporation, courtesy Tootsie Roll Industries).

in 1966 and converted him into a productive fullback. A deceptively fast deep threat who had played in the same backfield with Bob Hayes at Florida A&M, Dixon caught 59 passes as one of the AFL's leading receivers in 1967—while playing fullback. And Cannon enjoyed his best receiving year at tight end, catching 32 passes for 629 yards and 10 TDs.

General Manager Al Davis and coach John Rauch had seen great results after Davis had played a speedy halfback, Clem Daniels, at fullback through the early 1960s. Davis and Rauch wanted to inject speed into positions where it usually wasn't a prerequisite. The decisions with Dixon and Cannon helped lead to a 13–1 season in 1967, a 40–7 victory over the Oilers in the AFL championship game, and entrée to Super Bowl II, which the Raiders lost to the Green Bay Packers, 33–14.

"Again it was speed that intrigued Davis," wrote Glenn Dickey. "His idea was to put speed at positions where it wasn't expected. Tight ends were traditionally selected for their blocking, not their receiving—they had to be big enough and tough enough to block linebackers in order to make the running game work. But Davis wanted a receiver in that position. The safeties who had to cover Daniels, Dixon, and now Cannon were overmatched. On the 1967 Super Bowl team, Cannon became more of a deep threat than either of the wide receivers, Fred Biletnikoff and Bill Miller, and he caught ten touchdown passes."[24]

The Raiders eventually established great consistency at tight end with a continuum of long-serving stars: Cannon (1965–1969), Raymond Chester (1970–1972 and 1978–1981), Dave Casper (1974–1980 and 1984), Todd Christensen (1979–1988), Ethan Horton (1987–1993), Rickey Dudley (1996 to 2000), and Zach Miller (2007 through 2010). Of this group, both Casper and Christensen rank among the greatest tight ends in pro football history.

A favorite target of quarterback Kenny Stabler, Casper played 11 total seasons, including stints for the Oilers and Vikings, and ended up back with Al Davis' Los Angeles Raiders in 1984. Originally a defensive tackle at Notre Dame, Casper became a tight end in his junior year. A 6-foot-4, 240-pounder, he was appreciated for his intellectual approach to the game.

"He's always trying to figure out something that will help us," Stabler said during the 1976 season. "He's our 'thinking man's receiver.' He knows what the other team's coverage is. And he knows what to do against it.

Fifteen. Tight End: Biography of a Position

I'll call a play and he'll come up with something that will work even better. I don't resent that because I know he is sure it's a better way."[25] The John Madden-coached Raiders went 13–1 in 1976 and defeated the New England Patriots and Pittsburgh Steelers in the playoffs on their way to victory over Minnesota Vikings, 32–14, in Super Bowl XI. Casper caught four passes for 70 yards and a TD in that Super Bowl.

"Casper does everything well," Stabler elaborated. "But he's the worst-looking player I've ever seen in practice. He looks bad when he's running and warming up. He can't catch the ball in practice, but doesn't miss it once the game starts. To me, he looks like he won't come in out of the rain. When he's warming up, you look at him and think that every step he takes is going to be his last. You'd think he was on his last legs. You expect him to fall down, but once the game starts and the ball is snapped, there isn't a better tight end in football."[26]

In that championship year, Casper caught 53 passes for 691 yards and 10 TDs. Remarkably consistent for five years in a row, he was named first-team All Pro after four of those seasons. Casper caught 378 career passes for 5,216 yards and 52 TDs. He was inducted into the Pro Football Hall of Fame in 2002. Casper's central participation in two famous plays gave his career added importance.

"The Ghost to the Post" is the nickname for the 42-yard completion from Stabler to Casper on Christmas Eve, 1977, at Memorial Stadium in Baltimore that set up the game-tying field goal by Errol Mann in the final minute of the Raiders' double-overtime playoff victory, 37–31, over the Colts. Casper, nicknamed after the cartoon character of Casper, ran a deep post pattern on a play that was designed to go to a wide receiver breaking inside. Raiders offensive coordinator Tom Flores told Stabler to "take a look at the ghost to the post" before deciding on where to throw the ball.[27] The high-arc pass that came off Stabler's fingertips was overthrown and not toward the post, so Casper had to break off the pattern, turn his body right, speed up, and gather in the pass directly over his head with an almost superhuman effort. Errol Mann's 22-yard field goal tied the game at 31-all. Casper finished off the Colts after 43 seconds into the second overtime when Stabler hit him with a 10-yard TD pass.

The play most associated with Casper's career—and with Raiders gall—is "The Holy Roller," aka the "Immaculate Deception." With 10 seconds left in a September 1978 game against the Chargers at Jack Murphy Stadium in San Diego, and with the home team up, 20–14, the Raiders had the ball on the Chargers' 14-yard line. Stabler was about to be sacked by Chargers' linebacker Woodrow Lowe, and fumbled the ball forward where resourceful running back Pete Banaszak appeared to be trying to recover the dribbling oval when he lost his footing and virtually shoveled the pigskin toward the goal line. Casper was closest to the bouncing ball and, in his supposed recovery effort, batted and kicked it over the goal line—and fell on it. The play was ruled a Raiders touchdown to the consternation of 52,000 San Diego fans. Errol Mann's extra point made the difference in a 21–20 Raiders victory. The Holy Roller changed football rules. In the offseason, the NFL instituted the Casper Rule, which states that if a player fumbles forward in the last two minutes of either half or on fourth down, only the fumbling player can recover or advance the ball.

The tight end has become integral to the passing game with incremental gains made at the position by a succession of great players from Casper onward, including Ozzie Newsome, Kellen Winslow, Todd Christensen, Shannon Sharpe, Ben Coates, Tony Gonzalez, Antonio Gates, Jason Witten, and others. They have evolved the position into a receiving-game essential, often more important to the nature and outcomes of the game in the 21st century than their fleet-footed counterparts at wide receiver.

CHAPTER SIXTEEN

Running Backs as Receivers

Preston Pearson has led a charmed football life. For an athlete who never played a down of college football, and a running back in a league in which contemporaries are lucky to last five years, and usually not on playoff teams, Pearson played on 10 division-winning clubs in his 14-year career.

In a league in which it's rare for a player to make it to a Super Bowl, Pearson participated in *five*, with three teams—the Baltimore Colts, Pittsburgh Steelers, and Dallas Cowboys. He was a member of the winning teams of Super Bowl IX, Pittsburgh, and Super Bowl XII, Dallas. His good fortune by association included head coaches Don Shula, Chuck Noll, and Tom Landry, and quarterbacks Johnny Unitas, Terry Bradshaw, and Roger Staubach—all Pro Football Hall of Famers. Pearson led the NFL in kickoff return average in 1968 for the Colts, and played as an every-down back for both Pittsburgh and Dallas. But his greatest ability was as a clutch performer—one of the greatest third-down receivers of all time.

Landry and Pearson conspired in the invention of the "third-down back." Pearson became a situational specialist whose clutch grabs moved the chains. To later third-down backs, such as Rocky Bleier, Ronnie Harmon, John L. Williams, Larry Centers, Kevin Faulk, and Reggie Bush, Preston Pearson qualifies as a spiritual father—even though Pearson and Bleier played in the same backfield at Pittsburgh. Bleier became a third-down receiver after Pearson was claimed on waivers by Dallas, before the 1975 season. Pearson was used by the Cowboys to crack increasingly sophisticated zone defenses. The angular and durable former basketball player at the University of Illinois was often described as "knifing" through a hole. His lithe frame didn't give defenders any girth to latch onto. He possessed quick moves, speed into the secondary, and could stretch for that extra yard after the catch.

One playoff game virtually defined and affirmed both the value of the receiving back and the work-in-progress of the increased use of running backs to break defensive zones—when Pearson led the Cowboys into Super Bowl XII via a 37–7 victory over the Rams in the NFC championship game.

On January 4, 1976, in Los Angeles Memorial Coliseum, Pearson caught three touchdown passes from Roger Staubach. Pearson ran 18 yards with a screen pass for Dallas' initial score. He dove along the right end zone sideline to collect an overthrown 15-yarder in what could serve as the NFL's poster clip for playoff effort and athletic sacrifice. In the third quarter, he grabbed a shovel pass and slickly maneuvered 19 yards through defenders for a TD.

Pearson caught seven passes for 123 yards and three TDs, and he outgaining the Rams from scrimmage, 143 yards to 140.

While the Cowboys lost the Super Bowl to his old team, the Steelers, Pearson enjoyed newfound worth in Dallas after Franco Harris' stardom reduced him to a backup role in Pittsburgh. Pearson built toward his showcase championship game by rushing for 509 yards and catching 27 passes for 351 yards and four total TDs during the season. To get to the conference championship, Pearson provided the heroics the week before in a 17–14, come-from-behind, fourth-quarter victory over the Minnesota Vikings in the divisional playoff at Bloomington.

Dallas started its final drive from its own 15-yard line with 1:51 remaining. Staubach completed passes to Pearson on third-and-one and then on fourth-and-16, near midfield. With the final seconds ticking away, Staubach tossed up what's usually been described as a "desperation heave." Pearson caught it at the five, and ran it in for the winning TD.

"Getting Preston Pearson on waivers from the Steelers was a big deal, a great move," Staubach explained. "That helped us a tremendous amount. Preston really brought a great ability out of the backfield to catch the football. And we really weren't a backfield-type passing team. Our passing game was oriented more downfield because back then you couldn't hit the receivers downfield, so [defenders] were going back deeper, and linebackers were going back in support, so you were dumping the ball off a lot. And Preston brought with him the ability to come

Sixteen. Running Backs as Receivers

out of the backfield and catch passes. Also, we went to the shotgun formation where we could use him. And Preston was the sort of receiver who could adjust well to the defense. He'd turn in when he was supposed to, so he really took a lot of pressure off [star wide receiver] Drew Pearson."[1]

Dallas coach Tom Landry seemed to require backs who were not the feature back to possess excellent receiving skills, from Amos Marsh and Dan Reeves in the 1960s to Walt Garrison and Moose Johnston. Initially as an every-down setback beside the rugged Robert Newhouse, then as a situational performer when Tony Dorsett became the starting halfback, Pearson took the "other back" post to a new level. Then, off the bench on third-and-short (or -long), he nabbed quick passes to move the chains. Usually operating out of the shotgun formation on third down, Dallas sometimes positioned Pearson in the slot for a checkout or sideline route, sometimes for a curl-in. Even after defenses adjusted to Pearson on third down, his skills and quickness and the Cowboys' plays still conspired to make him the league's great situational player.

In 1977, as No. 1 draft pick Dorsett gradually took over at halfback, cutting Pearson's playing time, the latter still ranked as one of the NFC's top five receivers, with 46 catches for 535 yards and four TDs. He virtually replicated those numbers the next year with 47 receptions for 526 yards as a part-timer. "The Cowboys' Preston Pearson was ... amazing," Paul Zimmerman wrote. "In 1979, when he was 34 and getting ready to wind it up, he caught 26 passes, 23 of them for first downs. Sixteen of 17 passes turned a third down into a first down, and the 17th gained nine yards on a third-and-10 ... and that's with everybody in the place knowing he was going to get the ball."[2] That's the great aspect of Pearson's latter career: Fans watching on television and in the stadium and personnel on both sidelines knew that Pearson was out there again on third down and that he was getting the ball.

"See, Landry had it in his mind that he wanted Preston to be a third-down specialist," Drew Pearson told historian Peter Golenbock. "Football had become a game where on third-down situations the other teams were taking away the wide receivers, so to be effective on third down you had to have good inside receivers. ... and who's covering him? Linebackers. And he was killing them. And the thing was, Preston turned out to be better than Landry ever, ever imagined he would be at what he did. Because Preston was the type of guy he was, he took it and he studied it and he made it. He worked on his pass routes, and he invented pass routes from that position. His biggest pass route was the sideline route. He took it another step: turn-in. Faking here and going there. Preston made it happen. He was able to set up a defender and kill him with a pass route.... He knew that was his niche, and he took advantage of it and took it to its highest level. And now he's regarded as one of the greatest to ever play in third-down situations coming out of the backfield."[3]

Had the Colts not taken a chance and drafted Pearson, a Freeport, Illinois, steelworker's son, on the 12th round in 1967, this basketball player probably would not have become the idiosyncratic success that he became on the football field. Pearson concluded his career with 941 rushes for 3,609 yards and 13 TDs while he caught 254 passes for 3,095 yards and scored 17 TDs. He also caught 43 playoff passes for 505 yards. After football, Pearson and promoter Janie Tilford formed Pro-Style Associates, matching athletes to companies for marketing purposes. Pearson wrote a 1985 memoir, *Hearing the Noise, My Life in the NFL*.

Other running backs of the same era, led by the Colts' Lydell Mitchell and the Vikings' Chuck Foreman, rolled up bigger receiving numbers than Pearson. And, in fact, running backs led the NFL in receptions six times during the 1970s. But no running back was more notable for backfield receiving than Pearson, partially because he was more visible as a member of the perpetually nationally-televised Cowboys.

The zone coverage that took away a lot of the deep and medium-deep passing in the late 1960s and early 1970s was subverted by Pearson and other running backs and tight ends by intensifying the use of "underneath" routes—capitalizing on short tosses. Defenses also had perfected the roughhouse bump-and-run technique to deter wide receivers from getting deep. The bump-and-run was pioneered by cornerbacks Willie Brown and Kent McCloughan of the Oakland Raiders in the AFL.

This man-on-man, collision coverage was taken to extremes by the Pittsburgh Steelers so that the "Mel Blount rule" was enacted by the NFL in 1978 to protect receivers, specifically saying they can't be jostled more than five yards beyond the line of scrimmage. The powerful 6-foot-3 Blount, an eventual Pro Football Hall of Famer who intercepted 57 passes

Sixteen. Running Backs as Receivers

as an infamously physical Steelers cornerback, barely tolerated receivers on his side of the field. Blount's pounding of receivers sometimes resulted in bandages. "The Mel Blount rule" helped return the deep game from not exactly mothballs, but from the occasional try or desperation heave that it had become.

Between the zone sophistication of the 1960s and less wide receiver molestation in the 1980s was a window of opportunity for running backs to catch more passes. It might rightly be called a window of overwork. The reduction of deep and medium-long routes at the decade's outset put more emphasis on the running game, period. As an illustration of the reliance on running backs exhibited by NFL offenses in the 1970s, be advised that prior to 1970, pro running backs had gained 1,000 yards rushing in a season 42 times.

But in the first decade after the AFL-NFL merger, 1970 to 1979, backs gained 1,000 yards rushing 79 times—averaging about eight each year or not far from double the number than in the previous half-century of league play. A dozen backs rushed for 1,000 yards in 1976. The addition of two more games in 1978 to make the regular season 16 games helped sustain the high numbers of 1,000-yard rushers in 1978 (11 backs) and 1979 (12). Since then, it's been customary for half or most NFL teams to have a rusher gain 1,000 yards. The feature back has to average only 63 yards a game to attain 1,000 yards over 16 games. Twenty backs finished 1998 as 1,000-yard rushers, and in 2000 there were 23 of them—in a 32-team league. Seventeen runners accumulated 1,000 or more yards in 2010 as the emphasis shifted in the new century toward throwing the football more.

But in the 1970s, teams sought to fight battles incrementally, establishing drives with consistency in what became known as possession offense. Quarterbacks threw more short balls underneath zone defenses to running backs and tight ends—more than to wide receivers. The emphasis on running backs in the passing game showed up incrementally and sometimes off the main stage with struggling teams looking for the consistency that a star running back could give them.

The aerial action famous in the AFL was like a preamble to the 1970s. Once the AFL was underway, and passing became that league's scoring *modus operandi*, running backs received heavy reliance as receivers, both as safety-valves and as primary route runners. Abner

Haynes, an end-zone magnet out of North Texas State and an African American who helped integrate that institution, was an all-everything for coach Hank Stram's Dallas Texans. He led the AFL in rushing touchdowns in its first three seasons with, respectively, nine, nine, and 13 (19 total TDs in 1962 to lead the league, six through the air). Haynes also led the league in rushing in its inaugural year of 1960 with 875 yards while also registering as the AFL's fifth leading receiver with 55 catches (for 576 yards, and 12 TDs overall).

Haynes was the fledgling league's Player of the Year and Rookie of the Year in 1960. "He was a franchise player before they talked about franchise players," Stram said. "He did it all—rushing, receiving, kickoff returns, punt returns. He gave us the dimension we needed to be a good team in Dallas."[4] Retiring from football after the 1967 season, Haynes became an executive for Dallas-based Zale Corporation, and then a sports agent, representing such football players as Joe Greene, Rayfield Wright, Harvey Martin, and Hollywood Henderson.

Screen and flare passes were mixed with short routes and other backs caught substantial numbers of passes during the AFL years (1960 to 1969), including Dick Christy for the New York Titans in 1962 (62 for 538 yards and three TDs), Bo Dickinson for the Denver Broncos in 1962 (60 for 554 and four TDs), Ode Burrell for the Houston Oilers in 1965 (55 for 650 and four TDs), and Hewritt Dixon for the Oakland Raiders in 1966 (59 for 563 and two TDs).

George Allen's experimentation in his first year as the Los Angeles Rams head coach in 1966 produced the initial instance in the modern NFL of a setback becoming one of the league's leading receivers. With pint-sized Dick Bass rushing for 1,090 yards and the deep and outside routes handled by Tommy McDonald (55 catches for 714 yards and three TDs) and Jack Snow (34 for 634 yards and three TDs), quarterback Roman Gabriel's options were flexible. However, his most frequent target was Bass' running mate, Tom Moore, who slipped out of the backfield to make 60 receptions (for 433 yards and three TDs), leading the 8–6 also-ran Rams and good for fifth place in the NFL, following "Bullet Bob" Hayes.

After the 1970 AFL-NFL merger, running backs became integrated into the throwing game more than ever. Rookie fullback Lee Bougess out of the University of Cincinnati on the 3–11 hard-luck Philadelphia Eagles

Sixteen. Running Backs as Receivers

in 1970 grabbed 50 passes as one of the league's leading receivers. Ron Johnson of the second-division New York Giants caught 48 passes the same year for 487 yards to add to his 1,027 rushing yards—for a dozen total TDs. Rugged all-purpose back Art Malone of the 7–7 Falcons in 1972 grabbed 50 aerials for 585 yards to total 1,383 yards from scrimmage.

The first back after the merger to be a top rusher, then immediately a top receiver, was Preston Pearson's backfield mate on Chuck Noll's rebuilding Steelers, who were 1–13 in 1969, 5–9 in 1970, and 6–8 in 1971. Juke-possessed, bowling-ball fullback Frenchy Fuqua rushed in 1970 for 691 yards and an AFC-leading 5.0 yards per carry. The following year, Fuqua caught 49 balls for 427 yards (and 1,057 total yards from scrimmage) as one of the conference's leading receivers.

The Steelers' offense exploited blitz packages by deploying Fuqua for short tosses, many of them misdirection screens or dumps into the flat from quarterback Terry Bradshaw. Fuqua's career highlight was 218 yards rushing against the Eagles in 1970, most of it on TD runs of 72 and 85 yards. But he would become best known as the momentarily intended receiver on football's most legendary play, the "Immaculate Reception." Caught by Franco Harris, this juggernaut of sporting lore allowed Pittsburgh to beat the Oakland Raiders, 13–7, in a divisional playoff game at Three Rivers Stadium.

An ungodly fluke or divine intervention, it gave the Steelers their first playoff win in their 40-year history. That win propelled the team to a new confidence level. That confidence plus Noll's painstaking approach to detail—in drafting players, building the defense and establishing the run on offense—reinforced the greatest collection of players ever on one team, and an unprecedented four Super Bowl victories in a six-year period.

As perhaps the most re-examined and replayed single event in sports history, the Immaculate Reception remains, after four decades, one of the most controversial calls of all time. It came on fourth-and-long with 22 seconds left in the game and the Steelers down, 7–6, at their own 40-yard line. The intended throw was to go to rookie wide receiver Barry Pearson. But as Bradshaw scrambled away from Oakland's pass rush and the play was broken, he spotted Fuqua and threw a medium-deep dart toward the running back, who was crossing the field near the Raiders' 35-yard line.

The ball, Fuqua, and Oakland defensive back Jack Tatum collided at once, caroming the ball backward in an arc. It remained in the air long enough for Harris, chasing the play, to make a shoestring grab. After tucking the ball, Harris ran past linebacker Gerald Irons as tight end John McMakin blocked pursuing linebacker Phil Villapiano. Harris ran down the left sideline, stiff-armed cornerback Jimmy Warren, and appeared to score a touchdown, standing up. Back judge Adrian Burk, who had played quarterback for the Eagles in the 1950s, signaled for a touchdown. The hometown crowd erupted in pandemonium.

This all occurred, of course, way before officiating teams had instant replay on the sidelines. Referee Fred Swearingen stopped the proceedings, conferred with his team of officials on the field, and asked Steelers sideline official Jim Boston to be taken to a telephone. The issue was whether the defender, Tatum, had touched the ball before Harris gathered it in. If Tatum had not touched the ball, and it came to Harris directly from Fuqua, it would have been an incompletion. The rules at the time stated that once an offensive player touches a pass, he is the only offensive player who can catch that pass, unless the opposition touches it, too (the rule has since been changed).

Swearingen made a phone call from the baseball dugout to league official Art McNally in the press box. Swearingen told McNally that two of his officials believed that Tatum had touched the ball. McNally said that he told Swearingen, "Everything's fine then. Go ahead."[5] Swearingen went back out on the field and signaled touchdown. The hometown fans were ecstatic. It took 15 minutes to restore order so that Pittsburgh's special teams unit could line up and kick the extra point. Coach John Madden's Raiders, who had scored their go-ahead TD with 1:17 left to play, were nonplussed to say the least. Madden has said that the play has haunted him for years.

As sometimes happens with a big controversy, little controversies become barnacled to it: Did Harris actually catch the ball before it hit the ground? Did the officials actually look at an instant replay right after the play? What did the league officials actually say to one another that resulted in the TD? There's no existing conclusive footage showing whether Tatum touched the ball or not. There was some noise about local station WTAE-TV's "lost footage" of the play. Most conclusions say that Tatum did hit the ball, or the ball wouldn't have ricocheted

Sixteen. Running Backs as Receivers

backward as it did. Re-hashing of the play includes a study reprinted in Timothy Gay's *The Physics of Football* that concluded that the officials on the field made the correct call.[6] Fuqua remained coy about the issue until two decades after the fact. In a talk with Pittsburgh sports writer Jim O'Brien, Fuqua, who admitted to being something of a storyteller, said of Tatum, "Jack didn't touch [the ball]. It's the only secret that I have left in my life."[7]

Fuqua was one of the more flamboyant sporting figures of his time, known for capes, enormous hats, and platform shoes with clear acrylic heels containing live goldfish. A Morgan State product who had returned kicks for the Giants and later added blocking back for the mercurial Harris to his duties, Fuqua was hampered by hamstring and collarbone injuries, became a backup to Harris and Rocky Bleier, and played on the Steelers' Super Bowl–winning teams of 1973 and 1974. Christened John in Detroit, Fuqua retired after the 1976 season, and worked for the *Detroit News*. True to his singular nature, Fuqua devised a candy bar on the 35th anniversary of the Immaculate Reception, calling it the "Immaculate Confection."

The year after the Immaculate Reception, journeyman fullback Fred Willis of the Houston Oilers became the first running back to lead a conference in receptions. A Boston College alumnus acquired midway through the 1972 season by the Oilers from the Cincinnati Bengals, Willis led the AFC in 1973 with 57 catches. However, his success emerged from futility as an example of individual numbers meaning little as far as the team went, like a slugger blasting home runs on a cellar-dweller: Houston was 1–13 in 1973. Willis' 371 yards (6.5 yards per catch) and one TD didn't help the cause as much as either wide receiver, Ken Burrough or Billy Parks, both of whom caught 43 passes for more than 500 yards each and scored at least one TD apiece.

Backs were one-two in receptions in 1973. Willis was followed in the AFC receiving sweeps by the Kansas City Chiefs' all-purpose grinder, Ed Podolak, who caught 55 passes. The multi-dimensional Podolak's greatest game was also the longest game ever played, the divisional play-off on Christmas Day, 1971, against the Dolphins, won by Miami on Garo Yepremian's field goal in the second overtime period, after 82 minutes and 40 seconds had elapsed, exhausting even the TV viewers—but Podolak more than anyone. He famously ripped off 350 yards—in a 27–

24 loss. He caught eight passes for 110 yards, including a seven-yard TD toss from Lenny Dawson; carried 17 times for 85 yards and a TD, and returned five kicks and punts for 155 yards, including a 78-yard kickoff return.

Podolak arrived in the middle of the Chiefs' glory years, and played on the Super Bowl IV-winning club. He proved himself a gutsy and steady performer whose rugged persistence made him the Chiefs' feature back of the 1970s, outlasting such talents as Mike Garrett and Robert "The Tank" Holmes. In nine seasons he ran for 4,451 yards and caught 288 passes for 2,456 yards and scored 40 TDs. After football, he was in the broadcast booth for his alma mater, the University of Iowa.

Running backs were not gaining big yardage with their newfound extended roles in their teams' passing games, but they were establishing possession football, contributing to long drives—consuming five, seven, 10, and 15 yards or more at a time on screen and swing passes. Overworked, they ran on first and second downs, and then moved the chains with third-down catches. The repositioning of the hash marks closer to the middle of the field in 1972 also provided an offensive boost, giving the outside receivers more operating room and robbing the defense of its partner, the sideline.

The inevitable finally took place. The reliance on running backs to do the lion's share of offensive work meant that they weren't just among the league leaders in receptions. For the rest of the decade, in an unprecedented skein, they *were* the league leaders. Defensive disruptions deterred even medium-deep routes as DBs such as Mel Blount and Donnie Shell on the Steelers, George Atkinson and Jack Tatum on the Raiders, and Charlie Waters and Cliff Harris on the Cowboys were teeing off on wide-outs. Long bombs still were hurled, and things dramatically changed after the Mel Blount rule in 1978, but big-play football was squeezed back on the play-selection chart, and running backs stepped into the void and caught more balls.

For six straight years, a back led the NFL in receptions, three times by Colts, twice by Vikings: Lydell Mitchell of Baltimore in 1974 with 72 catches, and again in 1977 with 71; Chuck Foreman of Minnesota in 1975 with 73; MacArthur Lane of the Chiefs in 1976 with 66; Ricky Young of the Vikings in 1978 with 88, and Joe Washington of the Colts in 1979 with 82. In 1980, fullback Earl Cooper of coach Bill Walsh's San Francisco

Sixteen. Running Backs as Receivers

49ers caught 83 balls to pace the NFC as the "West Coast Offense" evolved out of possession football.

As zone defenses became the norm through the 1960s, occasionally in tandem with man-to-man coverage or double-teaming on star receivers, defensive backs and linebackers dropped more into zone coverage. Weak sides of rotated zone defenses actually created weak areas of defensive absence. As well, the three-four defense gradually began replacing the four-three alignment into the 1980s, meaning teams were showing a defensive front of three linemen and four linebackers rather than vice versa in the manner that had created such vaunted lines as the Rams' "Fearsome Foursome," Minnesota's "Purple Gang," and Pittsburgh's "Steel Curtain." Linebackers were converting from the roughhouse, run-stuffing era of Sam Huff, Joe Schmidt, Ray Nitschke, and Dick Butkus to a more adaptive breed of quick, athletic, and responsive LBs, personified by the Steelers' remarkable trio of Andy Russell, Jack Ham, and the lithe and lethal Jack Lambert in the middle.

Both the "underneath," created by deep-dropping linebackers and fewer up-front linemen, and the "weak" sides became areas of offensive attack by both the running game and short passing attack. Ball-control offenses with multifaceted star backs flourished in the 1970s, some of them with "downhill" fullbacks. The Miami Dolphins wielded Larry Csonka and the Houston Oilers wreaked havoc with the powerful Earl Campbell. Pittsburgh dominated with the steady Franco Harris. O.J. Simpson set rushing records with the Buffalo Bills.

Backs such as the Colts' Lydell Mitchell, the Rams' Lawrence McCutcheon, the Vikings' Chuck Foreman, and the Raiders' Mark Van Eeghen became the rocks of their offenses. Superior talents such as Walter Payton and Tony Dorsett were just getting started as pros. As well, tight ends during this period became consistent go-to receivers, integrating that position more than ever into the short, ball-control passing game.

Historian Tom Bennett pointed out that personnel shifts at the quarterback position on several teams as well as the influence of a new breed of players who grew up on televised pro football also made a difference. A generation of cagey veteran quarterbacks, who could pick zones apart, retired from the game: Johnny Unitas, Lenny Dawson, Sonny Jurgenson, Bart Starr, John Brodie, Daryle Lamonica,

Earl Morrall, Jackie Kemp, and Don Meredith.[8] As they left the field, there wasn't a near comparable group arriving to take over. As well, the backs and linemen coming into the pros from college were influenced by the pro running game depicted weekly on television as a matter of future employment and proficiency. The shift of emphasis onto runners in the 1970s was at all levels of football.

The way running backs figured into offensive schemes as pass receivers often wasn't that much different than their operational effectiveness as rushers. They were the recipients of short tosses from the quarterback, many of these catches behind the line of scrimmage. They advanced the ball much as if they would on running plays, through the line or around end, using their abilities as runners. The quarterback dropping into the pocket, often from a play-action fake to one of the backs into the line, could hold onto the ball as defenders charged, then dump it over their outstretched arms to a running back waiting in the flat.

Sometimes, on screen passes, running backs would be escorted by phalanxes of blockers that might include the fullback or the tight end or pulling guards. Sometimes, the back executed a quick chip block on a defensive end or blitzing linebacker, then slipped out of the pocket, and received a short, quick toss. Other times, backs scattered behind and parallel to the line of scrimmage as a safety valve for a short toss as the quarterback checked off covered receivers in the secondary. In these cases, backs were often the last resorts.

Although some running backs were dispatched as downfield receivers, this was not the norm. Some speedy backs possessed of sure hands could always be downfield threats: Preston Pearson, Herschel Walker, Joe Cribbs, James Brooks, Amp Lee, Charlie Garner, etc. However, the time it took for them to run from the offensive backfield into the secondary and then break off on routes wasn't conducive to proficient offenses playing swift-charging defensive ends and blitzing linebackers. It also wasn't conducive to quarterbacks' health. Scramblers like Fran Tarkenton and Roger Staubach welcomed multifaceted backs as downfield receivers. On the Vikings, Tarkenton counted on running backs Tommy Mason and Bill Brown as blockers, runners, and receivers. Both backs logged more than one season in which they each accumulated 500 yards both running and receiving.

Using running backs as receivers is a strategy nearly as old as pass-

Sixteen. Running Backs as Receivers

ing itself, and great runners in the halcyon years of pro football have excelled as their team's most effective receivers. Halfback Johnny Blood was the Packers' best deep threat before Don Hutson came on the Green Bay scene to virtually create the receiving record book. The legendary Red Grange was as important as the man-in-motion receiver for the Chicago Bears as he was a runner. In the 1940s, Harry Clarke became the versatile go-to receiver out of the Bears' backfield. The specialization of backfield roles in the T formation and the amelioration of two-way players—those who played 60 minutes or nearly that on both offense and defense—made such superior multiple-threat backs-of-all-trades as Washington's Sammy Baugh, Pittsburgh's Bill Dudley, and Brooklyn's Ace Parker a diminishing species after the Second World War.

However, one postwar running back made a singularly spectacular mark as a receiver—as well as a rusher—before he left the National Football League for better pay in the Canadian Football League. Gene Roberts enjoyed a nova-like career as a star on the New York Giants before he abruptly left the club in 1951 because of a contract dispute with owner Wellington Mara, and played his final four pro seasons for the Ottawa Rough Riders.

Roberts led the CFL in scoring with 88 points in 1953, his second Canadian season. It was an era when CFL salaries were competitive with those in the NFL, and some American players chased the bigger contracts, including premier receivers Bud Grant and Mac Speedie. Grant left the Philadelphia Eagles for the CFL's Winnipeg Blue Bombers after ranking second in receptions in the NFL in 1952 with 56 (for 997 yards and seven TDs). He returned to the NFL to become one of the league's legendary coaches, guiding the Minnesota Vikings to four Super Bowls (if four losses).

Before Roberts went north, he achieved stardom for outstanding exploits under the New York spotlight with the catchy nickname of "Choo Choo"—a moniker based on the Glenn Miller hit "Chattanooga Choo Choo," applied when he starred at the University of Tennessee–Chattanooga as a "swift, powerful halfback, and deft-handed receiver," in the words of *Ottawa Sun* writer Earl McRea.[9]

An eighth-round draft pick by the Giants in 1947, Roberts played in New York through 1950. In 1949, he tied fullback/kicker Pat Harder of the Chicago Cardinals for the NFL scoring title with 102 points.

Roberts' scores were all touchdowns—17 total, nine rushing, eight receiving—in a 12-game season. As the main offensive force in football in 1949, Roberts led the league with 1,345 yards from scrimmage, 711 on 35 receptions, and 634 yards on 152 carries. In terms of yardage, he was the NFL's fourth-leading receiver and fourth-leading rusher.

Coach Steve Owen's Giants were led by quarterback Charlie Conerly and premiere defensive back Emlen Tunnell. "Owen was not surprised by Conerly and Tunnell," recalled Barry Gottehrer. "He was amazed by Choo Choo Roberts.... A disappointing rookie in 1947, Roberts, playing every backfield position except quarterback, scored 17 touchdowns in '49, just one short of the NFL record.... In four different games, he tied the Giant record of 3 touchdowns. Against the Bears, he went 85 yards with a Conerly pass in the closing minutes for the winning touchdown. Against the Redskins, he injured his shoulder early in the game and headed for the dressing room. Popping his shoulder back in place, he returned to the field, substituted himself back into the game, and scored two touchdowns."[10]

Roberts was the first NFL running back to total more than 200 yards *receiving* in a game—and he did it twice in one season. On October 23, 1949, Roberts caught four passes for 201 yards in a 35–28 Giants victory over the Chicago Bears at the Polo Grounds. The winning 85-yarder from Conerly was the longest play of that NFL season. Roberts caught the opening TD pass of 29 yards and added a 62-yard score after the half. Roberts was the first player to gain 200 yards with so few receptions, a mark tied by wide receivers—two generations later by Gary Clark of the Washington Redskins in a 1991 game (four catches for 203 yards), and another generation after that by DeSean Jackson of the Philadelphia Eagles in 2010 (four receptions for 210 yards).

Three weeks after Roberts' first 200-yard receiving afternoon, on November 14, 1949, he was again the force in a 30–10 Giants defeat of the Packers at Lambeau Field. He hauled in seven passes from Conerly for 212 yards and touchdowns of 45, 44, and 10 yards. Roberts remains the only NFL running back in history with two games of more than 200 yards receiving in a single season. The following season, Roberts became the fourth pro back in history—after Cliff Battles, Spec Sanders, and Steve Van Buren—to gain 200 yards on the ground in one game, specifically 218 yards on 26 carries, including TD runs of 62 and 35 yards, in a 51–

21 defeat of the Chicago Cardinals at the Polo Grounds. This Giants team rushing record stood until Tiki Barber gained 220 yards in a 2005 game.

Choo Choo Roberts refused to scrimmage in practice as a collegiate player, and his coaches went along with his decision. His single-season record of 18 rushing TDs at Tennessee-Chattanooga still stands as a testimony to his prowess and his understanding of what his body could take. He was of premium value to the Steve Owen-coached Giants, but they wouldn't pay him what he felt he was worth, so he walked away from Big Apple stardom. He played with arthritic knees throughout his career, and preferred to prepare and apply his own ice packs instead of relying on the Rough Riders' trainer. Roberts became a chiropractor, and scorned medical advice later in life. Ottawa journalist McRea found evidence of Roberts' reclusiveness in old age.[11] A native Kansan, Eugene O. Roberts passed away from complications of a urinary infection on July 6, 2009, in Independence, Missouri. He was 86. Roberts remains the only player to lead both the NFL and CFL in scoring.

Experimentation in the NFL with backfield receivers and ends split wide, which intensified under coach Clark Shaughnessy on the Los Angeles Rams in 1949, was continued by most teams through the 1950s. The newfangled passing game was mostly recognizable to the public through the flashy positions of flanker and split end. The other end, who mostly remained lined up next to a tackle, played the same as he always had, but was about to adopt a new nomenclature: tight end. Shaughnessy listened to the advice of his assistant coach, Red Hickey, a former end for the Steelers and Rams, and converted Elroy "Crazy Legs" Hirsch from a halfback to a full-time flanker. Untold success made the laboratory work mighty conspicuous: Hirsch scored 30 touchdowns in his first three seasons at flanker, gaining nearly 1,500 yards in 1951.

Switching from halfbacks to flankers and sometimes back again—often on the very next play or from game to game—as the 1950s dissolved into the 1960s were such NFL stars as Lenny Moore of the Colts, Frank Gifford of the Giants, Hugh "King" McElhenny of the San Francisco 49ers, Tommy McDonald of the Eagles, Ray Renfro of the Browns, and Ollie Matson of the Cardinals and Rams. The codification was slow to catch up. These players were mostly still identified as halfbacks, occasionally as flankers, and sometimes as ends, which they, in fact, were not.

Categorization was in flux as flip charts, programs, and newspaper rosters still identified flankers as halfbacks and still abbreviated split or tight ends as either "E" or "OE," for offensive end—making no distinction between 180-pound speed merchants on the outside and 235-pound virtual third tackles.

The Giants exploited the many talents of Gifford in and out of the flanker position as he became the first player to log multiple seasons in which he gained both 500 yards rushing and 500 receiving. Gifford achieved these numbers in the Giants' NFL championship year of 1956, when he was named the league's Most Valuable Player. He also achieved the dual marks in 1957 and 1959.

In 1956, Gifford rushed for 819 yards on 159 carries for five touchdowns, and caught 51 passes for 603 yards and four TDs, leading the Jim Lee Howell-coached, 8–3 Eastern Division-champions through to a dominating 47–7 victory over the Bears in the title game. Gifford's versatility made him something of a throwback player in an age of increasing NFL specialization. In fact, he also played defensive back in some seasons, and was selected for the Pro Bowl as a DB in 1953. An option passer of consistency, he completed 46 percent of his passes over 12 seasons.

"Gifford is one of the most versatile athletes I have

Hugh McElhenny represented the 1954 San Francisco 49ers' "Million Dollar Backfield" with Y.A. Tittle, Joe Perry, and John Henry Johnson—Hall of Famers all. McElhenny four times caught 30-plus passes in a season for 3,247 career yards on aerials (compared to 5,281 rushing) (Topps® Bowman® courtesy The Topps Company, Inc.).

Sixteen. Running Backs as Receivers

ever seen," said the often taciturn Steve Owen, the longtime Giants head coach who drafted him on the first round in 1952 out of the University of Southern California. "He has hard-running ability. He is an accurate passer, a strong blocker, a sensational receiver, a superior defensive back. He returns kicks and even place-kicks."[12] Vince Lombardi once claimed that Gifford could "burst through a line faster than any player I've seen."[13]

Gifford retired after the 1960 NFL championship game, in which Eagles linebacker Chuck Bednarik hit him with a devastating tackle. Gifford lost consciousness and had to be taken off the field with a concussion. After a year of retirement in the prime of his career, Gifford mulled over his options. He decided to return to the Giants in 1962, and coach Allie Sherman made him primarily a flanker. He played three more strong seasons, all of which found the Giants back in the NFL championship game (losing them all). In 1962, Gifford caught 39 passes for 796 yards and seven touchdowns.

In half of Gifford's dozen seasons with the Giants, the team won the NFL's Eastern Division. He ran the ball 840 times for 3,609 yards and 34 touchdowns, but he was more valuable as a receiver, catching 367 passes for 5,434 yards and 43 TDs (78 TDs in all). Gifford remained an icon of football for generations as the longtime anchor of *Monday Night Football* on ABC, putting in years as both the play-by-play man and an analyst, exhibiting an ease and facility as a communicator and a versatility that mirrored his grace and skill as an athlete. Gifford was elected to the Pro Football Hall of Fame in 1977.

The one other halfback of the postwar era whose multifaceted skills—particularly his receiving abilities—were often directly responsible for the success of his winning team was the spectacular Lenny Moore. As a fleet runner and superb receiver, Moore helped the Baltimore Colts win NFL Championships in 1958 and 1959. He was instrumental in keeping the Colts among the league's elite for a generation, from the Weeb Eubank era into the Don Shula stint.

Quarterback Johnny Unitas commanded a formidable arsenal, including fullback Alan "The Horse" Ameche, the often underrated tight end Jim Mutscheller and outside threat Raymond Berry. But the most versatile player on the team was Moore. Especially during their championship years, Moore and Unitas perfected and exploited the quick slant pass over the middle, dangerous ground for the receiver and often episodes of needle-threading for the quarterback. With Moore's speed and evasive capabilities, the slant sometimes led to big gains or touchdowns. When he retired after the 1967 season, Moore was one of three players in pro history to score more than 100 touchdowns, 113–63 on runs, 48 on receptions, and two on returns. The other two great TD scorers were the greatest running back of all time, Jim Brown, and the greatest receiver to that time, Don Hutson.

The 6-foot-1 and 191-pound Moore smoothly adapted to Baltimore's in-the-moment needs with a premium skill set. The second player after Gifford to rush and catch for more than 500 yards in the same year in multiple years, Moore was so versatile that, in his 12-year career, he gained more than 900 yards in receptions twice, in 1958 and 1960, and rushed for 16 touchdowns in another year. That was 1964, in which he scored 20 TDs in all, and was named the NFL's Most Valuable Player. The testimonies to Moore's talents are legion, and Berry once identified him as "probably pound for pound, the best offensive weapon—scoring weapon—that I've ever seen."[14] Legendary coach Joe Paterno, who was an assistant to Rip Engle during Moore's college years at Penn State, has consistently vowed throughout his long career that Moore was "probably the best player I've coached, all-around."[15]

The Colts selected Moore on the first round. Moore led the NFL with a rookie rushing average of 7.5 yards per carry (86 carries for 649 yards and eight TDs). Two years later, in another impressive statistic, Moore again led the NFL in yards per carry with a 7.3 average (82 carries for 598 yards) *and gained* 938 yards on 50 receptions.

"He's so quick and shifty," averred Giants quarterback Charlie Conerly, "that it's almost impossible to defend against him."[16] Moore's distinctions on the field included the mummy-like wrapping of his socks with adhesive tape firmly to his cleats. He was nicknamed "Spats" because of this idiosyncrasy, which developed in his Penn State days to hide the fact that he wasn't wearing Engle-ordered high-top cleats. The Colts had no problem footing his adhesive-tape bills for a generation.

Had it not been for Moore, the Colts would not have made it into the "Greatest Game Ever Played," the 1958 NFL championship game with the Giants at Memorial Stadium in Baltimore. And they probably would not have won it, either. But Baltimore prevailed, 23–17, when Ameche plunged in from a yard out in overtime in a televised event that could

Sixteen. Running Backs as Receivers

have been scripted by suspense master Rod Serling and was as riveting as anything on the home tube. That game's drama on TV was instrumental in affirming the national fascination for pro football.

To win the Western Division in 1958 with an eventual 9–3 record, the Colts jumped out to an 8–1 start and were pursued through the season by the Bears and Rams, both of whom ended the season at 8–4. Moore scored 14 TDs that year, seven rushing and seven receiving, ranking second in the league in scoring to Jim Brown, who scored 18 TDs. Had the Colts not won the November 30 game against the San Francisco 49ers, the division would have concluded in a three-way 8–4 tie, since the Colts flagged at the season's close and lost their last two regular-season games. The Colts trailed the 49ers, 27–7, at halftime, but Unitas mounted a second-half comeback that reached its crescendo in the fourth quarter when Moore ran 73 yards in and out of several would-be tacklers' grasps to a TD that put the Colts ahead to stay.

"When the final gun sounded, Memorial Stadium erupted in a celebration as wild as any football stadium has ever seen," Andy Piascik wrote. "The Colts players were swarmed over by fans who began lining the sidelines as the game wound down, and Moore, among others, was carried off the field in triumph. It was not only a great Colts moment but one of the great moments in football history."[17]

In the championship game, fans rightly remember Berry's superb performance, catching 12 passes for 178 yards and a TD—and catching them during the last regulation-time drive to tie the game with a field goal to send it into overtime, and during the OT drive that ended in Ameche's run. But Lenny Moore also caught six passes in that game for 101 yards, including a 60-yarder from Unitas.

When Moore came into the league, he was a bit recalcitrant at Eubanks' efforts to convert him from a full-time runner into a part-time runner and part-time flanker, but his success speaks for itself. After establishing himself as one of the most difficult backs to cover in the league, the Colts shook up the status quo prior to the 1961 season by trading Big Daddy Lipscumb, Buzz Nutter, and Johnny Sample to the Pittsburgh Steelers for Jimmy Orr, Billy Ray Smith (Sr.), and Joe Lewis. Orr, a premiere flanker, gave Unitas—with Berry and Moore—one of the finest receiving corps in NFL history. Consequently, Moore was back at halfback, and nagged by injuries in 1962 and 1963. Reinvigorated in

1964, Moore set the single-season TD record of 20 and was Comeback Player of the Year as well as league MVP—in the *only year* that a Jim Brown-fronted Cleveland team won the NFL title.

"I really wish that I could have spent my whole career as a flanker," Moore said in the sports classic, *The Running Backs*, by Murray Olderman. "I wish I would have said no when Weeb came to me and asked to make the change [back to halfback]. But the way it was put to me, for the good of the team, I couldn't say no."[18]

By vacillating between the two posts, Moore never ran up big running or catching career numbers. Yet, he scored all those TDs. NFL sages in Moore's time and after remarked about the uncanny abilities of contemporaries Moore and Green Bay's Paul Hornung as scorers who seemed to smell pay-dirt, who played at increased levels of quickness, ruggedness, and proficiency the closer their teams got to the end zone. That notion, especially about Moore, still abides half a century later. Lenny Moore was elected to the Pro Football Hall of Fame in 1983.

Previous to Gifford and Moore, the only backfield men to have made the 500–500 club in pro ball did it only once: Harry Clarke of the Bears in 1943, Chet Mutryn of the All American Football Conference's Buffalo Bills in 1948, Choo Choo Roberts of the Giants in 1949, and Ollie Matson of the Chicago Cardinals in 1954. Halfback Matson was a remarkably consistent rusher and receiver in the 1950s, and had a couple of good years after Rams General Manager Pete Rozelle traded nine players for him in 1959.

Matson finished his career with a season's stop in Detroit and three years in Philadelphia as a backup. His 73 touchdowns on runs, receptions, returns, and a fumble recovery over 14 years in the NFL was a major factor in his induction in 1972 into the Pro Football Hall of Fame. He scored 23 receiving TDs, and 3,285 of his 12,884 career yards were on receptions.

The one other back to achieve the 500–500 mark through the 1960 season, after which the NFL year went from 12 to 14 games, was Tom "The Bomb" Tracy of the Pittsburgh Steelers, in 1958. The 14-game season made the 500–500 achievement not exactly commonplace, but not that much of a criterion for measuring backfield versatility. In fact, in the decade-long American Football League, which instituted a 14-game schedule a year before the NFL, in 1960, two running backs achieved the

Sixteen. Running Backs as Receivers

Ollie Matson of the Chicago Cardinals was one of the postwar era's great broken-field runners and was as effective as a flanker as he was as a runningback. In 1954, for instance, he gained 506 yards rushing and 611 receiving. He was elected to the Hall of Fame in 1972 (Topps® Bowman® courtesy The Topps Company, Inc.).

dual marks four times, Abner Haynes and the Oakland Raiders' Clem Daniels. AFL backs reached the 500–500 marks 15 times, and a dozen NFL setbacks also reached the 500–500 plateaus in the 1960s.

Not readily receivers as much as halfbacks, fullbacks still have displayed some distinction as pass catchers. The Kansas City Chiefs' 6-foot-3 and 232-pound bruiser of the AFL era, Curtis McClinton, holds the distinction of catching the first AFL touchdown pass in Super Bowl play, a seven-yarder from Lenny Dawson against the Green Bay Packers in Super Bowl I. But McClinton also played one of the oddest games ever for a fullback—the final contest of 1965. He rushed seven times for 15 yards—11 of that on a TD lug. But McClinton caught five passes from Lenny Dawson for 213 yards in a 45–35 shootout win over the Denver Broncos at Municipal Stadium. The fullback's longest catch on the day went for 69 yards.

McClinton's achievement was to have made the fewest number of catches to gain more than 200 yards in one game, or since since Choo Choo Roberts gained 201 on four grabs in 1949. The closest any running back has come to McClinton's still-record receiving yardage total for running backs occurred in a 1999 game when Marshall Faulk of the St. Louis Rams rolled up 204 yards. But Faulk required 12 receptions to accumulate that much real estate. McClinton was so readily deployed as a blocker to protect Dawson or escort halfback Mike Garrett that he slipped out of the backfield with ease.

Relatively forgotten, even by AFL terms, McClinton played from 1962 through 1969, and was integral to the Texans-Chiefs success. He was named the league's Rookie of the Year in 1962 when he rushed 111 times for 604 yards (leading the league with 5.4 yards a carry) and caught 29 passes for 333 yards. His best year was 1965 when he carried 175 times for 665 yards and a league-leading six rushing TDs, and caught 37 passes for 590 yards and nine total TDs.

McClinton was fast enough to run the high hurdles at the University of Kansas, and he was a versatile big man, blocking with the best of them and possessing a receiver's soft hands. His counterpart on the Buffalo Bills, the self-promotional fullback Cookie Gilchrist, wasn't in the habit of talking about other players when he himself would do, but once said of McClinton, "He's got the tools, and the intelligence to use them. He's got more wrinkles than me once he's underway."[19] After football, McClinton graduated from Harvard University's Kennedy School of Government, and served in Department of Commerce posts as well as deputy mayor of Washington, D.C.

Some running backs' versatility was ignited by more involvement in the passing game. But others were switched permanently to receiver from running back. Within a couple

Bobby Mitchell, a spectacular broken-field runner, and Jim Brown formed a classic one-two backfield punch for the Cleveland Browns (1958 to 1961). Then, Mitchell and Charley Taylor became spectacular one-two deep threats on the Washington Redskins (1962 to 1968) (Philadelphia Gum Company, courtesy Tootsie Roll Industries).

Sixteen. Running Backs as Receivers

of years, the Washington Redskins converted two of the league's best running backs, Bobby Mitchell and Charley Taylor, into, eventually, two of the greatest receivers of all time. Before the 1964 season, Washington acquired quarterback Sonny Jurgenson from the Philadelphia Eagles. One of the best deep throwers of his era, Jurgenson fully exploited his superbly talented receivers, who rolled up many spectacular touchdowns, if for not all that many wins.

Mitchell arrived in Washington two years prior to the QB via an unusual trade. Washington dealt its No. 1 draft choice, Syracuse University All American halfback Ernie Davis, to the Browns for Mitchell. But Davis died of leukemia before he played a down. The Mitchell acquisition had a far deeper context than a pro-sports trade, and its ramifications have been covered better and with more detail elsewhere. Suffice it to say that the Redskins were the last all-white team in the NFL— through the 1961 season, and Mitchell was their first black player. The all-white Redskins had been an embarrassment in the nation's capital for the Kennedy administration which assumed office in 1960.

Kennedy had partially ridden to the presidency as the Civil Rights candidate. He was a football fan, and for the team in D.C. to remain segregated was a blight on his administration. Blacks picketed the federally-owned D.C. Stadium (later renamed RFK Memorial Stadium). The local press treated the situation as a joke. Sam Lacy, writing in the *Baltimore Afro-American*, referred to the Redskins as football's "lone wolf in lily-whiteism."[20] In *The Washington Post*, Shirley Povich brought his sarcastic streak to bear, writing that Jim Brown "integrated" the end zone, making the score "separate but unequal."[21] Through the persistence of Secretary of the Interior Stewart Udall, the feds threatened to revoke the Redskins' 30-year lease on the stadium. The integration of the team was sanctioned by other NFL owners and was propelled by the activism of the D.C.-area black community against the Redskins' racist owner George Preston Marshall.

The major player brought to Washington for this twilight episode in pro-sports integration was Mitchell. Accompanying him from Cleveland in the trade was rookie back Leroy Jackson, who, with guard John Nisby, brought in from the Steelers, and draftees Ron Hatcher and Joe Hernandez, were the other black players who integrated the Redskins in 1962. The star attention in the situation was focused on Mitchell.

From 1958 through 1961, Mitchell had been the most talented second-choice runner in football as Jim Brown's backfield mate. Despite that, Mitchell never rushed for less than 500 yards a season in Cleveland. In 1961, Mitchell led the NFL with a 5.4 yards-per-carry average. Brown and Mitchell were as formidable as any backfield talent tandem in football annals, but Brown was such a superior player that Mitchell's Cleveland exploits have been obscured by time.

Not only did Mitchell have a new team in 1962, and a greater cultural role than he had ever expected, he also had a new position. Coach Bill McPeak converted the 6-foot, 192-pound, University of Illinois product to flanker—and Mitchell flourished, leading the NFL with 72 catches and 1,384 yards. He also scored 11 touchdowns. That brilliant first year in Washington "only underlined the stupidity of Marshall's previous all-white policy," Bob Carroll wrote.[22] Away from the Jim Brown legend, Mitchell was finally a full-fledged star, even if he was on the perennially second-division Redskins. "Once he left Jim's planet-sized shadow, Mitchell demonstrated that his skills were as formidable as any offensive talent to play football," wrote Brown biographer Mike Freeman.[23]

In 1963, Mitchell caught 69 passes for a league-leading 1,436 yards, and seven TDs, one of 99 yards against the Browns. In 1964, Mitchell led the NFL in receiving TDs with 10 (on 60 catches for 904 yards). From 1965 through 1967, Mitchell never caught less than 58 balls and never gained less than 866 yards as one of the two or three best flankers in the NFL. He finished his career with 14,078 all-purpose yards, 7,954 on 521 receptions for 65 TDs. A brilliant runner after the catch, with great evasive capabilities and reserves of speed, Mitchell was one of the finest all-around players of any era. He scored 91 touchdowns in 11 years—five of those on kickoff returns and three on punt returns. When the NFL Network selected an unofficial top 10 "elusive runners" of all time in 2009, Mitchell was ranked No. 5.

Mitchell retired before the 1969 season. The Redskins' new coach, Vince Lombardi, asked him to stay on as a scout. Mitchell eventually moved up to assistant general manager. While Mitchell never played on an NFL champion during the Redskins' perennial also-ran era of the 1960s, he was a member of the front-office team for coach Joe Gibbs' Super Bowl-winning Washington clubs of 1982, 1987, and 1991. Mitchell was inducted into the Pro Football Hall of Fame in 1983. When he retired

Sixteen. Running Backs as Receivers

in 2003 after 40 years with the Redskins, Mitchell blamed owners Edward Bennett Williams and Jack Kent Cooke for not hiring him as general manager, especially in 1978, when Bobby Beathard was appointed GM.[24]

Mitchell's playing career overlapped those of Frank Gifford and Lenny Moore, without any of the team success enjoyed by them. Mitchell may have been the most spectacular player to have been converted from running back to flanker in NFL history—unless that's Charley Taylor. When the two were operating as the wide-outs on the Redskins, from 1966 through 1968, they formed one of the greatest receiving tandems in pro football annals. For a player who was the "other guy" as a running back with Brown, Mitchell flourished along with Taylor.

Taylor was drafted on the first round in 1964 by Washington out of Arizona State, and he made an immediate and spectacular impact as the 6-foot-3, 210-pound starting halfback, rushing for 755 yards and five touchdowns on 199 carries, *and* catching 53 passes for 814 yards and five more TDs. Taylor was named NFL Rookie of the Year (by United Press International). When Otto Graham arrived in Washington as head coach in 1966, he switched Taylor to split end, and, again, the impact was immediate. Taylor caught 72 passes to lead all NFL receivers, for 1,119 yards and

When Charley Taylor retired after the 1977 season, his 13th with the Washington Redskins, his 649 receptions were the most by any player in history, including Don Maynard (633) and Raymond Berry (631). Taylor was elected to the Pro Football Hall of Fame in 1973 (Philadelphia Gum Company, courtesy of Tootsie Roll Industries).

12 TDs. He led the league again the following year with 70 receptions, good for 990 yards and nine TDs. Taylor remained at wide receiver, playing 13 years, all with Washington. Taylor was a main component of the "Over the Hill Gang," the Redskins' 11–3 adventure in 1972 under coach George Allen, who stockpiled veteran castoffs and free agents, reasoning that savvy counted for a lot: Speedy Duncan, Roy Jefferson, Billy Kilmer, Ron McDole, Clifton McNeil, and several ex-Rams.

The "Over the Hill Gang" won the NFC Championship, defeating the Dallas Cowboys, 26–3, as Taylor caught seven passes from Kilmer for 146 yards, and touchdowns of 15 and 45 yards (the Redskins lost the Super Bowl to the Miami Dolphins). Taylor lasted through the George Allen period in Washington, retiring when Allen left after the 1977 season.

Charley Taylor caught 649 career passes for 9,110 yards and 79 TDs. He accumulated 10,598 yards from scrimmage, and scored a total of 90 TDs. At the time of his retirement, he had caught more passes than any other player in history. The similarity of his overlapping career with teammate Mitchell's is rather uncanny as they were both high-caliber wide receivers on the Redskins who were both welcomed into the Pro Football Hall of Fame a year apart from each other. Taylor was inducted in 1984, the year after Mitchell. Taylor followed Mitchell into the Redskins front office. Initially, like Mitchell, he was hired as a scout.

"With a hard thrower like Sonny Jurgenson, you're going to let your hands ride with the ball, because he throws so hard," Taylor told Paul Zimmerman. "You can't do it facing him. Unless you have huge hands, the ball will bounce off. With Fran Tarkenton, my teammate in the Pro Bowl one year, if you try to ride the ball into your hands, it'll fall short, because he throws a soft pass. You've got to catch him facing him, like Homer Jones used to [on the Giants]. Homer can catch that way with practically anybody, though, because his hands are so large. He sort of clamps the ball."[25]

When Joe Gibbs became head coach in 1981, he named Taylor the Redskins' receivers coach. Taylor stayed in the post through 1994, sharing in the three Redskins' Super Bowl titles. Taylor coached such outstanding Redskins receivers as Art Monk, Charlie Brown, Gary Clark, and Ricky Sanders. Both Mitchell and Taylor remain the most outstanding players to have evolved into receivers who had started their pro careers as running backs.

Sixteen. Running Backs as Receivers

Another Mitchell took the backfield's involvement in the passing game to a new level as far as numbers were concerned. When he caught 72 balls in 1974, it was the most that any running back had caught in a season to that time. Lydell Mitchell had much more than his initials and college and pro teams in common with Lenny Moore in the great lineage of Penn State running backs, which included, between the two L.M. careers, Dick Hoak, Bob Campbell, Charlie Pittman, and Franco Harris.

At 5-foot-11 and 204 pounds, Mitchell was two inches shorter and about 15 pounds heavier than Moore, but he was gifted in the same manner, reminiscent of Moore in his swift but strong and shifty running style. Mitchell was drafted by the Colts on the second round in 1972, and became one of the NFL's best runners and certainly top receiving threats. He was so talented in college that he set the NCAA scoring record in 1971 with 29 touchdowns and set the Penn State seasonal rushing record with 1,567 yards. He was so much the star for Joe Paterno's Nittany Lions that future Pro Football Hall of Famer Franco Harris toiled as his blocking back, and soon-to-be Heisman Trophy-winning (in 1973) running back John Cappelletti elected to play defense in 1971 so that he could play at all.

After arriving in Baltimore, Mitchell could never complain about not getting the ball. Mitchell's frequency of use on Colts teams less talented than in Moore's day made him into a pounder, more of a short-yardage back than his predecessor. Instead of being any sort of Moore-like deep threat on a team with other weapons, Mitchell became a workhorse. Even though memories of him as broken-field college performer were still fresh, Mitchell's receptions in the NFL were ball-control grabs out of the backfield, possession plays. They worked like solid rushes as he only averaged 8.5 yards per catch throughout his career.

For a guy who led the NFL twice in receptions in nine years, Mitchell gained 100 yards receiving in a game only once—125 yards on eight receptions for a TD against his future employers, the San Diego Chargers, in 1976. Three times he caught passes for double figures in a game—and didn't accumulate 100 yards, including 13 grabs for 82 yards and two TDs against the New York Jets in 1974.

Mitchell was very like his college backfield mate, Harris, who also became his post-football business partner and lifelong friend. Harris preserved his body and extended his career against quite a bit of criticism in working-class Pittsburgh by not exerting full effort all the time. Both Mitchell and Harris often elected to step out of bounds rather than gut it out for a few more yards. It's as if the two Nittany Lions made a pact at some point not to let the pros grind them down. To his credit, Harris was integral to four Super Bowl-champion Steelers teams, and was deservedly inducted into the Pro Football Hall of Fame in 1990.

"I see well all around me and I can sense when I'm about to get hit, so I protect myself," Mitchell told Lou Sahadi. "It's very seldom that anybody gets a real solid, head-on shot at me. That's where runners get hurt. I take a shot on my arm or side. And when I see I'm about the get hit hard, I sell out. I go down. You see too many runners get hurt when they're hopelessly stopped and still struggling. Then somebody else hits them and they get hurt. The biggest factor is that I always keep my legs moving, and that prevents injuries. It is when the leg is planted that knees and ankles give way on tackles. I've got to carry the ball at least 20 times a game to be effective. I get better; I am more conscious of what is going on the more I carry the ball."[26]

Mitchell falls short of being a borderline case for Hall of Fame induction. In six of his nine years, he was the feature back, five with the Colts and one with the Chargers. However, during that period, 1973 through 1978, Mitchell was one of the most overworked backs in the league. In the years that he led the league in receptions, he rushed 214 times for 757 yards, and 301 occasions for 1,159 yards. He led the league in touches in 1976 with 349 and 1977 with 372, ending up second in yards from scrimmage both years (to O.J. Simpson and Walter Payton, respectively).

A knee injury eventually led to his retirement after a final season with the Rams. He played on some good teams, but they never got past the first round of the playoffs as the Colts were smothered by the Pittsburgh Steelers twice and haunted by Oakland's "Ghost to the Post" play in 1977, when tight end Dave Casper burned Baltimore deep to force overtime late in the game, then a win.

Roger Craig was a beneficiary of the West Coast offense. At the University of Nebraska, Craig spent most of his time as a backup, first to Jarvis Redwine, then to Heisman Trophy winner Mike Rozier. Still a premium prospect, Craig was drafted on the second round in 1983 by the 49ers, which had acquired Wendell Tyler from the Rams that year

Sixteen. Running Backs as Receivers

to be the feature back. However, coach Bill Walsh saw the obvious all-around value in the rookie and split his running backs' duties. In their first year as backfield mates, they each carried the ball 176 times—feature back Tyler for 856 yards for four TDs with 34 receptions for 285 yards and two more TDs, while the former Cornhusker and designated "blocking back" gained 725 yards on the ground for eight TDs and caught 48 passes for 427 yards and four TDs. This healthy rivalry went on for two more seasons, with Tyler rushing for 1,262 yards and scoring nine TDs from scrimmage in 1984, Craig's second season, in which the blocking back gained 600-plus yards both rushing and receiving and scored 10 TDs. In an era when feature backs almost exclusively did it all, the Tyler-Craig combo was both an exception and exceptional.

Craig's breakout season, 1985, had a superhuman aspect as he became the first player in NFL history to gain 1,000 yards rushing and 1,000 receiving in a single season. He literally combined two great years into 16 games: 214 carries for 1,050 yards and nine TDs, and 92 receptions for 1,016 yards, and six TDs. The 92 receptions led all NFL receivers.

As the most beneficial talent to a winning club using his great all-around talent, Marshall Faulk was a spectacular runner with reserves of surprising power and evasive technique when situations called for them, and belongs with the great and truly versatile talents who powered the engines of championship-winners: Red Grange, Sid Luckman, Sammy Baugh, Frank Gifford, and Lenny Moore.

Faulk was drafted by the Indianapolis Colts in 1994 on the first round out of San Diego State as the second player selected overall (after defensive tackle Dan "Big Daddy" Wilkinson). A 5-foot-10, 211-pound halfback, Faulk had durability and quick maneuverability. Unlike similar sized backs, Faulk's low center of gravity and strength belied uncommon speed. He became an immediate star, for five years with the Colts, and then seven—1999 through 2005—with the St. Louis Rams. Faulk rushed for 1,000 or more yards in seven of his 12 seasons.

He gained just over 1,300 yards rushing in four consecutive and amazingly productive years, straddling the NFL centuries from 1998 to 2001, in which his *receiving* stats were, respectively, 86 for 908 yards and four TDs; 87 for 1,048 yards and five TDs; 81 for 830 yards and eight TDs, and 80 for 765 yards and nine TDs. In each of those four years, Faulk gained more than 2,100 yards from scrimmage. In 1999, he became the second running back in history after Roger Craig to gain 1,000 yards rushing and receiving in the same season. Faulk was named by at least one media organization as the league MVP in 1999, 2000, and 2001. In the same three years, he led the NFL in rushing yards per carry, with averages of 5.5, 5.4, and 5.3 yards, respectively. He led the league in touchdowns with 26 in 2000 and 21 in 2001.

It's a measure of the elusive Faulk's essential toughness as a running back that he notched 100 touchdowns on the ground and 36 through the air as one of pro football's great scorers. Unlike many backs who were superlative receivers, Faulk battled for 12,279 career yards rushing and still managed to grab 767 passes for 6,875 yards.

The natural extension of the evolution of running backs catching more and more passes was running backs who did that not necessarily to the exclusion of everything else, but to the point where it became their main career preoccupation. By the 1990s, Larry Centers and Ronnie Harmon evolved into go-to receivers on different teams no matter what defenses seemed to do or what else their team used to advance the ball. Setbacks both, playing on teams with every-down flankers, Centers and Harmon played to their strengths. They were possession players, often every-down players, but mostly situational receivers. Each was often used on third down on screen passes or flare routes to move the chains.

At 5-foot-11 and 200 pounds, Harmon was a first-round draft choice by the Buffalo Bills out of the University of Iowa. He played on five teams from 1986 to 1997 with his best years, 1990 through 1995, with the San Diego Chargers. Only once did Harmon rush 100 times in a season (116 for 485 yards in 1987 for the Bills), but he never gained less than 500 yards in receptions for the Chargers, and rolled up 914 in 1992 (on 79 passes for one TD). These were the post–Air Coryell years, playing on hot and cold teams, mostly for coach Bobby Ross, and in the same backfield as fullback Natrone Means. Harmon ran 615 times for 2,774 yards and 10 TDs in his career, but caught 582 balls for 6,076 yards and 24 TDs.

Centers' career is even more tilted toward the pass, and he has the numbers to be considered the greatest receiver out of the backfield of all time. A six-foot, 225-pound fullback out of Stephen F. Austin, Centers was a fifth-round pick in 1990 by the Phoenix Cardinals. He played 14 seasons, most of those, 1990 to 1998, with the Phoenix-cum-Arizona

Sixteen. Running Backs as Receivers

Cards, two with the Redskins, two with the Bills, and a final career capper as member of the 2003 Super Bowl Champion New England Patriots. He was used by Pats coach Bill Belichick mostly in reserve, behind Antowain Smith and Kevin Faulk. Centers' most remarkable years were in 1995, when he caught 101 passes for 962 yards and two TDs, and 1996, when he grabbed 99 balls for 766 yards and seven TDs. Those two years were the only ones during which he gained more than 1,000 total yards from scrimmage. Over his career, Centers rushed 615 times for 2,188 yards and 14 TDs, but caught 827 passes for 6,797 yards and 28 TDs.

Centers is one of two running backs to have caught 100 passes in a season—LaDainian Tomlinson caught 100 in 2003 for the Chargers. Centers never led his team in any rushing category in 14 years. He was never the feature back. Only once, in 1995, did he lead his team in reception yards. Centers was noted for good footwork and was effective in short quarters after the catch. He had the misfortune of spending his prime years on mediocre teams. But it might be said that he took the specialized role of receiving running back to its zenith.

APPENDIX

Individual Honors

It doesn't make much sense to reiterate individual statistics when the easily accessed Pro-Football-Reference.com is such an excellent free web site for all aspects of team and individual receiving numbers throughout history. But there's value in listing those players thought to be the best by contemporaries and experts, regardless of receiving numbers. For instances, clutch performers—Paul Warfield and Lynn Swann in recent times—were regarded as supreme talents despite their often relatively low numbers in receptions, yardage, and touchdowns.

The Ohio League

A selection of Ohio League players from the top years of pre–NFL times was made by football historian Keith McClellan, author of *The Sunday Game*. The vicissitudes of the wild and woolly Ohio League didn't keep McClellan from framing his deeply researched book with rosters, schedules, and all-star selections, including 11 ends on a list of the 55 best pro players in the pre–NFL heyday—1915 to 1917—including:

John Devereaux, Dayton Triangles and Detroit Heralds
Bob Marshall, Minneapolis Marines
Bob "Nasty" Nash, Massillon Tigers
Alfred Earle "Greasy" Neale, Canton Bulldogs
Jesse Reno, Wabash Athletic Association
Knute Rockne, Fort Wayne Friars and Canton Bulldogs
Richard "Red" Shields, Detroit Heralds
Ernie Soucy, Canton Bulldogs

Earl "Dutch" Thiele, Cincinnati Celts, Massillon Tigers, and Detroit Heralds

Samuel S. Willaman, Akron Indians, Cleveland Indians, and Canton Bulldogs

Pro Football Hall of Fame

The inductees into the Pro Football Hall of Fame in Canton, Ohio, who played at end or wide receiver or were exceptional receiving backfield players—and whose careers started before 1970—are (induction year in parentheses):

Lance Alworth (1978) San Diego Chargers, Dallas Cowboys, 1962–1972.

Morris "Red" Badgro (1981) New York Yankees, New York Giants, Brooklyn Dodgers, 1927–1928 and 1930–1936.

Raymond Berry (1973) Baltimore Colts, 1955–1967.

Fred Biletnikoff (1988) Oakland Raiders, 1965–1978.

Guy Chamberlin (1965) Canton/Cleveland Bulldogs, Frankford Yellow Jackets, Chicago Cardinals, 1920–1927.

Mike Ditka (1988) Chicago Bears, Philadelphia Eagles, Dallas Cowboys, 1961–1972.

"Bullet Bill" Dudley (1966) Pittsburgh Steelers, Detroit Lions, Washington Redskins, 1942 and 1945–1953.

Tom Fears (1970) Los Angeles Rams, 1948–1956.

Ray Flaherty (1976) New York Yankees, New York Giants, 1927–1935.

Frank Gifford (1977) New York Giants, 1952–1960 and 1962–1964.

Harold "Red" Grange (1963) Chicago Bears, New York Yankees, 1925, 1927, and 1928–1934.

Bob Hayes (2009) Dallas Cowboys, San Francisco 49ers, 1965–1975.

Bill Hewitt (1971) Chicago Bears, Philadelphia Eagles/Phil-Pitt "Steagles," 1932–1939 and 1943.

Elroy "Crazy Legs" Hirsch (1968) Chicago Rockets, Los Angeles Rams, 1946–1957.

Don Hutson (1963) Green Bay Packers, 1935–1945.

Dante Lavelli (1975) Cleveland Browns, 1946–1956.

John Mackey (1992) Baltimore Colts, San Diego Chargers, 1963–1972.
Ollie Matson (1972) Chicago Cardinals, Los Angeles Rams, Detroit Lions, Philadelphia Eagles, 1952–1966.
Don Maynard (1987) New York Giants, New York Titans/Jets, St. Louis Cardinals, 1958 and 1960–1973.
Tommy McDonald (1998) Philadelphia Eagles, Dallas Cowboys, Los Angeles Rams, Atlanta Falcons, Cleveland Browns, 1957–1968.
Johnny "Blood" McNally (1963) Milwaukee Badgers, Duluth Eskimos, Pottsville Maroons, Green Bay Packers, Pittsburgh Pirates, 1925–1938.
Wayne Millner (1968) Boston/Washington Redskins, 1936–1941 and 1945.
Bobby Mitchell (1983) Cleveland Browns, Washington Redskins, 1958–1968.
Lenny Moore (1975) Baltimore Colts, 1956–1967.
Pete Pihos (1970) Philadelphia Eagles, 1947–1955.
Charlie Sanders (2007) Detroit Lions, 1968–1977.
Jackie Smith (1994) St. Louis Cardinals, Dallas Cowboys, 1963–1978)
Charley Taylor (1984) Washington Redskins, 1964–1977.
Jim Thorpe (1963) Canton/Cleveland Bulldogs, Oorang Indians, Toledo Maroons, Rock Island Independents, New York Giants, Chicago Cardinals, 1920–1926 and 1928.
Doak Walker (1986) Detroit Lions, 1950–1955.
Paul Warfield (1983) Cleveland Browns, Miami Dolphins, 1964–1977.

Annual Honors

Most Valuable Player or Player of the Year (MVP) honors for receivers are recorded here in descending order along with Rookie of the Year and other significant or distinctive accolades for players who played before 1970. The league named MVPs from 1938 through 1946, after which various publications named their own MVPs, including the United Press (UP), Newspaper Enterprise Association (NEA), *The Sporting News* (TSN), *Pro Football Weekly* (PFW) and the Associated Press (AP) as well as the Pro Football Writers of America (PFWA) and the Maxwell Club (MX) of Philadelphia.

Appendix

The Most Valuable Players

1941 NFL—**Don Hutson**, end, Green Bay Packers.
1942 NFL—**Don Hutson**, end, Green Bay Packers.
1946 NFL—**Bill Dudley**, halfback, Pittsburgh Steelers.
1955 NEA—**Harlon Hill**, end, Chicago Bears.
1956 UP, NEA & TSN—**Frank Gifford**, halfback/flanker, New York Giants.
1960 UP & TSN (AFL)—**Abner Haynes**, halfback/flanker, Dallas Texans.
1963 UP (AFL)—**Lance Alworth**, flanker, San Diego Chargers.
1964 NEA (NFL)—**Lenny Moore**, halfback/flanker, Baltimore Colts.
1964 UP & TSN (AFL)—**Gino Cappelletti**, split end, Boston Patriots.
1965 MX (NFL)—**Pete Retzlaff**, tight end, Philadelphia Eagles.
1971 UP (AFC)—**Otis Taylor**, wide receiver, Kansas City Chiefs.
1971 PFW Offensive MVP (NFL)—**Otis Taylor**, wide receiver, Kansas City Chiefs.

The Rookies of the Year

1956 UP—**Lenny Moore**, halfback/flanker, Baltimore Colts.
1958 UP & AP—**Jimmy Orr**, split end, Pittsburgh Steelers.
1958 TSN—**Bobby Mitchell**, halfback, Cleveland Browns.
1959 UP—**Boyd Dowler**, split end, Green Bay Packers.
1960 UP & TSN (AFL)—**Abner Haynes**, halfback/flanker, Dallas Texans.
1960 UP, AP & TSN (NFL)—**Gail Cogdill**, split end, Detroit Lions.
1961 UP, AP & TSN (NFL)—**Mike Ditka**, tight end, Chicago Bears.
1962 UP &TSN (AFL)—**Curtis McClinton**, fullback, Dallas Texans.
1963 UP, AP & TSN (NFL)—**Paul Flatley**, split end, Minnesota Vikings.
1964 AP, UP, TSN & NEA (NFL)—**Charley Taylor**, halfback, Washington Redskins.
1966 UP & TSN (AFL)—**Bobby Burnett**, halfback/flanker, Buffalo Bills.
1968 AP Offensive (NFL)—**Earl McCullouch**, wide receiver, Detroit Lions.

Individual Honors

NFL All-Time Team and All-Decade Teams

The NFL sanctioned the selection of an All-Time Team and All-Decade Teams at the turn of the 21st century, highlighting them in *The NFL Century*. The teams were picked by a committee of top football journalists and executives, including Curt Gowdy, Will McDonough, Paul Zimmerman, Peter King, John Steadman, Harold Rosenthal, Bill Polian, and Bucko Kilroy. The **All-Time NFL Team** selections at the receiving spots up to 1999 were, at wide receiver, Lance Alworth, Raymond Berry, Don Hutson, and Jerry Rice; at tight end, Mike Ditka and Kellen Winslow, and, at running back, Jim Brown, Marion Motley, Bronko Nagurski, Walter Payton, Gale Sayers, O.J. Simpson, and Steve Van Buren.

The selections of ends and significant receiving backs on the All-Decade Teams through the 1960s were:

The 1920s: LaVern Dilweg and Guy Chamberlin at ends, and Paddy Driscoll, Red Grange, and Jim Thorpe in the backfield.

The 1930s: Don Hutson and Bill Hewitt at ends, and Cliff Battles and Earl "Dutch" Clark in the backfield.

The 1940s: Dante Lavelli and Pete Pihos at ends, and George McAfee and Marion Motley among the backfield selections.

The 1950s: Tom Fears and Raymond Berry at ends, Elroy "Crazy Legs" Hirsch at flanker, and Ollie Matson and Hugh McElhenny among the backfield selections.

The 1960s: Lance Alworth and Charley Taylor at wide receivers, John Mackey at tight end, and Jim Brown and Gale Sayers among the backs.

Total Football's "300 Greatest Players Plus"

The editors of the *Total Football: The Official Encyclopedia of the National Football League* selected 320 players as the greatest in history for the second edition in 1999. Players who started their pro careers after 1970 are listed in italics, so the reader can make comparisons between more recent and perhaps familiar talents and those of bygone eras.

The ends or wide receivers who made the list include: Morris "Red" Badgro, Raymond Berry, *Cris Carter*, Guy Chamberlin, LaVern Dilweg, Tom Fears, Bob Hayes, Charley Hennigan, Bill Hewitt, Don Hutson,

Michael Irvin, Billy "White Shoes" Johnson, Charlie Joiner, Ken Kavanaugh, Dante Lavelli, *James Lofton,* Tommy McDonald, Wayne Millner, *Drew Pearson, Andre Reed, Jerry Rice, Sterling Sharpe,* Mac Speedie, *John Stallworth, Lynn Swann,* Charley Taylor, Lionel Taylor, Otis Taylor, *Rick Upchurch,* and Paul Warfield. The kick- and punt-returning specialties of Johnson and Upchurch were factored into their selections.

Flankers or backs who were notable receivers who made the cut include: *Marcus Allen,* Lance Alworth, Fred Biletnikoff, Jim Brown, *Roger Craig,* Paddy Driscoll, "Bullet Bill" Dudley, *Chuck Foreman,* Frank Gifford, Harold "Red" Grange, Elroy "Crazy Legs" Hirsch, Ollie Matson, Don Maynard, Hugh McElhenny, Johnny "Blood" McNally, Bobby Mitchell, Lenny Moore, Marion Motley, Gale Sayers, Jim Thorpe, Doak Walker, and *Herschel Walker.*

Tight ends on the list are: *Dave Casper,* Mike Ditka, Ron Kramer, John Mackey, *Ozzie Newsome,* Pete Pihos, Charlie Sanders, *Shannon Sharpe,* Jackie Smith, and *Kellen Winslow.*

All Pro Selections

Since the NFL was created in 1920 as the American Professional Football Association, various publications have selected All Pro teams, including newspapers, magazines, press syndicates, the league, the Pro Football Hall of Fame, the Professional Football Writers of America, and contemporaries. Often first-, second-, and third-team selections were made at all the positions. All-Conference teams were selected by some entities in some years. The below list reflects any split end or tight end or wide receiver or back known for his receiving prowess to make as many as four All Pro teams at any level from 1920 through 1970, including in the short-lived first AFL in 1926 as well as AAFC and the AFL of the 1960s. Running backs who are designated (RB) on the list. Tight ends or players who played that position, even before it entered the football lexicon, are designated (TE).

Eleven—Don Hutson, Green Bay Packers (1935–45).
Ten—Clarke Hinkle, Green Bay Packers (RB: 1932–41).
Nine—Jim Brown, Cleveland Browns (RB: 1957–65); Charley Taylor, Washington Redskins (1966–70 and 1972–75).

Individual Honors

Eight—Paddy Driscoll, Chicago Staleys/Bears and Chicago Cardinals (RB: 1920 and 1922–28); LaVern Dilweg, Green Bay Packers (1926–33), and Paul Warfield, Cleveland Browns and Miami Dolphins (1964 and 1968–74).

Seven—Ray Flaherty, New York Yankees and New York Giants (1926, 1928–29, and 1931–34); Pete Pihos, Philadelphia Eagles (TE: 1947–50 and 1953–55); Ollie Matson, Chicago Cardinals and Los Angeles Rams (RB: 1952 and 1954–59); Lenny Moore, Baltimore Colts (RB: 1956–61 and 1964); and Lance Alworth, San Diego Chargers (1963–69).

Six—Earl "Dutch" Clark, Portsmouth Spartans/Detroit Lions (RB: 1931–32 and 1934–37); Bill Hewitt, Chicago Bears and Philadelphia Eagles (1932–34 and 1936–38); Cliff Battles, Boston/Washington Redskins (RB: 1932–37); Bill Dudley, Pittsburgh Steelers, Detroit Lions, and Washington Redskins (RB: 1942 and 1946–51); Dante Lavelli, Cleveland Browns (TE: 1946–49, 1951, and 1953); Mac Speedie, Cleveland Browns (RB: 1946–50 and 1952); Pat Harder, Chicago Cardinals and Detroit Lions (RB: 1946–50 and 1952); Frank Gifford, New York Giants (RB: 1953 and 1955–59); Raymond Berry, Baltimore Colts (1957–61 and 1965); Jim Taylor, Green Bay Packers (RB: 1960–64 and 1966); Art Powell, New York Titans and Oakland Raiders (1960 and 1962–66); Mike Ditka, Chicago Bears (TE: 1961–66); Fred Arbanas, Kansas City Chiefs (TE: 1962–67); Fred Biletnikoff, Oakland Raiders (1969–74); and Charlie Sanders, Detroit Lions (TE: 1969–71 and 1974–76).

Five—Vern Lewellen, Green Bay Packers (RB: 1925–29); Ken Strong, Staten Island Stapletons and New York Giants (RB: 1929–31 and 1933–34); Bill Smith, Chicago Cardinals (1934–36 and 1938–39); Jim Benton, Cleveland/Los Angeles Rams (1939 and 1944–47); Marion Motley, Cleveland Browns (RB: 1946–50); Bob "Hunchy" Hoernschmeyer, Chicago Rockets/Hornets and Detroit Lions (RB: 1946, 1949, and 1951–53); Tom Fears, Los Angeles Rams (1948–51 and 1955); Billy Howton, Green Bay Packers and Cleveland Browns (1952, 1955–57, and 1959); Hugh McElhenny, San Francisco 49ers (RB: 1952–54 and 1956–57); Billy Wilson, San Francisco 49ers, (1954–58); Pete Retzlaff, Philadelphia Eagles (TE: 1958–59, 1963–64, and 1966); Del Shofner, Los Angeles Rams and New York Giants (1958–59 and 1961–63); Bobby Mitchell, Cleveland Browns and Washington Redskins (RB: 1959–60 and 1962–64); Lionel Taylor, Denver Broncos (1960–63 and 1965); Don Maynard, New York Titans/Jets

(1960, 1965, and 1967–69); Dave Koucorek, San Diego Chargers (TE: 1961–65); Gale Sayers, Chicago Bears (RB: 1965–69); Leroy Kelly, Cleveland Browns (RB: 1966–69 and 1971); and Jackie Smith, St. Louis Cardinals (TE: 1966–70).

Four—Guy Chamberlin, Decatur Staleys and Canton/Cleveland Bulldogs (1920 and 1922–24); Tillie Voss, Rock Island Independents and Akron Pros, Toledo Maroons, Green Bay Packers, and Detroit Panthers (1922–25); Paul Goebel, Columbus Tigers (1923–26); Duke Hanny, Chicago Bears (1923–26); Luke Johnsos, Chicago Bears (1929–32); Morris "Red" Badgro, New York Giants (1930–31 and 1933–34); Glenn Presnell, Portsmouth Spartans/Detroit Lions (RB: 1931–34); Jim Poole, New York Giants (1938–40 and 1946); Perry Schwartz, Brooklyn Dodgers (1939–42); George Wilson, Chicago Bears (1941–44); Joe Aguirre, Washington Redskins and Los Angeles Dons (1943–46); Alyn Beals, San Francisco 49ers (1946–49); Jack Russell, New York Yankees and New York Yanks (1946–47 and 1949–50); Joe "The Jet" Perry, San Francisco 49ers (RB: 1949, 1953–54, and 1958); Elroy "Crazy Legs" Hirsch, Los Angeles Rams (1951–53 and 1956); Rick Casares, Chicago Bears (RB: 1955–58); Don Perkins, Dallas Cowboys (RB: 1961–62 and 1967–68); Gino Cappelletti, Boston Patriots (1961, 1963–64, and 1966); Charley Hennigan, Houston Oilers (1961–64); Bob Hayes, Dallas Cowboys (1965–68); Otis Taylor, Kansas City Chiefs (1966–67 and 1971–72); Gary Garrison, San Diego Chargers (1968 and 1970–72); and Gene Washington, San Francisco 49ers (1969–72).

The Pro Bowl

A professional football all-star game was first played in 1939, known as the Pro All-Star Game. The New York Giants defeated the Pro All-Stars, 13–10, at Wrigley Field, a Pacific Coast League baseball stadium in Los Angeles. In both 1940 and 1942, two Pro All-Star Games were played in January and December. The NFL Pro Bowl actually began play in 1951 at Los Angeles Memorial Coliseum.

Ends or flankers or frequent receivers among running backs who played before 1970 and were selected more than four times for the Pro Bowl or AFL All-Star Game (including players whose careers extended

Individual Honors

beyond 1970) are tallied here. Some players, such as Don Hutson, were selected to both games in 1940 and 1942. But these lists really can be read as monitors of the 1950s and 1960s. Also, the fewer teams in the AFL—eight and then 10 over the decade of the 1960s—makes for a preponderance of AFL players on these lists, since the NFL had a bigger field and stiffer competition from which to pick all-stars. It was tougher to make the Pro Bowl multiple times than it was for AFL stars to make that league's All-Star Game roster. Occasionally, some players were selected, but did not play for varying reasons, including injuries. Running backs or halfbacks who also played flanker and fullbacks are designated (RB) on the list. Tight ends or players who played that position, even before it entered the football lexicon, are designated (TE).

Nine—Jim Brown, Cleveland Browns (RB: 1957–65)

Eight—Charley Taylor, Washington Redskins (RB: 1965–68 and 1973–76); Paul Warfield, Cleveland Browns and Miami Dolphins (1965, 1969–75).

Seven—Frank Gifford, New York Giants (RB: 1954–57, 1959–60, and 1964); Lenny Moore, Baltimore Colts (RB: 1957, 1959–63, and 1965); Lance Alworth, San Diego Chargers (1964–70); and Charlie Sanders, Detroit Lions (TE: 1969–72 and 1975–77).

Six—Pete Pihos Philadelphia Eagles (TE: 1951–56); Hugh McElhenny, San Francisco 49ers and Minnesota Vikings (RB: 1953–54, 1957–59, and 1962); Billy Wilson, San Francisco 49ers (1955–60); Tommy McDonald, Philadelphia Eagles and Los Angeles Rams (1959–63 and 1966); Don Perkins, Dallas Cowboys (RB: 1962–64 and 1967–69); Leroy Kelly, Cleveland Browns (RB: 1966–71); and Fred Biletnikoff, Oakland Raiders (1968, 1970–72, and 1974–75).

Five—Doak Walker, Detroit Lions (RB: 1951–52 and 1954–56); Ollie Matson, Chicago Cardinals (RB: 1953 and 1955–58); Rick Casares, Chicago Bears (RB: 1955–59); Raymond Berry, Baltimore Colts (1959–60, 1962 and 1964–65); Pete Retzlaff, Philadelphia Eagles (TE: 1959, 1961, and 1964–66), Del Shofner, Los Angeles Rams and New York Giants (1959–60 and 1962–64); Jim Taylor, Green Bay Packers (RB: 1961–65); Mike Ditka, Chicago Bears (TE: 1962–66); Charley Hennigan, Houston Oilers (1962–66); Gino Cappelletti, Boston Patriots (1962 and 1964–67); Fred Arbanas, Kansas City Chiefs (TE: 1963–66 and 1968); Keith Lincoln,

San Diego Chargers and Buffalo Bills (RB: 1963–66 and 1968); Jackie Smith, St. Louis Cardinals (TE: 1967–71); and Harold Jackson, Philadelphia Eagles, Los Angeles Rams, and New England Patriots (1970, 1973–74, 1976, and 1978).

Four—Don Hutson, Green Bay Packers (both games in 1940 and both in 1942); Billy Howton, Green Bay Packers (1953 and 1956–58); Kyle Rote, New York Giants (1954 and 1955–57); John David Crow, St. Louis Cardinals and San Francisco 49ers (RB: 1960–61, 1963, and 1966); Sonny Randle, St. Louis Cardinals (1961–63 and 1966); Bobby Mitchell, Cleveland Browns and Washington Redskins (RB: 1960 and 1962–64); Dave Kocourek, San Diego Chargers (TE: 1962–65); Larry Garron, Boston Patriots (RB: 1962, 1964–65, and 1968); Art Powell, Oakland Raiders (1964–67); Clem Daniels, Oakland Raiders (RB: 1964–67); Bill Brown, Minnesota Vikings (RB: 1965–66 and 1968–69); Gale Sayers, Chicago Bears (RB: 1966–68 and 1970); Don Maynard, New York Jets (1966 and 1968–70); Ken Willard, San Francisco 49ers (RB: 1966–67 and 1969–70); Hewritt Dixon, Oakland Raiders (RB: 1967–69 and 1971); George Sauer, New York Jets (1967–70); Gary Garrison, San Diego Chargers (1969, 1971–73), and Bob Trumpy, Cincinnati Bengals (TE: 1969–71 and 1974).

Receivers who were named Pro Bowl Player of the Game or AFL All-Star Game Player of the Game prior to the 1970 season are: Billy Wilson of the San Francisco 49ers (1955), Ollie Matson of the Chicago Cardinals (RB: 1956), Hugh McElhenny of the San Francisco 49ers (RB: 1958), Frank Gifford of the New York Giants (RB: 1959), Curtis McClinton of the Kansas City Chiefs (RB: AFL, 1963), Keith Lincoln of the San Diego Chargers (RB: AFL, 1964 and 1965), Gale Sayers of the Chicago Bears (RB: 1967 and 1968), and Don Maynard of the New York Jets (AFL, 1968, in a tie with teammate QB Joe Namath).

NFL Network's NFL Top 10

The NFL Network telecasts NFL Top 10 documentaries in an hour-long format with commentary by various sportswriters and sportscasters. Occasionally, these lists, compiled by the network, seem skewed or lacking, and the commentators often make forceful mention of that.

Individual Honors

Mostly, the lists seemed thoughtfully weighed. Among these dozens of lists, all compiled in the 2000s, were:

Top Passing Combinations (air date July 25, 2007): (1) Peyton Manning to Marvin Harrison, Indianapolis Colts; (2) Steve Young to Jerry Rice, San Francisco 49ers; (3) Joe Montana to Jerry Rice, San Francisco 49ers; (4) Johnny Unitas to Raymond Berry, Baltimore Colts; (5) Jim Kelly to Andre Reed, Buffalo Bills; (6) Troy Aikman to Michael Irvin, Dallas Cowboys; (7) Arnie Herber to Don Hutson, Green Bay Packers; (8) Ken Stabler to Fred Biletnikoff, Oakland Raiders; (9) John Hadl to Lance Alworth, San Diego Chargers; and (10) Jim Zorn to Steve Largent, Seattle Seahawks.

Top 10 Receiving Corps (air date May 20, 2007): (1) San Diego Chargers of the early 1980s, with John Jefferson, Charlie Joiner, and Kellen Winslow; (2) St. Louis Rams of the early 2000s, with Torry Holt, Isaac Bruce, and Marshall Faulk; (3) Los Angeles Rams of the early 1950s, with Elroy "Crazy Legs" Hirsch, Tom Fears, and Bobby Boyd; (4) San Francisco 49ers, late 1980s and early 1990s, with Jerry Rice, John Taylor, Roger Craig, and Brent Jones; (5) Washington Redskins of the 1960s, with Charley Taylor, Bobby Mitchell, and Jerry Smith; (6) Oakland Raiders of the 1970s, with Fred Biletnikoff, Dave Casper, and Cliff Branch; (7) Miami Dolphins of the 1980s, with Mark Duper, Mark Clayton, and Tony Nathan; (8) Washington Redskins, 1980s, with Art Monk, Gary Clark, and Ricky Sanders; (9) Minnesota Vikings of the late 1990s and early 2000s, with Cris Carter, Randy Moss, and Jake Reed; (10) Indianapolis Colts of the early 2000s, with Marvin Harrison, Reggie Wayne, Dallas Clark, and Edgerrin James.

Top 10 Best Hands (air date July 24, 2009): (1) Cris Carter, Minnesota Vikings; (2) Raymond Berry, Baltimore Colts; (3) Steve Largent, Seattle Seahawks; (4) Larry Fitzgerald, Arizona Cardinals; (5) Fred Biletnikoff, Oakland Raiders; (6) Kellen Winslow, San Diego Chargers; Jerry Rice, San Francisco 49ers; Sterling Sharpe, Green Bay Packers; Lynn Swann, Pittsburgh Steelers; Marvin Harrison, Indianapolis Colts.

Top 10 Tight Ends (air date June 17, 2010): (1) John Mackey, Baltimore Colts; (2) Kellen Winslow, San Diego Chargers; (3) Mike Ditka, Chicago Bears, Philadelphia Eagles, and Dallas Cowboys; (4) Shannon Sharpe, Denver Broncos and Baltimore Ravens; (5) Ozzie Newsome, Cleveland Browns; (6) Jackie Smith, St. Louis Cardinals, Dallas Cowboys;

(7) Dave Casper, Oakland Raiders; (8) Tony Gonzalez, Kansas City Chiefs and Atlanta Falcons; (9) Mark Bavarro, New York Giants; and (10) Antonio Gates, San Diego Chargers.

The Pro Football Historical Abstract

Author and football historian Sean Lahman compiled the greatest wide receivers and tight ends in descending order in 2008 in his book *The Pro Football Historical Abstract*, published by The Lyons Press. Most of its top 75 wide receivers are from post–1970 times.

Lahman's top 10 wide receivers, in descending order, are: Jerry Rice, Don Hutson, Marvin Harrison, Steve Largent, James Lofton, Randy Moss, Lance Alworth, Don Maynard, Terrell Owens, and Michael Irvin.

Players on the list who began their careers before 1970 are: Raymond Berry (18), Billy Howton (19), Paul Warfield (22), Art Powell (26), Del Shofner (27), Gene Washington (49ers) (28), Charley Taylor (29), John Gilliam (32), Gary Garrison (38), Fred Biletnikoff (39), Charlie Joiner (40), Bobby Mitchell (44), Mac Speedie (45), Dave Parks (49), Otis Taylor (50), Bob Hayes (52), Jim Benton (54), Jimmy Orr (60), Dante Lavelli (62), Billy Wilson (66), and Elroy "Crazy Legs" Hirsch (69).

Lahman's top 10 tight ends from a 2007 perspective, in descending order, are: Tony Gonzalez, Shannon Sharpe, Ozzie Newsome, Jackie Smith, Pete Retzlaff, Kellen Winslow, Mike Ditka, Todd Christensen, Jerry Smith, and Riley Odoms.

The position solidified in the 1960s. Still there might have been some other reasons for the absence of Ron Kramer in the top 50 tight ends. No mention was made of any pre–1960s players. The TEs on the list who began their careers before 1970s are: Jackie Smith, Retzlaff, Ditka, and Jerry Smith, as well as Bob Trumpy (18), Charlie Sanders (20), Jim Mitchell (22), John Mackey (23), Billy Cannon (25), Willie Frazier (29), Jim Whalen (31), Milt Morin (32), Dave Kocourek (33), Preston Carpenter (35), Ted Kwalick (40), and Fred Arbanas (42).

Chapter Notes

Almost all of the statistics, standings, and other numerical data as well as playoff information and All Pro data were taken from, or corroborated by www.Pro-Football-Reference.com; Bob Carroll et al., eds., *Total Football II: The Encyclopedia of the National Football League* (New York: HarperCollins, 1999); and Pete Palmer et al., eds., *ESPN Pro Football Encyclopedia*, 2d ed. (New York: Sterling, 2007).

Chapter One

1. Frank Presbey and James Hugh Moffatt, *Athletics at Princeton: A History* (New York: Frank Presbey, 1901), p. 284.
2. Caspar Whitney, "Sports," *Harper's Weekly*, March 5, 1892.
3. Walter Camp and Lorin F. Deland, *Football [Rules of the Season of 1896]* (Cambridge: Riverside Press, 1896), p. 411.
4. John W. Heisman, "Fast and Loose," *Collier's Weekly*, October 20, 1928.
5. John Sayle Watterson, *Journal of Sport History* 27, no. 2 (Summer 2000), p. 297.
6. Edward Wagenknecht, *The Seven Worlds of Theodore Roosevelt* (Guilford, CT: Globe Pequot, 2009), p. 48.
7. Scott A. McQuilkin and Ronald A. Smith, "The Rise and Fall of the Flying Wedge: Football's Most Controversial Play," *Journal of Sport History* 20, no. 1 (Spring 1993), pp. 57–64.
8. Bernard M. Corbett and Paul Simpson, *The Only Game That Matters: The Harvard/Yale Rivalry* (New York: Crown, 2004), p. 74.
9. Coit Howard Conant, *The Evolution of Offensive Football in American Colleges, 1800–1913*, dissertation, University of Wisconsin-Madison, 1962, p. 57.
10. John Sayle Watterson, *College Football: History, Spectacle, Controversy* (Baltimore: Johns Hopkins University Press, 2000), p.100.
11. Wiley Lee Umphlett, *Creating the Big Game: John W. Heisman and the Invention of American Football* (Westport, CT: Greenwood Press, 1992), pp. 88–95.
12. Watterson, *College Football*, pp. 100–108.
13. David M. Nelson, *The Anatomy of a Game: Football, the Rules and the Men Who Made the Game* (Cranbury, N.J.: Associated University Presses, 1994), p. 122.

Chapter Two

1. Watterson, *College Football*, p. 103.
2. William Barry Furlong, "The Reincarnation of Woody Hayes," *Life*, November 21, 1969, p. 52. For the record, concerning this rather famous quotation, the original statement ended in "ain't good." That was changed in this article and many places to "are bad," because of the midcentury notion that "ain't" just ain't good English; the original was restored here by the author.
3. Michael Quinion, *Why Is Q Always Followed by U?* (New York: Particular Books, 2009).
4. Watterson, *College Football*, p. 106.
5. Nelson, *The Anatomy of a Game*, p. 128.
6. Philip L. Brooks, *Forward Pass: The Play That Saved Football* (Yardley, PA: Westholme, 2007), p. 73.
7. Allison Danzig, *The History of Amer-*

ican Football: Its Great Teams, Players, and Coaches (Englewood Cliffs, N.J.: Prentice-Hall, 1956), p. 34.
8. Harold Keith, "Pioneer of the Forward Pass," *Esquire* 22 (1944), p. 54.
9. Danzig, *The History of American Football*, p. 34.
10. Danzig, *The History of American Football*, p. 35.
11. Eddie Cochems, "The Forward Pass and the On-Side Kick," in Walter Camp, ed., *Spalding's How to Play Foot Ball* (New York: American Sports Publishing, 1907), p. 51.
12. Bob Carroll et al., eds., *Total Football II: The Official Encyclopedia of the National Football League* (New York: HarperCollins, 1999), pp. 9–10.
13. Carroll, *Total Football*, p. 7; David Finoli and Tom Aikens, *The Birthplace of Professional Football: Southwestern Pennsylvania* (Charleston, S.C.: Arcadia, 2004).
14. Frederick P. Miller, Agnes F. Vandome, and John McBrewster, eds., *Howard R. Reiter* (Berlin: VDM, 2010).
15. "First Forward Pass Thrown by Wesleyan Team in 1906," *Bridgeport* (CT) *Post*, November 5, 1955.
16. "'Mon' Gets Good Start: Use a Long Forward Pass with Good Effect," *Des Moines Daily News*, October 3, 1906.
17. "Tigers Brilliant Against Stevens: New Rules Seem to Please Princeton Players," "Indians Swamp Susquehanna," "Kicking Wins for Harvard," and "Williams Wins with Forward Pass," *Trenton* (N.J.) *Times*, October 4, 1906, collected in "Forward Pass," http://en.wikipedia.org/wiki/Forward_pass, December 19, 2014.
18. George Sullivan, *All About Football* (New York: G.P. Putnam's Sons, 1987), introduction.
19. Danzig, *The History of American Football*, p. 37.
20. Danzig, *The History of American Football*, p. 37.
21. Danzig, *The History of American Football*, p. 37.
22. Ellis Lucia, *Mr. Football: Amos Alonzo Stagg* (South Brunswick, N.J.: A.S. Barnes, 1970), p. 150.
23. Lucia, *Mr. Football*, p. 151.
24. Tom Bennett, *The Pro Style* (Englewood Cliffs, N.J.: Prentice-Hall, 1976), p. 20.
25. Watterson, *College Football*, p. 123.
26. Danzig, *The History of American Football*, p. 36.
27. Danzig, *The History of American Football*, p. 38.
28. Camp, ed., *Spalding's How to Play Football*, p. 51.

Chapter Three

1. Robert M. Quackenbush and Steve Bynum, *Knute Rockne: His Life and Legend* (New York: October Football Corporation, 1988), p. 64.
2. Lars Anderson, *Carlisle vs. Army: Jim Thorpe, Dwight Eisenhower, Pop Warner (and the Forgotten Story of Football's Greatest Battle)* (New York: Random House, 2007), p. 145.
3. Anderson, *Carlisle vs. Army*, p. 145.
4. Nelson, *The Anatomy of a Game*, p. 133.
5. Nelson, *The Anatomy of a Game*, p. 133.
6. Anderson, *Carlisle vs. Army*, p. 145.
7. Anderson, *Carlisle vs. Army*, p. 145.
8. Anderson, *Carlisle vs. Army*, p. 145.
9. Danzig, *The History of American Football*, p. 38.
10. Nelson, *The Anatomy of a Game*, p. 131.
11. Nelson, *The Anatomy of a Game*, p. 131.
12. Nelson, *The Anatomy of a Game*, p. 131.
13. Nelson, *The Anatomy of a Game*, p. 131.
14. Nelson, *The Anatomy of a Game*, p. 131.
15. Danzig, *The History of American Football*, p. 37.
16. Anderson, *Carlisle vs. Army*, p. 194.
17. Anderson, *Carlisle vs. Army*, p. 194.
18. Watterson, *College Football*, pp. 123–129.
19. Mike Thompson and Wesley Stout. "The Villain of the Piece," *Saturday Evening Post*, October 31, 1931, p. 29.

20. Watterson, *College Football*, pp. 127–128.
21. Watterson, *College Football*, pp. 130–131.

Chapter Four

1. Ray Robinson, *Rockne of Notre Dame: The Making of a Legend* (New York: Oxford University Press, 1999), p. 41.
2. Danzig, *The History of American Football*, p. 41.
3. Danzig, *The History of American Football*, p. 42.
4. Robinson, *Rockne of Notre Dame*, p. 45.
5. Danzig, *The History of American Football*, p. 42.
6. Harry Cross, "Inventing the Forward Pass, November 1913," in William Taaffe and David Fischer, eds., *Sports of the Times: A Day-by-Day Selection of the Most Important, Thrilling, and Inspired Events of the Past 150 Years* (New York: The New York Times, 2003), p. 347.
7. Taaffe and Fischer, eds., *Sports of the Times*, p. 347.
8. Frank P. Maggio, *Notre Dame and the Game That Changed Football: How Jesse Harper Made the Forward Pass a Weapon and Knute Rockne a Legend* (New York: Carroll & Graf, 2007), p. 9.
9. *Collier's Weekly*, October 25, 1930; Fred Eisenhammer and Eric Sondheimer, *College Football's Most Memorable Games*, 2d ed. (Jefferson, N.C.: McFarland, 2010), p. 11.
10. Robinson, *Rockne of Notre Dame*, p. 47.
11. Robert Bruckner screenplay, *Knute Rockne, All American*, Warner Bros., 1940.
12. Danzig, *The History of American Football*, p. 41.
13. Robert C. Zuppke and Milton Martin Frithiof Olander, *Football Techniques and Tactics* (Champaign, IL: Bailey and Himes, 1924), pp. 161–177.
14. Paul Zimmerman, *A Thinking Man's Guide to Pro Football* (New York: E.P. Dutton, 1970), p. 89.
15. Danzig, *The History of American Football*, p. 41.

16. Raymond Schmidt, *The Shaping of College Football: The Transformation of a National Sport, 1919–1930* (Syracuse: Syracuse University Press, 2007), p. 235.

Chapter Five

1. *Professional Football Researchers Association (PFRA) Annual* 1 (1971), pp. 1–2.
2. Keith McClellan, *The Sunday Game: At the Dawn of Professional Football* (Akron: Akron University Press, 1998), p. 18.
3. Bennett, *The Pro Style*, p. 32.
4. McClellan, *The Sunday Game*, p. 117.
5. McClellan, *The Sunday Game*, p. 120.
6. McClellan, *The Sunday Game*, p. 117.
7. McClellan, *The Sunday Game*, p. 92.
8. McClellan, *The Sunday Game*, p. 127.
9. McClellan, *The Sunday Game*, p. 127.
10. McClellan, *The Sunday Game*, p. 62.
11. "History of the Football Helmet," Past Time Sports, http://www.pasttimesports.biz/history.html, December 28, 2014, and Beau Riffenburgh, "Tools of the Trade," in Carroll et al., *Total Football*, p. 36.
12. Bob Curran, *Pro Football's Rag Days* (Englewood Cliffs, N.J.: Prentice-Hall, 1969), pp. 33–35.
13. Curran, *Pro Football's Rag Days*, pp. 33–38; Matthew Algeo, *Last Team Standing: How the Steelers and the Eagles—"The Steagles"—Saved Pro Football During World War II* (Cambridge, MA: Da Capo, 2006), pp. 58–62; John Thorn et al., eds., *Total Baseball: The Official Encyclopedia of Major League Baseball* (New York: Total Sports, 1999), p. 336.
14. McCllelan, *The Sunday Game*, p. 106.
15. McClellan, *The Sunday Game*, p. 106.
16. McClellan, *The Sunday Game*, p. 195.
17. McClellan, *The Sunday Game*, p. 195.
18. McClellan, *The Sunday Game*, p. 197.
19. McClellan, *The Sunday Game*, p. 200.
20. McClellan, *The Sunday Game*, pp. 200–201.

Chapter Six

1. Chris Willis, *The Man Who Built the National Football League: Joe F. Carr* (Lanham, MD: Scarecrow Press, 2010).

2. Dr. L.H. Baker, *Football Facts and Figures* (New York: Farrar & Rinehart, 1945), p. 657.
3. Danzig, *The History of American Football*, pp. 38–39.
4. Will McDonough, et al., *The NFL Century: The Complete Story of the National Football League, 1920-2000* (New York: Smithmark and the National Football League, 1999), pp. 40–41.
5. John Maxymuk, *Strong Arm Tactics: A History and Statistical Analysis of the Professional Quarterback* (Jefferson, N.C.: McFarland, 2008), p. 79.
6. Algeo, *Last Team Standing*, p. 63.
7. John D. McCallum and Charles H. Pearson, *College Football U.S.A. 1869-1971—Official Book of the National Football Foundation* (New York: Hall of Fame Publishing and McGraw-Hill, 1972), p. 248.
8. Chad Livingston, "The Nebraska 100: No. 39, Guy Chamberlin," http://data omaha.com/neb100/player/39, November 24, 2014.
9. Richard M. Cohen, Jordan A. Deutsch, and David S. Neft, *The Scrapbook History of Pro Football, 1893-1979* (Indianapolis: Bobbs-Merrill, 1979), p. 29.
10. Carroll Jett, *Here Come the Big Reds: Information & Stories about Parkersburg High School Football* (Parkersburg, W.V: Parkersburg High School, 2014), p. 50; "Former Pitt Star Faces Grave Charges," *New Castle (PA) News*, December 9, 1948.
11. Richard Whittingham, *What a Game They Played: An Inside Look at the Golden Era of Pro Football* (Lincoln: University of Nebraska Press, 1984), p. 137.
12. Whittingham, *What a Game They Played*, p. 45.
13. Whittingham, *What a Game They Played*, p. 45.
14. Whittingham, *What a Game They Played*, p. 45.
15. Whittingham, *What a Game They Played*, p. 45.

Chapter Seven

1. Maxymuk, *Strong Arm Tactics*, p. 80.
2. Carroll, et al., *Total Football II*, p. 50.
3. Whittingham, *What a Game They Played*, p. 94.
4. Myron Cope, *The Game That Was: The Early Days of Pro Football* (New York: World, 1970), p. 65.
5. Murray Olderman, *The Runningbacks* (Englewood Cliffs, N.J.: Prentice-Hall, 1969), p. 149.
6. Whittingham, *What a Game They Played*, p. 29.
7. Cope, *The Game That Was*, p. 94.
8. Dennis J. Gullickson, *Vagabond Halfback: The Life and Times of Johnny Blood McNally* (Madison, WI: Trails Books, 2006), p. 198.
9. Olderman, *The Runningbacks*, p. 150.
10. Olderman, *The Runningbacks*, p. 150.
11. Olderman, *The Runningbacks*, p. 150.
12. John Maxymuk, *NFL Head Coaches: A Biographical Dictionary, 1920-2011* (Jefferson, N.C.: McFarland, 2012), p. 193.
13. Olderman, *The Runningbacks*, p. 147.
14. Gullickson, *Vagabond Halfback*, book's title.
15. Gerald Holland, "Is That You Up There, Johnny Blood?" *Sports Illustrated*, September 2, 1963.

Chapter Eight

1. Robert Smith, *Pro Football: The History of the Game and the Great Players* (Garden City, N.Y.: Doubleday, 1963), p. 100.
2. Danzig, *The History of American Football*, p. 75.
3. Amos Alonzo Stagg, *Saturday Evening Post*, October 23, 1926.
4. George Halas, Gwen Morgan and Arthur Veysey, *Halas by Halas: The Autobiography of George Halas* (New York: McGraw-Hill, 1999), p. 139.
5. Joe King, *Inside Pro Football* (Englewood Cliffs, N.J.: Prentice-Hall, 1958), p. 161.
6. Bennett, *The Pro Style*, p. 30.
7. Halas et al., *Halas by Halas*, p. 139.
8. Danzig, *The History of American Football*, p. 78.
9. Danzig, *The History of American Football*, p. 74.

10. Danzig, *The History of American Football*, p. 77.
11. Clark Shaughnessy, Ralph Jones and George Halas, *The Modern T Formation with Man-in-Motion* (Chicago: Author, 1941).
12. Halas, et al., *Halas by Halas*, p. 139.
13. McDonough, et al., *The NFL Century*, p. 43.
14. McDonough, et al., *The NFL Century*, p. 43.
15. Halas, et al., *Halas by Halas*, p. 140.
16. Stephen Fox, *Big Leagues: Professional Baseball, Football, and Basketball in the National Memory* (New York: William Morrow, 1994), p. 245.
17. McDonough, et al., *The NFL Century*, p. 48.
18. Bennett, *The Pro Style*, p. 34.
19. McDonough, et al., *The NFL Century*, p. 52.
20. Bennett, *The Pro Style*, p. 34.
21. McDonough, et al., *The NFL Century*, p. 51.
22. Halas, et al., *Halas by Halas*, p. 180.

Chapter Nine

1. Sean Lahman, *The Pro Football Historical Abstract* (Guilford, CT: The Lyons Press, 2008), pp. 152–153.
2. Michael L. LaBlanc, ed., *Professional Sports Team Histories: Football* (Detroit: Gale Research, 1994), p. Q-96.
3. "Hall of Famers: Don Hutson, Biography." Pro Football Hall of Fame, http://www.profootballhof.com/hof/member.aspx?PLAYER_ID=104, December 13, 2014.
4. Whittingham, *What a Game They Played*, p. 118.
5. "Hall of Famers: Don Hutson, Biography."
6. Phil Barber and John Fawaz, *NFL's Greatest: Pro Football's Best Players, Teams and Games* (New York: Dorling Kindersley, 2000), p. 38.
7. Whittingham, *What a Game They Played*, p. 184.
8. Whittingham, *What a Game They Played*, p. 124.

9. Whittingham, *What a Game They Played*, p. 124.
10. Richard Whittingham, *Sunday's Heroes: NFL Legends Talk about the Times of Their Lives* (Chicago: Triumph Books, 2004), p. 140.
11. Whittingham, *What a Game They Played*, pp. 126–127.
12. Peter King, "The Greatest Player You Never Saw," in Rob Fleder, ed., *The Football Book* (New York: Time/Sports Illustrated, 2005), p. 162.
13. Algeo, *Last Team Standing*, p. 197.
14. LaBlanc, ed., *Professional Sports Team Histories*, p. Q-96.
15. Whittingham, *What a Game They Played*, p. 135.
16. Whittingham, *What a Game They Played*, pp. 127–128.

Chapter Ten

1. Frank Leahy, *Notre Dame Football—The T Formation* (New York: Prentice-Hall, 1949).
2. Roger Fimrite, "A Melding of Men All Suited to a T," *Sports Illustrated*, September 5, 1977.
3. Peter King, *Greatest Quarterbacks* (New York: Bishop Books, 1999), pp. 83–84.
4. Jeff Davis, *Papa Bear: The Life and Legacy of George Halas* (New York: McGraw-Hill, 2005), p. 139.
5. Davis, *Papa Bear*, pp. 139–140.
6. Sid Luckman, *Luckman at Quarterback: Football as a Sport and a Career* (Chicago: Ziff-Davis, 1949), p. 35.
7. Whittingham, *What a Game They Played*, p. 177.
8. Allison Danzig, ed., *Oh, How They Played the Game!: The Early Days of Pro Football and the Heroes Who Made It Great* (New York: Macmillan, 1971), p. 400.

Chapter Eleven

1. Peter King, *Greatest Quarterbacks*, p. 83.
2. Frank Leahy, *Notre Dame Football—*

The T Formation (New York: Prentice-Hall, 1949).

3. Luckman, *Luckman at Quarterback*, p. 140.

4. Luckman, *Luckman at Quarterback*, p. 137.

5. Harold U. Ribalow and Meir Z. Ribalow, *The Jew in American Sports* (New York: Hippocrene Books, 1985), p 180.

6. Ribalow and Ribalow, *The Jew in American Sports*, p. 280.

7. Ribalow and Ribalow, *The Jew in American Sports*, p 180.

8. Howard Roberts, *The Story of Pro Football* (New York: Rand McNally, 1953), p. 28.

9. Paul Zimmermann, "The Bronk and the Gazelle: Fifty Years Ago, Bronko Nagurski and Don Hutson Dominated Pro Football. But How Would They Do Today?" *Sports Illustrated*, September 11, 1989.

10. Gerald Holland, "Greasy Neale: Nothing to Prove, Nothing to Ask," *Sports Illustrated*, August 24, 1964.

11. "A Brief History of Hash Marks," The Game Before the Money, http://www.thegamebeforethemoney.com/a-brief-history-of-hash-marks/, December 30, 2014.

12. Whittingham, *What a Game They Played*, p. 189.

13. "Ram Tough: Jim Benton Tops Them All," ESPN.com, July 16, 2010, accessed December 11, 2014.

Chapter Twelve

1. Fimrite, "A Melding of Men All Suited to a T."

2. Len Pasquarelli, "Shaughnessy Among All-Time Innovators," ESPN.com: NFL, September 29, 2009.

3. Michael MacCambridge, *America's Game: The Epic Story of How Pro Football Captured a Nation* (New York: Random House, 2004), p. 62.

4. Robert J. Scott and Myles A. Pocta, *Honor on the Line: The Fifth Down and the Spectacular 1940 Football Season* (Bloomington, IN: iUniverse, 2010), p. 17.

5. Cyclone Covey, *The Wow Boys: The Story of Stanford's Classic 1940 Football Season, Game by Game* (New York: Exposition Books, 1957), p. 22.

6. Heartley "Hunk" Anderson and Emil Klosinski, *Notre Dame, Chicago Bears, and "Hunk" Anderson: Football Memoirs in Highlight* (Oviedo, FL: Sun-Gator, 1976), p. 189.

7. Fimrite, "A Melding of Men All Suited to a T."

8. Lyons Yellin, "Legend Clark Shaughnessy Heads Inductees into Loyola Hall of Fame," NOLA.com and *New Orleans Times-Picayune*, January 26, 2012.

9. Whittingham, *What a Game They Played*, p. 177.

10. LaBlanc, ed., *Professional Sports Team Histories*, p. 199.

11. Ron Smith, *Pro Football's Heroes of the Hall* (St. Louis: The Sporting News, 2003), p. 103.

12. Stuart Leuthner, *Iron Men: Bucko, Crazylegs and the Boys Recall the Golden Days of Professional Football* (Garden City, N.Y.: Doubleday, 1988), p. 171.

13. Leuthner, *Iron Men*, p. 175.

14. Pasquerelli, "Shaughnessy Among All-Time Innovators."

15. Fimrite, "A Melding of Men All Suited to a T."

Chapter Thirteen

1. Jack Clary, *Great Teams' Great Years: The Cleveland Browns* (New York: Macmillan, 1973), p. 63.

2. Paul Brown and Jack Clary, *PB: The Paul Brown Story* (New York: Atheneum, 1979), p. 203.

3. Andy Piascik, *Coffin Corner* 27, no. 3 (2005).

4. Dan Rooney with Andrew E. Masich and David F. Halaas, *Dan Rooney: My 75 Years with the Pittsburgh Steelers and the NFL* (New York: Da Capo, 2008), p. 66.

5. Donald Steinberg, *Expanding Your Horizons: Collegiate Football's Greatest Team* (Pittsburgh: Dorrance, 1992), p. 96.

6. Piascik, *Coffin Corner*.

7. Steve Wulf, ed., *ESPN: The Mighty Book of Sports Knowledge* (New York: Ballantine, 2009), p. 133.

8. Dave Zirin, *A People's History of Sports in the United States: 250 Years of Politics, Protest, People, and Play* (New York: The New Press, 2008), p. 109.
9. Piascik, *Coffin Corner*.
10. Clary, *Great Teams' Great Years*, p. 18.
11. Clary, *Great Teams' Great Years*, p. 18.
12. Brown and Clary, *PB*, p. 136.
13. Chris Foster, "Speedie Turns Home Into a Hall," *Los Angeles Times*, September 12, 1991.
14. Foster, "Speedie Turns Home Into a Hall."
15. Brown and Clary, *PB*, p. 136.
16. Paul Zimmermann, "Revolutionaries," *Sports Illustrated*, August 17, 1998, p. 78.
17. Brown and Clary, *PB*, p. 137.
18. Clary, *Great Teams' Great Years*, p. 18.
19. Chuck Heaton, *Browns Scrapbook: A Fond Look Back at Five Decades of Football from a Legendary Cleveland Sportswriter* (Cleveland: Gray & Company, 2007), p. 172.
20. Brown and Clary, *PB*, p. 137.
21. Matt Maiocco, *The San Francisco 49ers: The Complete Illustrated History* (Minneapolis: MVP Books, 2013), p. 17.
22. George Cantor, *Paul Brown: The Man Who Invented Modern Football* (Chicago: Triumph Books, 2008), p. 2.

Chapter Fourteen

1. James P. Terzian, *Great Teams' Great Years: New York Giants* (New York: Macmillan, 1973), p. 133.
2. "Billy Wilson, Sure-Handed Receiver for 49ers, Dies at 81," *The New York Times*, January 28, 2009.
3. Daniel Brown, *100 Things 49ers Fans Should Know and Do Before They Die* (Chicago: Triumph Books, 2013), "No. 42: The Goose Is Loose."
4. Zimmerman *The Thinking Man's Guide to Pro Football*, pp. 87–88.
5. Red Smith, "Three for the Ages," in John Thorn, ed., *The Armchair Quarterback* (New York: Charles Scribner's Sons, 1982), p. 272.

Chapter Fifteen

1. *Film Classic: Mike Ditka and the 1963 Bears*, "Masterpiece Theatre NFL," NFL Videos.
2. Mike Ditka and Don Pierson, *Ditka: An Autobiography* (Chicago: Bonus Books, 1986), p. 90.
3. George Allen and Ben Olan, *Pro Football's 100 Greatest Players: Rating the Stars of Past and Present* (Indianapolis: Bobbs-Merrill, 1982), p. 49.
4. David Maraniss, *When Pride Still Mattered: A Life of Vince Lombardi* (New York: Simon & Schuster, 1999), p. 222.
5. Richard Goldstein, "Ron Kramer, Tight End with Packers and Lions, Dies at 75," *The New York Times*, September 12, 2010.
6. Bob Carroll, *When the Grass Was Real* (New York: Simon & Schuster, 1993), p. 196.
7. Sam DeLuca, *The Football Handbook* (New York: Jonathan David, 1978), p. 107.
8. DeLuca, *The Football Handbook*, p. 108.
9. Zimmerman, *A Thinking Man's Guide to Pro Football*, p. 194.
10. Allen and Olan, *Pro Football's 100 Greatest Players*, p. 54.
11. Ed Bouchette, "Elbie Nickel / Best Tight End in Steelers History," *Pittsburgh Post-Gazette*, March 2, 2007.
12. Paul Zimmerman, *The New Thinking Man's Guide to Pro Football* (New York: HarperCollins, 1987), p. 116.
13. Zimmermann, *The New Thinking Man's Guide to Pro Football*, p. 116.
14. Barber and Fawaz, *NFL's Greatest*, p. 47.
15. John Mackey and Thom Loverro, *Blazing Trails: Coming of Age in Football's Golden Era* (Chicago: Triumph Books, 2003), p. 95.
16. Zimmerman, *The Thinking Man's Guide to Pro Football*, pp. 95–96.
17. Thom Loverro, *Hail Victory: An*

Oral History of the Washington Redskins (Hoboken, N.J.: John Wiley & Sons, 2006), p. 158.

18. Loverro, *Hail Victory*, p. 158.

19. John Devaney, *Star Pass Receivers of the NFL* (New York: Random House, 1972), pp. 92–93.

20. Dave Anderson, *Great Pass Receivers of the NFL* (New York: Random House, 1966), pp. 60–62.

21. Bennett, *The Pro Style*, p. 109.

22. Jack Horrigan and Mike Rathet, *The Other League: The Fabulous Story of the American Football League* (Chicago: Follett, NFL Properties, and Rutledge, 1970), p. 62.

23. Mark Stallard, *Kansas City Chiefs Encyclopedia* (New York: Sports Publishing, 2002), p. 170.

24. Glenn Dickey, *Just Win, Baby: Al Davis and His Raiders* (New York: Harcourt Brace Jovanovich, 1991), p. 33.

25. Kenny Stabler and Dick O'Connor, *Super Bowl Diary: The Autobiography of Kenny "The Snake" Stabler* (Los Angeles: Pinnacle Books, 1977), p. 144.

26. Stabler and O'Connor, *Super Bowl Diary*, p. 145.

27. Paul Gutierrez, *100 Things Raiders Fans Should Know & Do Before They Die* (Chicago: Triumph Books, 2014), pp. 90–91.

Chapter Sixteen

1. Peter Golenbock, *Cowboys Have Always Been My Heroes: The Definitive Oral History of America's Team* (New York: Warner Books, 1997), p. 587.

2. Zimmermann, *The New Thinking Man's Guide to Pro Football*, p. 103.

3. Golenbeck, *Cowboys Have Always Been My Heroes*, p. 588.

4. Stallard, *Kansas City Chiefs Encyclopedia*, p. 132.

5. Ira Miller, "Cold Reception / Raiders-Steelers Rivalry Is Still Immaculate After All These Years," www.sfgate.com/sports, November 29, 2000, accessed December 17, 2014)

6. Timothy Gay, Ph.D., *Football Physics: The Science of the Game* (New York: Rodale Press, 2004, pp. 3–17.

7. Jim O'Brien, *Whatever It Takes: The Continuing Saga of the Pittsburgh Steelers—II* (Pittsburgh: James O'Brien, 1992), p. 138.

8. Bennett, *The Pro Style*, p. 72.

9. Earl McRea, "Choo Choo's Glory Blazed Across the Atlantic," *Toronto Sun*, January 6, 2010.

10. Barry Gottehrer, *The Giants of New York* (New York: G.P. Putnam's Sons, 1963), p. 217.

11. McRea, "Choo Choo's Glory Blazed Across the Atlantic."

12. Ron Smith, *Pro Football's Heroes of the Hall*, p. 116.

13. Jack Cavanaugh, *Giants Among Men: How Robustelli, Huff, Gifford, and the Giants Made New York a Football Town and Changed the NFL* (New York: Random House, 2008), p. 103.

14. Andy Piascik, "Lenny Moore," *The Coffin Corner* 24, no. 5 (2002), p. 2.

15. Joe Soprano, "All-Time Top 10 Penn Staters in the NFL," *Wilkes-Barre* (PA) *Times-Leader*, August 16, 2014.

16. George Sullivan, *The Great Running Backs* (New York: G.P. Putnam's Sons, 1972), p. 111.

17. Piascik, "Lenny Moore," p. 1.

18. Olderman, *The Runningbacks*, p. 364.

19. "Kansas City Chiefs," *Street & Smith's Pro Football Yearbook*, 1963, p. 59.

20. Thomas G. Smith, "Civil Rights on the Gridiron: The Kennedy Administration and the Desegregation of the Washington Redskins," in Patrick B. Miller and David K. Wiggins, eds., *Sport and the Color Line: Black Athletes in Twentieth Century America* (New York: Routledge, 2004), p. 296.

21. Shirley Povich, *All Those Mornings … at the Post* (New York: Public Affairs, 2005), p. 208.

22. Carroll, *When the Grass Was Real*, 53.

23. Mike Freeman, *Jim Brown: The Fierce Life of an American Hero* (New York: William Morrow, 2006), p. 118.

Notes—Chapter Sixteen

24. Mitchell disappointed in not being appointed general manager of the Redskins by two owner regimes. Thomas G. Smith, *Showdown: JFK and the Integration of the Washington Redskins* (Boston: Beacon Press, 2011), Epilogue.

25. Zimmermann, *A Thinking Man's Guide to Pro Football*, p. 96.

26. Lou Sahadi, *Pro Football's Gamebreakers* (Chicago: Contemporary Books, 1977), p. 52.

Bibliography

Books

Algeo, Matthew. *Last Team Standing: How the Steelers and the Eagles—"The Steagles"—Saved Pro Football During World War II*. Cambridge, MA: Da Capo, 2006.

Allen, George, and Ben Olan. *Pro Football's 100 Greatest Players: Rating the Stars of Past and Present*. Indianapolis: Bobbs-Merrill, 1982.

Anderson, Dave. *Great Pass Receivers of the NFL*. New York: Random House, 1966.

Anderson, Heartley "Hunk," and Emil Klosinski. *Notre Dame, Chicago Bears, and "Hunk" Anderson: Football Memoirs in Highlight*. Oviedo, FL: SunGator, 1976.

Anderson, Lars. *Carlisle vs. Army: Jim Thorpe, Dwight Eisenhower, Pop Warner (and the Forgotten Story of Football's Greatest Battle)*. New York: Random House, 2007.

Baker, Dr. L. H. *Football Facts and Figures*. New York: Farrar & Rinehart, 1945.

Barber, Phil, and John Fawaz. *NFL's Greatest: Pro Football's Best Players, Teams and Games*. New York: Dorling Kindersley, 2000.

Bennett, Tom. *The Pro Style*. Englewood Cliffs, N.J.: Prentice-Hall, 1976.

Berry, Raymond, and C.H. "Butch" Gilbert, Jr. *Raymond Berry's Complete Guide for Pass Receivers*. West Nyack, N.Y.: Parker, 1982.

Bishoff, Steve. *Great Teams' Great Years: The Los Angeles Rams*. New York: Macmillan, 1973.

Blanda, George, and Wells Twombly. *Blanda: Alive and Kicking*. Los Angeles: Nash, 1971.

Blount, Roy, Jr. *About Three Bricks Shy of a Load*. New York: Ballantine, 1974.

Bowden, Mark. *The Greatest Game Ever: Giants vs. Colts, 1958, and the Birth of the Modern NFL*. New York: Atlantic Monthly Press, 2008.

Brichford, Maynard. *Bob Zuppke: The Life and Football Legacy of the Illinois Coach*. Jefferson, N.C.: McFarland, 2009.

Brooks, Philip L. *Forward Pass: The Play That Saved Football*. ... Yardley, PA: Westholme, 2007.

Brown, Daniel. *100 Things 49ers Fans Should Know and Do Before They Die*. Chicago: Triumph Books, 2013.

Brown, Paul, and Jack Clary. *PB: The Paul Brown Story*. New York: Atheneum, 1979.

Buchanan, Lamont. *The Story of Football*. New York: Vanguard, 1947.

Camp, Walter, ed. *Spalding's How to Play Foot Ball*. New York: American Sports, 1907.

_____ and Lorin F. Deland. *Football*. Cambridge: Riverside Press, 1896.

Cantor, George. *Paul Brown: The Man Who Invented Modern Football*. Chicago: Triumph Books, 2008.

Carroll, Bob. *When the Grass Was Real: Unitas, Brown, Lombardi, Sayers, Butkus, Namath, and All the Rest: The*

Bibliography

Best Ten Years of Pro Football. New York: Simon & Schuster, 1993.

____, Pete Palmer, and John Thorn. *The Hidden Game of Football.* New York: Warner Books, 1988.

Carroll, John M. *Red Grange and the Rise of Modern Football.* Champaign: University of Illinois, 1999.

Cavanaugh, Jack. *Giants Among Men: How Robustelli, Huff, Gifford, and the Giants Made New York a Football Town and Changed the NFL.* New York: Random House, 2008.

Chrebet, Wayne, and Vic Carucci. *Every Down, Every Distance: My Journey to the NFL.* Garden City, N.Y.: Doubleday, 1999.

Claassen, Harold (Spiker). *The History of Professional Football.* Englewood Cliffs, N.J.: Prentice-Hall, 1963.

Clary, Jack T. *Great Teams' Great Years: The Cleveland Browns.* New York: Macmillan, 1973.

Coan, Howard. *Great Pass Catchers in Pro Football.* New York: Julian Messner, 1971.

Cohen, Richard M., Jordan A. Deutsch, and David S. Neft. *The Scrapbook History of Pro Football, 1893–1979.* Indianapolis: Bobbs-Merrill, 1979.

Conerly, Charlie, and Tom Meany. *The Forward Pass.* New York: E.P. Dutton, 1960.

Cook, William A. *Jim Thorpe: A Biography.* Jefferson, N.C.: McFarland, 2011.

Cope, Myron. *Broken Cigars.* Englewood Cliffs, N.J.: Prentice-Hall, 1969.

____. *The Game That Was: The Early Days of Pro Football.* New York: World, 1970.

Corbett, Bernard M., and Paul Simpson. *The Only Game That Matters: The Harvard/Yale Rivalry.* New York: Crown, 2004.

Covey, Cyclone. *The Wow Boys: The Story of Stanford's Classic 1940 Football Season, Game by Game.* New York: Exposition Books, 1957.

Crippen, Kenneth R. *The Original Buffalo Bills: A History of the All American Football Conference Team, 1946–1949.* Jefferson, N.C.: McFarland, 2010.

Curran, Bob. *Pro Football's Rag Days.* Englewood Cliffs, N.J.: Prentice-Hall, 1969.

Curtice, Jack C. *The Passing Game in Football.* New York: Ronald Press, 1961.

Daly, Dan. *The National Forgotten League: Entertaining Stories and Observations from Pro Football's First Fifty Years.* Lincoln: University of Nebraska Press, 2012.

Danzig, Allison. *The History of American Football: Its Great Teams, Players, and Coaches.* Englewood Cliffs, N.J.: Prentice-Hall, 1956.

____. *Oh, How They Played the Game: The Early Days of Pro Football and the Heroes Who Made it Great.* New York: Macmillan, 1971.

Davis, Jeff. *Papa Bear: The Life and Legacy of George Halas.* New York: McGraw-Hill, 2005.

DeLuca, Sam. *The Football Handbook.* Middle Village, N.Y.: Jonathan David, 1978.

Devaney, John. *Star Pass Receivers of the NFL.* New York: Random House, 1972.

DeVito, Carlo. *The Ultimate Dictionary of Sports Quotations: From Hank Aaron to the Zone.* New York: Facts on File, 2001.

Dickey, Glenn. *Just Win, Baby: Al Davis and His Raiders.* New York: Harcourt Brace Jovanovich, 1991.

Dicks, Rudy. *The '63 Steelers: A Renegade Team's Chase for Glory.* Kent, OH: Kent State University Press, 2012.

Ditka, Mike, and Don Pierson. *Ditka: An Autobiography.* Chicago: Bonus Books, 1986.

Donovan, Arthur J. *Fatso: Football When Men Were Really Men.* New York: William Morrow, 1987.

Dorsett, Tony, and Harvey Frommer. *Running Tough: Memoirs of a Football Maverick, Tony Dorsett.* New York: Doubleday, 1989.

Bibliography

Edwards, LaVell, and Norman Chow. *Winning Football with the Forward Pass*. Boston: Allyn and Bacon, 1985.

Eisenhammer, Fred, and Eric Sondheimer. *College Football's Most Memorable Games*, 2d ed. Jefferson, N.C.: McFarland, 2010.

Ellison, Glenn. *Run and Shoot Football*. West Nyack, N.Y.: Parker, 1985.

Ewbank, Weeb, and Neil Rotter. *Goal to Go: The Greatest Football Games I Have Coached*. New York: Hawthorn Books, 1972.

Finoli, David, and Tom Aikens. *The Birthplace of Professional Football: Southwestern Pennsylvania*. Charleston, S.C.: Arcadia, 2004.

Fleder, Rob, ed. *The Football Book*. New York: Time/Sports Illustrated, 2005.

Fox, Stephen. *Big Leagues: Professional Baseball, Football, and Basketball in the National Memory*. New York: William Morrow, 1994.

Freedman, Lew. *Clouds Over the Goalposts: Gambling, Assassination and the NFL in 1963*. New York: Sports Publishing, 2013.

Freeman, Mike. *Jim Brown: The Fierce Life of an American Hero*. New York: William Morrow, 2006.

Friedman, Benny. *The Passing Game*. New York: Steinfeld, 1931.

Gargano, Anthony L. *NFL Unplugged: The Brutal, Brilliant World of Professional Football*. Hoboken, N.J.: John Wiley & Sons, 2010.

Gay, Timothy, Ph.D. *Football Physics: The Science of the Game*. New York: Rodale Press, 2004.

Gems, Gerald R. *For Pride, Profit, and Patriarchy: Football and the Incorporation of American Cultural Values*. Lanham, MD: Scarecrow Press, 2000.

Gifford, Frank, and Peter Richmond. *The Glory Game: How the 1958 NFL Championship Changed Football Forever*. New York: HarperCollins, 2008.

Golenbock, Peter. *Cowboys Have Always Been My Heroes: The Definitive Oral History of America's Team*. New York: Warner Books, 1997.

Gottehrer, Barry. *The Giants of New York*. New York: G.P. Putnam's Sons, 1963.

Graham, Otto. *Otto Graham—'T' Quarterback*. New York: Prentice-Hall, 1953.

Grange, Harold "Red." *My Favorite Football Stories*. New York: A.S. Barnes, 1955.

_____ and Ira Morton. *The Red Grange Story: The Autobiography of Red Grange*. New York: G.P. Putnam, 1953.

Greenberg, Murray. *Passing Game: Benny Friedman and the Transformation of Football*. New York: Public Affairs, 2008.

Grobani, Anton. *Guide to Football Literature*. Detroit: Gale, 1975.

Gruver, Edward. *The American Football League: A Year-by-Year History, 1960–1969*. Jefferson, N.C.: McFarland, 1987.

Gullickson, Dennis J. *Vagabond Halfback: The Life and Times of Johnny Blood McNally*. Madison, WI: Trails Books, 2006.

Gutierrez, Paul. *100 Things Raiders Fans Should Know & Do Before They Die*. Chicago: Triumph Books, 2014.

Halas, George, Gwen Morgan, and Arthur Veysey. *Halas by Halas: The Autobiography of George Halas*. New York: McGraw-Hill, 1999.

Hand, Jack. *Heroes of the NFL*. New York: Random House, 1965.

Hanks, Stephen. *The Game That Changed Pro Football*. New York: Birch Lane Press, 1989.

Harman, Dan. *Carroll Dale Scores Again!* Anderson, IN: Warner Books, 1969.

Harris, David. *The Genius: How Bill Walsh Re-invented Football and Created an NFL Dynasty*. New York: Random House, 2008.

_____. *The League: The Rise and Decline of the NFL*. Toronto: Bantam, 1986.

Hayes, Bob, and Robert Pack. *Run, Bullet, Run. The Rise, Fall, and Recovery of Bob Hayes*. New York: Harper & Row, 1990.

Bibliography

Heaton, Chuck. *Browns Scrapbook: A Fond Look Back at Five Decades of Football from a Legendary Cleveland Sportswriter.* Cleveland: Gray & Company, 2007.

Heffelfinger, W.W. (Pudge), and John McCallum. *This Was Football.* New York: A.S. Barnes, 1954.

Heisman, John. *John Heisman's Principles of Football.* St. Louis: Sports Publishing Bureau, 1922 [Athens, GA: Hill Street Press, 2000].

Herskowitz, Mickey. *1950–1959: The Golden Age of Pro Football: A Remembrance of Pro Football in the 1950s.* Canton, OH: NFL Properties, 1974.

Higdon, Hal. *Pro Football U.S.A.* New York: G.P. Putnam's Sons, 1968.

Hollander, Zander, ed. *Strange But True Football Stories.* New York: Windward Books, 1967.

_____ and Paul Zimmerman. *Football Lingo.* New York: W.W. Norton, 1967.

Horrigan, Jack, and Mike Rathet. *The Other League: The Fabulous Story of the American Football League.* Chicago: Follett, NFL Properties, and Rutledge, 1970.

Jarrett, William S. *Timelines of Sports History: Football.* New York: Facts on File, 1993.

Jett, Carroll. *Here Come the Big Reds: Information & Stories about Parkersburg High School Football.* Parkersburg, W.V.: Parkersburg High School, 2014.

Johnson, Keyshawn, and Shelley Smith. *Just Give Me the Damn Ball! The Fast Times and Hard Knocks of an NFL Rookie.* New York: Warner Books, 1997.

Katzowitz, John. *Sid Gillman: Father of the Passing Game.* Covington, KY: Clerisy Press, 2012.

King, Joe. *Inside Pro Football.* Englewood Cliffs, N.J.: Prentice-Hall, 1958.

King, Peter. *Greatest Quarterbacks.* New York: Bishop Books, 1999.

_____. *Inside the Helmet: A Player's-Eye View of the NFL.* New York: Simon & Schuster, 1993.

LaBlanc, Michael L., ed. *Professional Sports Team Histories: Football.* Detroit: Gale, 1994.

Lahman, Sean. *The Pro Football Historical Abstract.* Guilford, CT: The Lyons Press, 2008.

Layne, Bobby, and Bob Drum. *Always on Sunday.* Englewood Cliffs, N.J.: Prentice-Hall, 1962.

Lazenby, Roland. *Going Deep: 100 Years of Football's Forward Pass.* Dulles, VA: Potomac, 2007.

Leahy, Frank. *Notre Dame Football—The T Formation.* New York: Prentice-Hall, 1949.

Leuthner, Stuart. *Iron Men: Bucko, Crazylegs and the Boys Recall the Golden Days of Professional Football.* New York: Doubleday, 1988.

Levy, Alan H. *Tackling Jim Crow: Racial Segregation in Professional Football.* Jefferson, N.C.: McFarland, 2003.

Lipman, Dave, and Ed Wilks. *The Speed King: Bob Hayes of the Dallas Cowboys.* New York: G.P. Putnam's Sons, 1971.

Loverro, Thom. *Hail Victory! An Oral History of the Washington Redskins.* Hoboken, N.J.: John Wiley & Sons, 2006.

Lucia, Ellis. *Mr. Football: Amos Alonzo Stagg.* South Brunswick, N.J.: A.S. Barnes, 1970.

Luckman, Sid. *Luckman at Quarterback: Football as a Sport and a Career.* Chicago: Zoff-Davis, 1949.

_____. *Passing for Touchdowns.* Chicago: Ziff-Davis, 1948.

MacCambridge, Michael. *America's Game: The Epic Story of How Pro Football Captured a Nation.* New York: Random House, 2004.

Mackey, John, and Thom Loverro. *Blazing Trails: Coming of Age in Football's Golden Era.* Chicago: Triumph Books, 2003.

Madden, John, and Dave Anderson. *One Knee Equals Three Feet (And Everything Else You Need to Know About Football).* New York: Villard, 1986.

Maggio, Frank P. *Notre Dame and the Game That Changed Football: How Jesse Harper Made the Forward Pass a Weapon and Knute Rockne a Legend.* New York: Carroll & Graf, 2007.

Maiocco, Matt. *The San Francisco 49ers: The Complete Illustrated History.* Minneapolis: MVP Books, 2013.

Maki, Allan. *Football's Greatest Stars.* Buffalo: Firefly Books, 2008.

Maltby, Marc. S. *The Origins and Early Development of Professional Football, 1890–1920.* New York: Routledge, 1987.

Maraniss, David. *When Pride Still Mattered: A Life of Vince Lombardi.* New York: Simon & Schuster, 2000.

March, Harry A. *Announcing the American Professional Football League for the Fall of 1936.* New York: American Professional Football League, 1935.

Marples, Morris. *A History of Football.* London: Secker & Warburg, 1954.

Maule, Tex. *The Game: The Official Picture History of the National Football League.* New York: Random House, 1963.

Maxymuk, John. *NFL Head Coaches: A Biographical Dictionary, 1920–2011.* Jefferson, N.C.: McFarland, 2012.

_____. *Strong Arm Tactics: A History and Statistical Analysis of the Professional Quarterback.* Jefferson, N.C.: McFarland, 2008.

McCallum, John D., and Charles H. Pearson. *College Football U.S.A. 1869–1971: Official Book of the National Football Foundation.* New York: McGraw-Hill, 1972.

McClellan, Keith. *The Sunday Game: At the Dawn of Professional Football.* Akron: University of Akron Press, 1998.

McCullough, Bob. *My Greatest Day in Football.* New York: St. Martin's Press, 2001.

McDonnell, Chris. *The Football Game I'll Never Forget: 100 NFL Stars' Stories.* Buffalo: Firefly Books, 2004.

McDonough, Will, and Peter King, et al. *The NFL Century: The Complete Story of the National Football League, 1920–2000.* New York: Smithmark, 1999.

Miller, Frederick P., Agnes F. Vandome, and John McBrewster, eds. *Howard R. Reiter.* Berlin: VDM, 2010.

Miller, Jeff. *Going Long: The Wild 10-Year Saga of the Renegade American Football League in the Words of Those Who Lived it.* Chicago: Contemporary Books, 2003.

Miller, Patrick B., and David K. Wiggins, eds. *Sport and the Color Line: Black Athletes in Twentieth Century America.* New York: Routledge, 2004.

Murray, Jim. *The Great Ones.* Los Angeles: Los Angeles Times Books, 1999.

Myers, Gary. *The Catch: One Play, Two Dynasties, and the Game That Changed the NFL.* New York: Crown, 2009.

Neft, David S., and Richard M. Cohen and Rick Korch. *The Football Encyclopedia.* New York: St. Martin's Press, 1994.

Nelson, David M. *The Anatomy of a Game: Football, the Rules and the Men Who Made the Game.* Cranbury, N.J.: Associated University Presses, 1994.

Newhouse, Dave. *Heisman: After the Glory.* St. Louis: The Sporting News, 1985.

Oates, Bob, Jr. *The First 50 Years: The Story of the National Football League.* New York: Simon & Schuster, 1969.

O'Brien, Jim. *Doing It Right: The Steelers of Three Rivers and Four Super Bowls Share Their Secrets for Success.* Pittsburgh: James O'Brien, 1991.

_____. *Whatever It Takes: The Continuing Saga of the Pittsburgh Steelers—II.* Pittsburgh: James O'Brien, 1992.

Olderman, Murray. *The Runningbacks.* Englewood Cliffs, N.J.: Prentice-Hall, 1969.

Oriard, Michael. *Reading Football: How the Popular Press Created an American Spectacle.* Chapel Hill: University of North Carolina Press, 1948.

Bibliography

Owens, Terrell, and Jason Rosenhaus. *T.O.* New York: Simon & Schuster, 2006.

Owens, Terrell, and Stephen Singular. *Catch This! Going Deep with the NFL's Sharpest Weapon.* New York: Simon & Schuster, 2004.

Page, Joseph S. *Pro Football Championships Before the Super Bowl.* Jefferson, N.C.: McFarland, 2011.

Palmer, Pete, and Ken Pullis, Sean Lahman, Todd Maher, Matthew Silverman, and Gary Gillette. *The ESPN Pro Football Encyclopedia*, 2d ed. New York: Sterling, 2007.

Parker, Raymond K. (Buddy). *We Play to Win!* Englewood Cliffs, N.J.: Prentice-Hall, 1955.

Peterson, Robert W. *Pigskin: The Early Years of Pro Football.* New York: Oxford University Press, 1977.

Povich, Shirley. *All Those Mornings ... at the Post.* New York: Public Affairs, 2005.

Presbrey, Frank, and James Hugh Moffatt. *Athletics at Princeton: A History.* New York: Frank Presbrey, 1901.

Pyle, Charles C. *Life and Football: History of Harold "Red" Grange.* New York: Bentley, Murray, 1926.

Quackenbush, Robert M., and Steve Bynum. *Knute Rockne: His Life and Legend.* New York: October Football Corporation, 1988.

Rand, Jonathan. *300 Pounds of Attitude: The Wildest Stories and Craziest Characters the NFL Has Ever Seen.* Guilford, CT: The Lyons Press, 2007

Rappaport, Ken. *The Little League That Could: A History of the American Football League.* Lanham, MD: Taylor Trade, 2010.

Rashad, Ahmad, and Peter Bodo. *Rashad: Vikes, Mikes, and Something on the Backside.* New York: Viking, 1988.

Reed, Herbert. *Football for Public and Player.* New York: Frederick A. Stokes, 1913.

Rentzel, Lance. *When All the Laughter Died in Sorrow.* New York: Saturday Review Press, 1972.

Reynolds, Neil. *Pain Gang: Pro Football's Fifty Toughest Players.* Washington, D.C.: Potomac, 2006.

Ribalow, Harold U., and Meir Z. Ribalow. *The Jew in American Sports.* New York: Block, 1948 [and New York: Hippocrene Books, 1985].

Rice, Jerry, and Brian Curtis. *Go Long! My Journey Beyond the Game and Fame.* New York: Ballantine, 2007.

Roberts, Howard. *The Story of Pro Football.* New York: Rand McNally, 1953.

Roberts, Jerry. *Roberto Clemente: Baseball Player.* New York: Facts on File, 2006.

Roberts, Randy, and David Welky, eds. *The Steelers Reader.* Pittsburgh: University of Pittsburgh Press, 2001.

Robinson, Ray. *Rockne of Notre Dame.* Oxford: Oxford University Press, 1999.

Rooney, Dan, with Andrew E. Masich and David F. Halaas. *Dan Rooney: My 75 Years with the Pittsburgh Steelers and the NFL.* New York: Da Capo, 2008.

Rosenthal, Harold. *American Football League Official History, 1960–1969.* New York: Elias Sports Bureau, 1970.

Sahadi, Lou. *The Long Pass.* New York: Bantam, 1969.

_____. *Pro Football's Gamebreakers.* Chicago: Contemporary Books, 1977.

Schmidt, Raymond. *The Shaping of College Football: The Transformation of a National Sport, 1919–1930.* Syracuse: Syracuse University Press, 2007.

Scott, Harry G. *Jock Sutherland: Architect of Men.* New York: Exposition Press, 1954.

Scott, Robert J., and Myles A. Pocta. *Honor on the Line: The Fifth Down and the Spectacular 1940 Football Season.* Bloomington, IN: iUniverse, 2010.

Shaughnessy, Clark. *Football in War & Peace.* New York: Jacobs Press, 1943.

Shaughnessy, Clark, Ralph Jones, and George Halas. *The Modern 'T' Forma-*

tion with Man in Motion. Chicago: Author Books, 1941.

Shula, Don, and Lou Sahadi. *The Winning Edge*. New York: E.P. Dutton, 1973.

Smith, Curt. *Of Mikes and Men: From Ray Scott to Curt Gowdy, Broadcasting Tales from the Pro Football Booth*. South Bend, IN: Diamond Communications, 1998.

Smith, Don. *Backfield in Motion!* New York: Galahad Books, 1973.

Smith, Robert. *Illustrated History of Pro Football*. New York: Madison Square Press—Grosset & Dunlap, 1977.

_____. *Pro Football: The History of the Game and the Great Players*. Garden City, N.Y.: Doubleday, 1963.

Smith, Ron. *Pro Football's Heroes of the Hall*. St. Louis: The Sporting News, 2003.

_____, Carl Moritz, Jim Brown, and John Rawlings. *The Sporting News Selects Football's Greatest Players: A Celebration of the 20th Century's Best*. New York: McGraw-Hill/NTC-Contemporary, 1999.

Smith, Thomas G. *Showdown: JFK and the Integration of the Washington Redskins*. Boston: Beacon Press, 2011.

Stabler, Kenny, and Dick O'Connor. *Super Bowl Diary: The Autobiography of Kenny "The Snake" Stabler*. Los Angeles: Pinnacle Books, 1977.

Stallard, Mark. *Kansas City Chiefs Encyclopedia*. New York: Sports Publishing, 2002.

Steidel, Dave. *Remember the AFL: The Ultimate Fan's Guide to the American Football League*. Cincinnati: Clerisy Press, 2008.

Steinberg, Donald. *Expanding Your Horizons: Collegiate Football's Greatest Team*. Pittsburgh: Dorrance, 1992,.

Stingley, Darryl, and Mark Mulvoy. *Darryl Stingley: Happy to Be Alive*. New York: Beaufort Books, 1983.

Sullivan, George. *All About Football*. New York: G.P. Putnam's Sons, 1987.

_____. *The Great Running Backs*. New York: G.P. Putnam's Sons, 1972.

_____. *Touchdown! The Pictorial History of the American Football League*. New York: G.P. Putnam's Sons, 1967.

Taaffe, William, and David Fischer, eds. *Sports of the Times: A Day-by-Day Selection of the Most Important, Thrilling, and Inspired Events of the Past 150 Years*. New York: The New York Times, 2003.

Terzian, James P. *Great Teams' Great Years: New York Giants*. New York: Macmillan, 1973.

Thorn, John, ed. *The Armchair Quarterback*. New York: Charles Scribner's Sons, 1982.

_____, et al., eds. *Total Baseball: The Official Encyclopedia of Major League Baseball*. New York: Total Sports, 1999.

Thorne, Ian. *Meet the Receivers*. Mankato, MN: Creative Education, 1975.

Treat, Roger. *The Encyclopedia of Football*, 16th rev ed. South Brunswick, N.J.: A.S. Barnes, 1979.

Tuckman, Michael W., and Jeff Schultz. *The San Francisco 49ers: Team of the Decade*. Rocklin, CA.: Prima, 1990.

Tunnell, Emlen, and Bill Gleason. *Footsteps of a Giant*. Garden City, N.Y.: Doubleday, 1966.

Umphlett, Wiley Lee. *Creating the Big Game: John W. Heisman and the Invention of American Football*. Westport, CT: Greenwood Press, 1992.

Valenzi, Kathleen D. *Champion of Sports: The Life of Walter Camp, 1859–1925*. Charlottesville, VA: Howell Press, 1990.

Vecchione, Joseph J., ed. *The New York Times Book of Sports Legends*. New York: Times Books, 1991.

Wagenknecht, Edward. *The Seven Worlds of Theodore Roosevelt*. Guilford, CT: The Globe Pequot Press, 2009.

Watterson, John Sayle. *College Football: History, Spectacle, Controversy*. Baltimore: Johns Hopkins University Press, 2000.

Weyland, Alexander M. *Football Immortals*. New York: Macmillan, 1962.

Whittingham, Richard. *Rites of Autumn: The Story of College Football*. New York: The Free Press, 2001.

_____. *Sunday Mayhem: A Celebration of Pro Football in America*. Dallas: Taylor, 1987.

_____. *Sunday's Heroes: NFL Legends Talk About the Times of Their Lives*. Chicago: Triumph Books, 2003.

_____. *What a Game They Played*. Lincoln: University of Nebraska Press, 1984.

Willis, Chris. *The Man Who Built the National Football League: Joe F. Carr*. Lanham, MD: Scarecrow Press, 2010.

_____. *Old Leather: An Oral History of Early Pro Football in Ohio, 1920–1935*. Lanham, MD: Scarecrow Press, 2005.

Wismer, Harry. *The Public Calls It Sport*. Englewood Cliffs, N.J.: Prentice-Hall, 1965

Wulf, Steve, ed. *ESPN: The Mighty Book of Sports Knowledge*. New York: Ballantine, 2009.

Zimmerman, Paul. *The New Thinking Man's Guide to Pro Football*. New York: HarperCollins, 1987.

_____. *A Thinking Man's Guide to Pro Football*. New York: E.P. Dutton, 1970.

Zirin, Dave. *A People's History of Sports in the United States: 250 Years of Politics, Protest, People, and Play*. New York: The New Press, 2008.

Zordich, Cynthia, and Bill Lyon. *When the Clock Runs Out: 20 NFL Greats Share Their Stories of Hardship and Triumph*. Chicago: Triumph Books, 1999.

Zuppke, Robert C., and Milton Martin Frithiof Olander. *Football Techniques and Tactics*. Champaign, IL: Bailey and Himes, 1924.

Newspapers, Magazines, Journals, Dissertations

"Billy Wilson, Sure-Handed Receiver for 49ers, Dies at 81." *The New York Times*, January 28, 2009.

Bouchette, Ed. "Elbie Nickel / Best Tight End in Steelers History." *Pittsburgh Post-Gazette*, March 2, 2007.

"A Brief History of Hash Marks." The Game Before the Money, http://www.thegamebeforethemoney.com/a-brief-history-of-hash-marks/.

Conant, Coit Howard. *The Evolution of Offensive Football in American Colleges, 1800–1913*. Diss., University of Wisconsin-Madison, 1962.

Fimrite, Roger. "A Melding of Men All Suited to a T." *Sports Illustrated*, September 5, 1977.

"First Forward Pass Thrown by Wesleyan Team in 1906." *Bridgeport* (CT) *Post*, November 5, 1955.

"The First Pro Pass." *Professional Football Researchers Association (PFRA) Annual* 1 (1971), pp. 1–2.

Foster, Chris. "Speedie Turns Home Into a Hall." *Los Angeles Times*, September 12, 1991.

Furlong, William Barry. "The Reincarnation of Woody Hayes." *Life*, November 21, 1969.

Goldstein, Richard. "Ron Kramer, Tight End with Packers and Lions, Dies at 75." *The New York Times*, September 12, 2010.

Heisman, John W. "Fast and Loose." *Collier's Weekly*, October 20, 1928.

"History of the Football Helmet." Past Time Sports, http://www.pasttimesports.biz/history.html.

Holland, Gerald. "Greasy Neale: Nothing to Prove, Nothing to Ask." *Sports Illustrated*, August 24, 1964.

_____. "Is That You Up There, Johnny Blood?" *Sports Illustrated*, September 2, 1963.

Keith, Harold. "Pioneer of the Forward Pass," *Esquire* 22 (1944).

Livingston, Chad. "The Nebraska 100: No. 39, Guy Chamberlin." http://dataomaha.com/neb100/player/39.

McQuilkin, Scott A., and Ronald A. Smith. "The Rise and Fall of the Flying Wedge: Football's Most Controversial

Play," *Journal of Sport History* 20, no. 1 (Spring 1993), pp. 57–64.

McRea, Earl. "Choo Choo's Glory Blazed Across the Atlantic." *Toronto Sun*, January 6, 2010.

Miller, Ira. "Cold Reception / Raiders-Steelers Rivalry Is Still Immaculate After All These Years." www.sfgate.com/sports, November 29, 2000 (December 17, 2014).

"'Mon' Gets Good Start: Use a Long Forward Pass with Good Effect." *Des Moines Daily News*, October 3, 1906.

"Packer Pass Beats Racine in Last Period." *Milwaukee Journal*, November 3, 1924.

Pasquarelli, Len. "Shaughnessy Among All-Time Innovators." ESPN.com: NFL, September 29, 2009.

Piascik, Andy. *Coffin Corner* 27, no. 3 (2005).

———. "Lenny Moore." *Coffin Corner* 24, no. 5 (2002).

"Ram Tough: Jim Benton Tops Them All." ESPN.com, July 16, 2010, accessed December 11, 2014.

Soprano, Joe. "All-Time Top 10 Penn Staters in the NFL." *Wilkes-Barre* (PA) *Times-Leader*, August 16, 2014.

Stagg, Amos Alonzo. *Saturday Evening Post*, October 23, 1926.

Street & Smith's Pro Football annuals.

Thompson, Mike, and Wesley Stout. "The Villain of the Piece." *Saturday Evening Post*, October 31, 1931.

"Tigers Brilliant Against Stevens: New Rules Seem to Please Princeton Players," "Indians Swamp Susquehanna," "Kicking Wins for Harvard," and "Williams Wins with Forward Pass," *Trenton* (N.J.) *Times*, October 4, 1906, collected in "Forward Pass," http://en.wikipedia.org/wiki/Forward_pass, December 19, 2014.

Watterson, John Sayle. *Journal of Sport History* 27, no. 2 (Summer 2000), p. 297.

Whitney, Caspar. "Sports." *Harper's Weekly*, March 5, 1892.

Yellin, Lyons. "Legend Clark Shaughnessy Heads Inductees into Loyola Hall of Fame." NOLA.com and *New Orleans Times-Picayune*, January 26, 2012.

Zimmermann, Paul. "The Bronk and the Gazelle: Fifty Years Ago, Bronko Nagurski and Don Hutson Dominated Pro Football. But How Would They Do Today?" *Sports Illustrated*, September 11, 1989.

———. "Revolutionaries." *Sports Illustrated*, August 17, 1998.

Web Sites

http://cnnsi.com
http://jcfb.com
http://sfgate.com
http://sports.espn.go.com
http://www.dataomaha.com
http://www.hickocksports.com
http://www.profootballhof.com

Index

AAFC *see* All American Football Conference
Abramowicz, Danny 117
Acme Packing Company 53
Adamle, Tony 131
Adams, George C. 9
Addison, Tom 169
AFL *see* American Football League
Akron Indians 34, 41, 44
Akron Pros 42, 48, 130
Albert, Frankie 112, 121, 136, 137
Aldrich, Ki 88
Algeo, Matthew 82
All America Football Conference (AAFC) 65, 98, 105, 112, 119, 124–139, 140, 194
Allegheny Athletic Association 16
Allegheny Mountains 21, 44
Allen, George 48, 121, 150–151, 158–159, 165, 180, 200
"Alley-Oop" 147
Altoona, Pa. 35
Alworth, Lance 1, 2, 3, 78, 137, 143, 147
Ameche, Alan "The Horse" 191, 183
American Basketball Association (1925–28) 41
American Football League (AFL) 1, 56, 105, 137, 152, 160, 163, 168, 171, 178, 179
American Professional Football Association (APFA) 34, 41–44, 52
Anderson, Dave 167
Anderson, Heartley "Hunk" 55, 97, 99, 111
Anderson, Lars 21–23
Anderson, Willie Lee "Flipper" 108
Angsman, Elmer 102
APFC *see* American Professional Football Association
Arbanas, Fred 161, 169–171
Arizona Cardinals 204–205
Arizona State University 164, 199
Army *see* West Point Academy
Arnsparger, Bill 139
Artoe, Lee 94, 106
Ashbaugh, Busty 38
Associated Press 161

Athletics at Princeton—A History 5
Atkinson, George "Butch" 184
Atlanta Falcons 117
Auburn University 7, 21

Badgro, Morris "Red" 50–51, 73
Bagarus, Steve 113
Baker, Dr. L.H. 43
Baldwin, Al 136
Ballman, Gary 168
Baltimore Afro-American 197
Baltimore Colts 1, 100, 106, 120, 124, 134, 136, 137, 138, 140, 143–145, 148, 156, 160, 161–164, 165, 173, 175, 178, 184, 185, 189, 191–194, 201–202
Banszak, Pete 174
Barber, Red 91
Barclay, George "Deerfoot" 37
Barrymore, John 57
Bartlesville, Okla. 24
Bass, Dick 180
Bass, Mike 166
Battles, Cliff 188
Baugh, Sammy 49, 71, 76, 83, 87, 91, 94, 98, 99, 100, 103, 105, 113–114, 121, 148, 187, 203
Bavaro, Mark 104
Baylor University 33
Bazaar, Kansas 33
Beals, Alyn 135, 136
Bednarik, Chuck 191
Belichick, Bill 205
Bell, DeBenneville "Bert" 10, 70, 72
Bell, John C., Jr. 10
Bell, John C., Sr. 10
Bell, Ricky 169
Beloit College 111
Bennett, Tom 19, 36, 62, 75, 169, 185
Benton, Jim 71, 80, 99, 100, 107–108, 117
Benwood, W.Va. 35–36
Bergman, Dutch 42
Berry, Charlie 54
Berry, Connie Mack 99
Berry, Dave 16

237

Index

Berry, Raymond 1, 3, 78, 134, 138, 140, 143–145, 160, 161, 164, 191, 193, 199
Bertelli, Angelo 96
Berwanger, Jay 110
Bezdek, Hugo 24–25, 42, 97
Bierman, Bernie 61
Big Leagues: Professional Baseball, Football and Basketball in the National Memory 70
Biletnikoff, Fred 1, 2, 172
Billick, Brian 139
"Black Sox Scandal" 38
Blagden, Crawford 26
Blanda, George 98, 105
Blazing Trails 162
Bleier, Rocky 175, 183
Blood, Johnny *see* McNally, Johnny "Blood"
Blood and Sand 56
Blount, Mel 1, 178–179, 184
Boston, Mass. 12
Boston Beaneaters 37
Boston Braves (football) 67
Boston College 61, 86, 104, 183
Boston Patriots 160, 168–169
Boston Redskins 42, 77
Boston University 89
Boston Yanks 94
Bouchette, Ed 159
Bougess, Lee 180
Bowdoin College 17
Bowser, Arda 44
Box, Cloyce 140
Boyd, Bob 116, 121, 157
Bradshaw, Terry 49, 87, 168, 175, 181
Brady, Tom 32
Bray, Ray 106
Breese, Drew 32
Brewer, Charlie 9
Briggs, Windy 40
Briggs Stadium 107
Brodie, John 148, 185
Brooker, Tommy 169
Brooklyn Dodgers (football) 67, 72, 74, 80, 83, 98, 99, 187
Brooks, James 186
Brown, Bill 186
Brown, Charlie 200
Brown, Jim 3, 79, 136, 138, 192, 193, 196, 197, 198
Brown, Johnny Mack 46
Brown, Larry 168
Brown, Paul 3, 65, 105, 109, 124–139, 144, 146
Brown, Willie 178
Brown County, Wis. 55
Brown University 12

Bruckner, Robert 32
Brumbaugh, Carl 63
Bryant, Paul "Bear" 80
Bucknell University 12, 16, 20, 23, 44
Buffalo, N.Y. 35, 41, 44
Buffalo All Americans 42, 48, 54
Buffalo Bills (AAFC) 124, 136, 194
Buffalo Bills (AFL/NFL) 168, 170, 185, 196, 204, 205
Buffalo Bison 48, 130
Bumgardner, Rex 126
Buoniconti, Nick 169
Bureau of Indian Affairs 24
Burford, Chris 170
Burk, Adrian 98, 182
Burnett, Dale 73, 74
Burrell, Ode 180
Burress, Plaxico 147
Burrough, Ken 183
Bush, Reggie 175
Butkus, Dick 185
Byrne, Eugene 25

Cagle, Chris 46
Camp, Walter 5, 6–10, 11, 15, 19, 20, 26, 27, 36, 43, 60, 70
Camp Kearney 47
Campbell, Bob 201
Campbell, Earl 185
Canadian Football League 133, 148, 156, 187, 189
Cannon, Billy 171–172
Canton, Ohio 41
Canton Bulldogs 16, 35, 37, 38–40, 42, 44, 47
Cantor, George 137
Capers, Dom 139
Cappelletti, John 201
Carfego, George 100
Carlisle Indian Industrial School 16, 17, 21–23, 24, 28, 33
Carnegie Tech University 62
Carpenter, Preston 161
Carr, Joe 41, 67, 70, 80
Carroll, Bob 198
Carroll College 13, 17
Carson, Bud 139
Carter, Joe 51
Casey, Bernie 121
Casper, Dave 25, 155, 166, 172–174, 202
Cassidy, Howard "Hopalong" 141
Cedar Point Amusement Park 28, 29
Centers, Larry 175, 204–205
CFL *see* Canadian Football League
Chamberlin, Guy 46–48, 158
Cherry, Boyd 40
Chester, Raymond 172

Index

Chicago, Ill. 27, 67, 85
Chicago Bears 12, 42, 43, 45, 46, 48, 54, 59–77, 72, 73, 79–80, 81, 83, 84–95, 96–106, 107–108, 109, 111, 112, 114, 115, 117, 118, 121, 122, 126, 127, 131, 145, 146, 148, 149–152, 157, 160, 187, 193, 194
Chicago Cardinals 42, 43, 47, 54, 67, 71, 88, 93, 98, 102, 118, 120, 128, 156, 161, 187, 189, 194, 195
Chicago Daily News 118–119
Chicago Herald and Examiner 43, 123
Chicago Hornets 136
Chicago Rockets 98, 119, 136
Chicago Stadium 68
Chicago Staleys 54
Chicago Tigers 43
Chicago Tribune 8, 124
Chicago White Sox 38
Christensen, Todd 172, 174
Christian, Archer 25
Christman, Paul 102, 103
Christy, Dick 180
Cincinnati, Ohio 35, 44, 67
Cincinnati Bengals 139, 171
Cincinnati Celts 35, 36
Cincinnati Enquirer 36
Cincinnati Reds (football) 38, 72
Clabby, Jimmy 42
Clark, Dutch 67
Clark, Dwight 143
Clark, Gary 188, 200
Clark, Potsy 68, 70
Clarke, Harry 81, 91, 97–98, 99, 100, 121, 187, 194
Clary, Jack 131, 132
Clayton, Mark 79, 82
Clemson University 7, 13
Cleveland, Ohio 35, 41
Cleveland Browns 65, 105, 106, 115, 120, 124–139, 140, 143, 157, 189, 198
Cleveland Bulldogs 45, 47, 50, 58
Cleveland Indians (Ohio League) 37
Cleveland Municipal Stadium 126, 128
Cleveland Rams 25, 71, 93, 105, 106, 107–108, 113, 117, 119, 156
Cleveland Rebels 134
Clooney, George 57
Coates, Ben 174
Cochems, Eddie 13–15, 18, 20, 21, 22, 24
Coffin Corner 126
Cohen, Abe 76
Cohen, Leonard 99
College Football All Star Game 124
College Football Hall of Fame 24, 48, 89, 118, 123
College Football Rules Committee 6, 8, 9, 10, 25, 26, 27

College of Idaho 147
College of the Pacific 19
Collier, Blanton 138
Collier's 8
Collins, Gary 138
Colorado College 67
Columbia University 12, 88, 98, 130
Columbus Panhandles 37, 38, 41, 42
Comnock, Arthur 7
Comp, Irv 82
Conerly, Charlie 106, 188, 192
Conzelman, Jimmy 102
Cooke, Jack Kent 199
Cooper, Earl 184
Cope, Myron 57
Corbett, Bernard M. 9, 17
Cornell University 12, 20, 21
Coryell, Don 109, 147, 169, 204
Cosbie, Doug 155
Coslet, Bruce 139
Costa, Paul 168
Coy, Ted 24
Craft, Russ 125
Craig, Roger 202–203, 204
Crazylegs 119
Cribbs, Joe 186
Cross, Harry 30
Csonka, Larry 185
Cumberland County, Pa. 21
Cusack, Jack 40

Dale, Carroll 138
Dallas Cowboys 148, 152, 155, 163, 164, 165, 175–178, 184, 200
Dallas Texans 168, 169, 180, 196
Dalrymple, Jerry 33
Daniels, Clem 172, 195
Danowski, Ed 76
Danzig, Allison 13, 18, 20, 23, 32, 57
Dartmouth College 11, 12, 26, 46, 61
Dashiell, Paul 10
Davenport, Iowa 35
Davis, Al 147, 171
Davis, Ernie 197
Davis, Fred 106
Davis, Glenn 115, 157
Davis, Jeff 89
Davis, Lamar 136
Davis, Parke 24
Dawson, Lenny 169, 170–171, 184, 185, 195, 196
Dayton Gym-Cadets 36, 41, 42
Dayton Oakwoods 36
Dayton Triangles 37, 42, 48
D.C. Stadium 197
Decatur, Ill. 41
Decatur Staleys 43, 47

Index

DeGroot, Dudley 113
Deland, Lorin F. 7, 9
DeLuca, Sam 154
Dempsey, Jack 44–45
Denison University 12
Denver Broncos 99, 133, 155, 171, 180, 195
Des Moines Daily News 17
Detroit, Mich. 35, 44
Detroit Lions 42, 58, 81–82, 83, 90, 98, 101, 104, 106, 107, 109, 115, 140–142, 145, 153, 164, 166, 168, 194
Detroit Mercy College 48
Detroit News 183
Detroit Tigers (baseball) 134
Detroit Tigers (Ohio League) 37
Detroit Wolverines 48, 50
Devaney, John 166
Dickey, Glenn 172
Dickinson, Bo 180
Dickinson College 24
Didier, Clint 169
Dietz, Lone Star *see* Lone Star Dietz, William
Dilweg, LaVerne "Lavvie" 47, 55–56, 58, 74
Dimancheff, Babe 102
Ditka, Mike 3, 109, 149–152, 154, 155, 160, 161, 162, 163, 164, 166, 167
Dixon, Hewritt "Hewie the Freight" 171–172, 180
Dorais, Gus 28, 30, 31, 32, 38–40, 42, 82
Doran, Jim 105, 141
Dorsett, Tony 49, 177, 185
Dowler, Boyd 138
Dreyfuss, Barney 16
Driscoll, Paddy 42, 43, 111
Driving Park 39–40
Dudley, "Bullet Bill" 187
Dudley, Rickey 172
"Duke" (football) 74–75
Duke University 92
Duluth Eskimos 46, 56, 57
Duluth Kelleys 45
Duncan, Leslie "Speedy" 200
Dungy, Tony 139
Dunn, Red 52, 54
Duper, Mark 138
Dupree, Billy Joe 148, 155

East 26th Street Liberties 56
Easton, Pa. 37
Eckersall, Walter 18, 19
Eichenlaub, Ray 30
Engle, Rip 192
Erasmus High School, N.Y. 88
Erickson, Hal 54
Esquire 14
Evashevski, Forrest "Evy" 33

Ewbank, Weeb 134, 138, 139, 144, 148, 191
Exendine, Albert 22, 23, 24, 28, 34

Fairmont College *see* Wichita State
Farkas, Andy 94, 100
"Father of American Football" 6
Faulk, Kevin 175, 205
Faulk, Marshall 195, 203–204
Faulkner, Jack 147
Fayetteville, Ark. 24
Fears, Tom 2, 103, 114, 115–118, 119, 121, 139, 142, 146, 155–157, 158
"Fearsome Foursome" 185
Feather, Tiny 50
Feathers, Beattie 60, 75, 81
Ferrente, Jack 148
Filchock, Frankie 101, 105
Fimrite, Ron 112
Flaherty, Ray 2, 49–51, 74, 76
Fleming, Red 38, 39
Flores, Tom 173
Florida A&M University 172
Flying wedge 9
Folwell, Bob 44
Football Digest 86
Football fatalities 8
Football Guide 23
Forbes, R.W. 17
Forbes Field 62
Fordham University 12
Foreman, Chuck 178, 184, 185
Fort Wayne Friars 34
Fortman, Danny 106
"Four Horsemen of Notre Dame" 28, 42, 46
Fox, John 139
Fox, Stephen 70
Francis, Russ 160
Frankford Yellow Jackets 45, 47
Franklin, Ike 76
Franklin & Marshall College 24
Franklin Field 23
Frazier, Willie 147, 171
Freeman, Mike 198
Friedman, Benny 33, 49–50, 51, 52
Fuqua, John "Frenchy" 181–183

Gabriel, Roman 180
Gallerneau, Hugh "Duke" 92, 93, 101, 112, 121
Garner, Charlie 186
Garrett, Mike 169, 184, 196
Garrison, Gary 147
Garrison, Walt 177
Gates, Antonio 174
Gatski, Frank "Gunner" 131
Gay, Timothy 183
Georgetown University 24

240

Index

Georgia Tech 7, 12
"Ghost to the Post" 173, 202
Gibbs, Joe 169, 200
Gibron, Abe 131, 139
Gifford, Frank 120, 189, 190–191, 194, 199, 203
Gilchrist, Cookie 196
Gillman, Sid 146–147
Gipp, George 32, 33, 52
Glaver, Bill 48
Goldberg, Marshall "Biggie" 88, 102
Goldenberg, Buckets 74, 78, 82–83
Golenbock, Peter 177
Gonzaga University 76
Gonzalez, Tony 163, 174
Goodell, Roger 25
Goodwin, Russ 38
Goodwin, Tod 77
Gotteher, Barry 188
Graham, Otto 65, 87, 106, 115, 125, 126, 127, 129, 130, 131, 132, 124, 135, 138, 139, 140, 144, 199
Grambling University 118
Grange, Harold "Red" 2, 45, 46, 49, 51, 55, 60, 63, 68, 69, 73, 75, 121, 187, 203
Grant, Bud 187
Great Lakes Naval Training Station 42, 97, 119, 127, 128, 129
Green, A.J. 147
Green, Dennis 139
Green Bay, Wis. 52, 55
Green Bay Blues 53
Green Bay Packers 3, 33, 45, 47, 48, 50, 51, 52–58, 62, 67, 71, 72, 74, 76, 77, 78–83, 84, 86, 87, 90, 92–93, 94, 97, 98, 100, 103, 105, 113, 117, 118, 126, 135, 137–138, 145, 149, 150, 151, 152–154, 160, 172, 187, 188, 194, 195
Green Bay Press-Gazette 55
Greene, "Mean Joe" 180
Greensburg, Pa. 16
Gregg, Forrest 139, 153–154
Grove, Roger 72, 74
Groza, Lou "The Toe" 115, 125, 126, 131
Gushurst, Fred 30
Gutkowsky, Ace 68
Guyon, "Indian Joe" 35

Hackett, Horatio B. "Stuffy" 14
Halas, George 2, 3, 12, 42, 43, 47, 48, 54, 61, 62, 63, 64, 65, 66, 68, 69, 70, 73, 76, 79–80, 84, 85, 86–92, 93, 94, 97, 101, 103, 104, 105, 106, 107, 108, 109, 110, 111, 112, 120, 121, 122, 127, 149, 152, 156
Hall, Edward K. 26
Ham, Jack 185
Hammond, Indiana 41, 42
Hammond Clabbys 42

Hanny, Duke 54
Hapes, Merle 101
Harder, Pat 102, 187
Hardy, Jim 156
Harmon, Ronnie 175, 204
Harper, Jesse 29, 30, 31
Harper's Weekly 6
Harris, Cliff 184
Harris, Franco 181–184, 185, 201–202
Harrison, Marvin 163
Hart, Jim 164
Harvard University 7, 8, 9, 11, 12, 14, 15, 17, 23–24, 25, 26, 27, 111
Hatcher, Ron 197
Haughton, Percy 26, 27
Hauser, Pete 23
Hay, Ralph 41
Hayes, "Bullet Bob" 137, 172, 180
Hayes, Woody 12
Haynes, Abner 179–180, 195
Hearing the Noise: My Life in the NFL 178
Hefflefinger, W.W. "Pudge" 7, 16
Hein, Mel 73
Heisman, John W. 2, 7–8, 10, 12, 21
Heisman Trophy 8, 33, 88, 105, 110, 115, 140, 201, 202
Henderson, Thomas "Hollywood" 180
Henry, Howard 26
Herber, Arnie 54, 58, 72, 74, 77, 81
Hering, Frank 60
Hernandez, Joe 197
Hewitt, Bill 73, 76, 156
Heyman, Fred 38
Hickey, Red 116, 120, 148, 155, 189
Hill, Harlon 145, 146
Hillenbrand, Billy 136
Hinkle, Clarke 53, 57, 93
Hinton, Eddie 163, 164
Hirsch, Elroy "Crazy Legs" 2, 78, 114, 115, 116, 118–121, 142, 146, 155–157, 158, 189
The History of American Football 18
Hoak, Dick 149, 201
Hoboken, N.J. 5
Hoerner, Bob 115, 118, 121, 157
Hoernschmeyer, Bob "Hunchie" 141
Holland, Gerald 58, 106
Holmes, Robert "The Tank" 169, 184
Holmgren, Mike 54
Holub, E.J. 169
Holy Cross University 89
"Holy Roller" 25, 173–174
Hoover, Herbert 33
Hornung, Paul 152, 153–154, 194
Horrigan, Joe 129
Horton, Ethan 172
Houston Oilers 98, 133, 146, 151, 171, 172, 180, 183, 185

241

Index

Howell, Dixie 33, 80
Howell, Jim Lee 104, 190
Howton, Billy 145
Huff, Sam 185
Hughitt, Tommy 42, 129
Hutchins, Dr. Robert Maynard 111
Hutson, Don 1-2, 32, 33, 54, 57, 71, 77, 78-83, 84, 86, 87, 92, 93, 94, 97, 107, 115, 118, 125, 135, 136, 158, 187, 192

IAAUS *see* Intercollegiate Athletic Association of the United States
IFA *see* Intercollegiate Football Association
"Immaculate Deception" 173-174
"Immaculate Reception" 163, 181-184
Indian Packing Company 53
Indiana Normal School *see* Indiana University of Pennsylvania
Indiana University of Pennsylvania 24
Indianapolis Colts 203
Inside Pro Football 62
Intercollegiate Athletic Association of the United States (IAAUS) 8, 10, 12, 15, 25
Intercollegiate Football Association (IFA) 7, 8, 19
"Iron Men of the North" 46, 56
Irons, Gerald 182
Isabel, Cecil 81, 98, 105
Ivy League 12, 88

Jack Murphy Stadium 173
Jackson, DeSean 188
Jackson, Leroy 197
Jackson, Mark 138
Jauron, Dick 139
Jeannette, Pa. 16
Jefferson, John 147
Jefferson, Roy 2, 164, 165-166, 200
John Carroll University 138
Johnson, Bill 139
Johnson, Calvin 147
Johnson, John Henry 130, 141, 143, 149, 190
Johnson, Ron 181
Johnson, Walter 100
Johnsos, Luke 74, 97, 99, 108, 111
Johnston, Moose 177
Joiner, Charlie 147
Jones, Edgar "Special Delivery" 131
Jones, Homer 200
Jones, Ralph 62-63, 64, 66-67, 69, 84, 87, 121
Jones, William "Dub" 125, 126, 127, 131-132
Julian, Carp 39
Jurgenson, Sonny 49, 185, 197, 200

Kalmanir, Tommy 157
Kansas City Blues 45

Kansas City Chiefs 108, 169-171, 183-184, 195-196
Kapp, Joe 99
Karr, Bill 73, 74, 76
Kavanaugh, Ken 84, 91, 92, 93, 101, 102, 103-104, 108
Keane, Jim 101, 102, 103
Keith, Harold 14
Kelley, Larry 33
Kelly, Shipwreck 72, 74, 80
Kemp, Jackie 186
Kemp, Ray 128
Kenosha, Wis., Maroons 45
Kezar Stadium 137
Kieran, John 31
Kiesling, Walt 46, 56
Kiley, Roger 33
Kilmer, Billy 148, 200
King, Fay 136
King, Joe 62
King, Peter 78, 96
Kirksville Normal School *see* Truman State University
Knafelc, Gary 152
Knute Rockne, All American 31-32
Kocourek, Dave 160, 161, 168
Kramer, Jerry 153
Kramer, Ron 138, 151, 152-154, 155, 160, 161
Kutner, Mal 102, 146

Lacy, Sam 197
Lafayette University 12, 37
Lahr, Warren 125
Lake Beulah, Wis. 13
Lake Erie 28
Lake Forest, Ill., Academy 69
Lambeau, Earl Louis "Curly" 2, 48, 52-54, 56, 58, 61, 67, 77, 80, 81, 83, 92
Lambeau Field 188
Lambert, Jack 138, 185
Lammons, Pete 171
Lamonica, Daryle 185
Landry, Tom 104, 148, 152, 175, 177
Lane, Dick "Night Train" 129, 159
Lane, MacArthur 184
Largent, Steve 78, 79
Latrobe, Pa. 16
Latrobe (Pa.) Clipper 16
Lavelli, Dante 125, 126, 127, 132, 134-135, 140, 141, 144
Layden, Elmer 42
Layne, Bobby 105, 106, 140, 141
League Baseball Park 39
Leahy, Frank 86
Leatherheads 57
Lebanon Valley College 23
LeBeau, Dick 109

242

Index

LeClerc, Roger 150
Lee, Amp 186
Leemans, Alphonse "Tuffy" 93
Lehigh University 9, 12
Leuthner, Stuart 120
Lewellen, Verne 54–56, 58
Lewis, Joe 193
Lewis, Woodley 161
Lewisburg, Pa. 44
Lillard, Joe 128
Lincoln, Keith 147
Lipscumb, Eugene "Big Daddy" 148, 193
Livingston, Pat 81
Lombardi, Vince 48, 54, 55, 94, 104, 117, 137, 139, 152–153, 191
Lone Star Dietz, William 42
Los Angeles Chargers 146
Los Angeles Dons 98
Los Angeles Express 118
Los Angeles Memorial Coliseum 128, 176
Los Angeles Rams 103, 106, 107, 108, 114–121, 122, 126, 129, 134, 135, 146, 150, 155–157, 159, 161, 176, 180, 185, 189, 193, 194, 200, 202
Louisiana State University 103
Lowe, Paul 147
Lowe, Woodrow 174
Loyola of the South 109, 110
Lucia, Ellis 18–19
Luckman, Estelle 89
Luckman, Sid 84, 87–90, 93, 94–95, 96–103, 105, 106, 108, 111, 112, 113, 121, 122, 203
Lujack, Johnny 96, 103, 105, 115

MacCambridge, Michael 110
MacCracken, Henry 8
Mack, Connie 15, 16
Mackey, John 3, 138, 161–164, 166, 168
MacLeod, Bob 90
Madden, John 48, 173, 182
Magnani, Dante 81, 100, 101
Mahrt, Alphonse H. 36–37
Malone, Art 181
Malone, Charley 77
Man o' War 44
Manhattan College 76
Maniaci, Joe 90
Mann, Bob 145
Mann, Errol 173
Manning, Peyton 32, 96, 99, 122
Manske, Edgar "Eggs" 88–89
Manual Arts High School 117
Mara, Wellington 50, 70, 74, 83, 187
Maraniss, David 153
Mare Island Marines 25, 42, 97
Marino, Dan 82, 138
Marsh, Amos 177

Marshall, Bob "Rube" 42
Marshall, George Preston 70, 76, 113, 197, 198
Martin, Harvey 180
Martz, Mike 109
Mason, Tommy 186
Massachusetts Agricultural College see University of Massachusetts
Massillon (Ohio) Independent 16
Massillon Tigers 16, 34, 35, 38–40, 41, 127
Masterson, Bat 25
Masterson, Bernie 89
Mathews, Ray 120
Mathewson, Christy 16
Matson, Ollie 120, 189, 194, 195
Maxymuk, John 52
Maynard, Don 1, 3, 138, 148, 199
McAfee, George 81, 84, 92, 93, 97, 121
McBride, Arthur B. " Mickey" 128
McCarthy, Mike 54
McClellan, Keith 34, 36, 37, 38, 39, 40
McClinton, Curtis 169, 195–196
McCloughan, Kent 178
McCormick, Mike 139
McCutcheon, Lawrence 185
McDole, Ron 200
McDonald, Tommy 120, 180, 189
McElhenny, Hugh "King" 143, 189, 190
McGee, Max 138, 154
McGillicuddy, Cornelius see Mack, Connie
McKay, John 169
McKeesport Olympics 35, 38
McLean, Ray "Scooter" 79, 84, 93–94, 97, 101
McMakin, John 182
McNally, Art 182
McNally, Johnny "Blood" 2, 46, 51, 55, 56–58, 72, 74, 77, 81, 187
McNeil, Clifton 200
McPeak, Bill 198
McRea, Earl 187
Means, Natrone 204
"Mel Blount rule" 178–179
Memorial Stadium (Baltimore) 192
Meredith, "Dandy Don" 186
Meyer, Dutch 76
Miami Dolphins 75, 82, 105, 138, 183, 185, 200
Miami Seahawks 128, 136
Michaels, Walt 139
Michigan Agricultural College see Michigan State University
Michigan State University 40, 170
Midway Plaisance 85
Miller, Bill 172
Miller, Heinie 54
Miller, Zach 172

243

INDEX

Millner, Wayne 71, 77, 158
Milwaukee Badgers 55, 56, 130
Milwaukee Journal 48
Minneapolis Marines 35, 54
Minneapolis Star-Tribune 57
Minnesota Vikings 99, 170, 172, 173, 176, 178, 184, 185, 186, 187
Mitchell, Bobby 3, 120, 165, 196–199, 200
Mitchell, Lydell 178, 184, 185, 201–202
The Modern T Formation 66
Molenda, Bo 54
Molesworth, Keith 73
Monday Night Football 191
Monk, Art 200
"Monsters of the Midway" 84–95
Montana, Joe 87
Moore, Harold 8
Moore, Lenny 79, 120, 138, 144, 164, 189, 191–194, 199, 201, 203
Moore, Nat 138
Moore, Sammy 15, 17
Moore, Tom 180
Moore, Wilbur 94
Morgan, Bill 76
Morgan State University 183
Morrall, Earl 186
Morris, Johnny 151
Moss, Paul 33
Moss, Randy 147
Motley, Marion 87, 127, 128–130, 131
Moundsville, W.Va. 36
Mount Pleasant, Frank 22, 23, 24
Muncie, Ind. 41
Muskegon, Mich., High School 44
Musso, George 106
Mutryn, Chet 194
Mutscheller, Jim 138, 144, 160
Mutual Broadcasting System 91
Myhra, Steve 145

Nagurski, Bronislau "Bronko" 60, 63, 68, 69, 73, 75, 76, 97, 100, 109
Namath, "Broadway Joe" 138, 148, 171
National Basketball Association (NBA) 124
National Collegiate Athletic Association (NCAA) 8
National Football League (NFL) 1, 2, 3, 42, 56, 78, 84, 85, 86, 91, 93, 100, 124, 140, 149, 187
National Football League of 1902 15
Navy *see* U.S. Naval Academy
NBA *see* National Basketball Association
NCAA *see* National Collegiate Athletic Association
Neale, Alfred Earle "Greasy" 35, 38, 42, 44, 78, 86, 102, 106–107, 125, 148, 157
Nelson, David M. 13, 22, 23

Nesbitt, Dick 68
Nesser, Al 42
Nesser, Ted 42
Nesser brothers 41, 42
Nevers, Ernie 46, 55, 57, 75, 131
New England Patriots 75, 144, 160, 173, 205
New Haven, Conn. 17
New Mexico Military Institute 156
New Orleans Saints 108, 117
New Richmond, Wis. 56
New York, N.Y. 8, 10, 12, 23, 26
New York Brickley Giants 45
New York Giants (baseball) 16
New York Giants (football) 1, 46, 48, 49–51, 58, 67, 69, 73, 74, 75, 76, 77, 83, 93, 96, 98–99, 100, 101, 104, 105, 106, 120, 125, 144, 148, 150, 151, 155, 181, 183, 187–189, 190–191, 194
New York Herald-Tribune 12, 28, 46, 91
New York Jets 138, 154, 170, 171, 201
New York Morning Telegraph 25
New York Post 99
New York Times 8, 18, 29–30, 31, 99, 153
New York Titans 180
New York University 8, 12
New York World Telegram & Sun 62
New York Yankees (baseball) 44
New York Yankees (football) 49, 55, 118, 135, 136
Newhouse, Robert 177
Newman, Harry 51, 74
Newsome, Ozzie 2, 166, 174
NFL *see* National Football League
NFL Films 1
NFL Network 3, 163, 198
NFL Players Association (NFLPA) 163–164, 168
NFL Properties 19
NFL-Reference.com 130
Niagara County, N.Y. 24
Nickel, Elbie 151, 159
Nisby, John 197
Nitschke, Ray 185
Noll, Chuck 109, 131, 138, 139, 147, 168, 175, 181
Nolting, Ray 90
Norman, Pettis 155
North Dakota State University 13
North Texas State University 180
Northeast Missouri State University *see* Truman State University
Northumberland County, Pa. 44
Northwest Oklahoma State University 24
Northwestern Louisiana University 164
Northwestern University 88, 89, 104, 130
Norton, Marty 54
Notre Dame Box 52, 86

Index

Notre Dame Football—The T Formation 86
Notre Dame University 21, 27, 28–33, 34, 42, 47, 52, 61, 71, 86, 96, 105, 111, 113, 172
Novacek, Jay 155
Nowaskey, Bob 92
Nutter, Buzz 193

Oak Park, Ill., High School 44
Oakland Raiders 25, 104, 155, 170, 171–174, 178, 180, 181–184, 185, 195, 202
Oberlander, Swede 46
Oberlin College 111
O'Brien, Davey 88
O'Brien, Jim (Colts) 163
O'Brien, Jim (sports writer) 183
O'Brien, Pat 31–32
Occidental College 24
Odoms, Riley 155
Official NFL Football Encyclopedia 123
"Ohio League" 12, 21, 34–40, 41, 127
Ohio State Journal 41, 111
Ohio State University 128, 131, 134, 146, 156
Oklahoma A & M 24
Olderman, Murray 194
The Only Game That Matters 17
Oorang Indians 42, 47
Oosterbaan, Benny 33
O'Rourke, Charlie 93
Orr, Jimmy 120, 146, 161, 164, 193
Osmanski, Bill 91, 97, 104
Ottawa Rough Riders 187, 189
Ottawa Sun 187
Otterbein College 24
"Over the Hill Gang" 200
Owen, Steve 93, 98, 188, 190–191
Owens, R.C. 120, 147
Owens, Terrell 78, 117, 143, 147

Paige, Stephone 108
Parker, Ace 83, 187
Parker, Buddy 104, 140, 141, 149
Parkersburg, W.Va. 38
Parks, Billy 183
Parks, Dave 168
Parratt, George "Peggy" 35
Parseghian, Ara 139
Pasquarelli, Len 110, 122
Paterno, Joe 192, 201
Paul Brown Stadium 138
Payton, Walter 185, 202
Pearson, Barry 181
Pearson, Drew 2, 148, 177–178
Pearson, Preston 148, 175–178, 181, 186
Penn State *see* Pennsylvania State University
Pennsylvania State University 20, 23, 25, 61, 192, 201–202

Perry, Joe "The Jet" 87, 130, 136, 143, 190
Petitbon, Richie 110
Phil-Pitt "Steagles" 82, 98, 107
Philadelphia, Pa. 10, 12, 15, 26, 45
Philadelphia Athletics 15
Philadelphia Eagles 38, 42, 51, 72, 78, 86, 89, 98, 102, 106–107, 117, 120, 125, 128, 142, 148, 152, 157–159, 161, 167–168, 180, 182, 187, 188, 189, 191, 194, 197
Philadelphia Phillies 15
Phillips, O.A. "Bum" 147
Phoenix Cardinals *see* Arizona Cardinals
Piascik, Andy 126, 127, 130, 193
Pierce, Hawley 16
Pihos, Pete 106, 142, 148, 151, 157–159, 165
Pine Bluff, Ark. 80
Pitcairn Quakers 35, 38
Pitt *see* University of Pittsburgh
Pittman, Charlie 201
Pittsburgh, Pa. 16, 35, 57, 72, 149, 202
Pittsburgh Athletic Club 16
Pittsburgh Pirates (baseball) 16, 25
Pittsburgh Pirates (football) 56, 58, 72, 73, 88, 128
Pittsburgh Post-Gazette 159
Pittsburgh Press 81
Pittsburgh Stars 16
Pittsburgh Steelers 86, 88, 98, 107, 109, 120, 126, 128, 131, 135, 138, 141, 145, 146, 149–151, 159, 161, 164, 165, 168, 173, 175, 176, 178–179, 181–184, 185, 187, 189, 194, 197, 202
Plasman, Dick 90, 92, 93
Pliska, Joe 30
Podolak, Ed 183–184
Poe, Edgar Allan 7
Policowski, Dan 35
Pollard, Fritz 130
Polo Grounds 46, 75, 76, 98, 99, 188, 189
Pool, Hampton 97, 99, 157
Portsmouth, Ohio, Spartans 67–68, 74
Portsmouth (Ohio) Times 67
Post, Dickie 147
Pottsville, Pa., Maroons 54, 56
Povich, Shirley 197
Powell, Art 137
Powers, Francis 119
Prairie View A&M University 169
Presnell, Glenn 74
Princeton University 5, 6, 7, 9, 11, 12, 15, 17, 23, 24, 26, 27, 30
Pritchard, Bosh 106
Pro Football Hall of Fame 3, 35, 43, 47, 48, 53, 56, 67, 71, 78, 79, 81, 82, 92, 93, 105, 109, 114, 126, 128, 129, 131, 133, 134, 135, 137, 138, 141, 145, 152, 153, 156, 158, 163, 164, 165, 166, 173, 175, 178, 194, 195, 198, 199, 200, 202

245

Index

Pro-Football-Reference.com 48, 137
Professional Football Researchers Association (PFRA) 35
Providence Steam Roller 49
Purdue University 33, 69
"Purple Gang" 185
Pyle, C.C. "Cash & Carry" 89

Racine, Wis. 83
Racine, Wis., Legion 48
Rancho Mirage, Calif. 83
Rapp, Bob 48, 54
Rauch, John 172
Reagan, Ronald 31
Redwine, Jarvis 202
Reed, Alvin 171
Reeves, Dan (owner) 114
Reeves, Dan (player) 177
Reeves, George M. "Bull" 37
Reiter, Howard Rowland "Bosey" 15, 16, 17, 18, 21
Renfro, Mel 163
Renfro, Ray 120, 189
Retzlaff, Pete 120, 142, 161, 167–168
RFK Memorial Stadium 197
Rice, Grantland 28, 46
Rice, Jerry 2, 32, 78, 79, 137, 139, 143
Richards, Kink 74
Richardson, Willie 164
Rickey, Branch 103
Riggins, John 169
Riley, Bullet see Dan Policowski
Roberts, Gene "Choo Choo" 187–189, 194, 195
Robeson, Paul 130
Robinson, Bradbury 13–14
Robinson, Jackie 128
Rochester, N.Y. 41
Rock Island, Ill. 35, 41
Rock Island, Ill., Independents 48
Rockne, Knute 2, 21, 22, 27, 28–33, 34, 35, 39–40, 42, 43, 44, 52, 62
Roethlisberger, Ben 32
Rogers, John I. 15
Rogers, Will 72
Ronzani, Gene 75
Rooney, Art 58, 70, 72, 88–89, 126
Rooney, Dan 88, 126, 159
Roosevelt, Theodore 8
Roper, Bill 26, 27, 30–31
Rose Bowl 25, 42, 49, 80, 86, 97, 110, 127
Ross, Bobby 204
Rote, Tobin 118, 141
Rozelle, Pete 70, 121, 194
Rozier, Mike 202
Rugby Union Code 5–6
Rules of the Season of 1896 7

Running backs 175–205
The Running Backs 194
Russell, Andy 185
Rutgers University 12
Ruth, George Herman "Babe" 44, 78, 100
Ryan, Buddy 109, 139
Ryan, Kent 83
Rymkus, Lou 131, 139

Saban, Lou 139
Sacksteder, Norb 37
Sacrinty, Nick 102
St. Anselm College 94
St. Croix County, Wis. 58
St. George Cricket Field 5
St. Louis, Mo. 13, 18, 20
St. Louis Cardinals (baseball) 37, 103
St. Louis Cardinals (football) 147, 164–165
St. Louis Globe-Democrat 13
St. Louis Rams 115, 195, 203
St. Louis University 13–15, 17–18, 21, 24, 28, 33
Sample, Johnny 193
San Diego Chargers 108, 146–147, 154, 160, 168, 169, 171, 173–174, 201, 202, 204
San Diego State University 203
San Francisco 49ers 106, 112, 117, 118, 120, 124, 136, 137, 139, 140, 142, 147–148, 157, 160, 161, 168, 184–185, 189, 190, 202
San Francisco Polytechnic High School 137
San Jose State University 142
Sanders, Charlie 2, 164, 166–167
Sanders, Ricky 200
Sanders, Spec 188
Sandusky, John 139
Sandusky, Ohio 28
Santa Clara University 137
Saskatchewan Roughriders 133
Saturday Evening Post 26, 60
Sauer, George 138, 148
Sayers, Gale 132
Scarry, Mo 131
Schmidt, Francis "Close the Gates of Mercy" 146
Schmidt, Joe 185
Schneider, Jack 13–14, 28
Seifert, Gorge 139
Selisgrove, Pa. 19
Serling, Rod 193
Sharpe, Shannon 174
Shaughnessy, Clark 3, 19, 60, 61, 65, 66, 84, 85, 87, 88, 94, 103, 108, 109–123, 136, 155–157, 189
Shaw, Bob 116, 151, 156, 159
Shaw, Buck 136
Shell, Donnie 184
Sherman, Solly 87

246

Index

Shibe, Ben 15
Shibe Park 15
Shofner, Del 161
Shotgun formation 147–148
Shoving wedge 9
Shula, David 139
Shula, Don 138, 139, 143, 162, 175, 191
Siegal, John 93
Simpson, O.J. 169, 185, 202
Simpson, Paul 9, 17
Sinnock, Pomeroy 18
Skorich, Nick 167
Smith, Antowain 205
Smith, Billy Ray, Sr. 193
Smith, Charlie 40
Smith, Jackie 164–165, 166, 167
Smith, Jerry 164, 165–166, 167
Smith, Red 144
Smith, Robert 60
Smith, Verda "Vitamin" 116, 157
Snavely, Carl 20, 21
"Sneakers Game" 76
Snow, Jack 121, 180
Solon, Lorin 37
Soltau, Gordie 146
South Bend, Ind. 30
South Bend Silver Edges 34
South Carolina State University 129
South Dakota State College 167
Southern California Sun 117
Southern Methodist University 33, 140
Spalding's How to Play Foot Ball 15, 20
Speedie, Mac 2, 125, 126, 127, 132–134, 135, 140, 141, 144, 187
The Sporting News 161, 163
Sports Illustrated 58, 106, 112
Sportsman's Park 13, 18
Springfield College 19
Stabler, Kenny 172–173
Stagg, Amos Alonso 7, 12, 13, 18–19, 21, 24, 32, 43, 60, 64, 109, 110
Stallworth, John 138
Standlee, Norm 93, 97, 112
Stanford University 49, 61, 86, 93, 96, 112, 121, 122, 148
Stark County, Ohio 35
Starr, Bart 87, 100, 185
Staten Island Stapletons 67
Staubach, Roger 148, 164, 175, 176–177, 186
"Steel Curtain" 185
Steffen, Judge Walter P. 62
Stephen F. Austin State University 204
Stephens, George 7
Sternaman, Dutch 62
Stevens Institute of Technology 17
Stewart, Edward J. 16
Stewart, George A. 9

Stockton, Calif. 19
Stonesifer, Don 146
Storck, Carl "Scummy" 42
Stram, Hank 168–170, 180
Strode, Woody 128
Strong, Ken 76
Stuhldreher, Harry 28
Sturgeon Bay, Wis. 13
Stydahar, Joe 106, 114–115, 120, 155, 157
The Sunday Game: At the Dawn of Professional Football 34
Super Bowl era 1, 2, 3, 4, 85, 115, 138, 139
Susquehanna University 17, 19, 23
Sutherland, Jock 127
Swann, Lynn 2, 78, 138, 143
Swearingen, Fred 182
Syracuse University 23, 161, 164, 197

T formation 59–77, 80, 84, 85, 86, 87, 89–92, 94–95, 96–98, 104, 105, 106, 113–114, 117, 118, 120, 121, 122, 136, 140, 155, 157, 159, 187
Tarkenton, Fran 186, 200
Tatum, Jack 182–184
Taylor, Charley 165, 196, 197, 199–200
Taylor, Hugh 103
Taylor, Jim 152–153
Taylor, Lionel 3
Taylor, Otis 169, 170
Tennessee Titans 115
Texas A & M University 33
Texas Christian University 33, 76, 88, 148
Thiele, Dutch 42
A Thinking Man's Guide to Pro Football 32
Thomas, Clendon 150
Thompson, Lex 106
Thompson, Mike 26
Thompson, Oliver 5
Thompson, Tommy 106, 148, 158
Thorpe, Jim 22, 24, 35, 37, 38, 39, 41, 42, 47, 55, 75
Three Rivers Stadium 181–184
Thurston, Fuzzy 153
Tight end 149–174
Tinsley, Gaynell 71
Tittle, Y.A. 99, 106, 143, 147, 148, 190
Toledo Blade 37
Toledo Maroons 54
Tomlinson, LaDainian 205
Tonawanda Kardex 45
Total Football 130, 137
Towler, "Deacon Dan" 118, 121, 130, 157
Tracy, Tom "The Bomb" 194
Treat, Roger 123
Trenton (N.J.) Times 17
Trimble, Jim 158
Trippi, Charley 102

Index

Truax, Billy 121
Truman State University 17
Trumpy, Bob 171
Tucker, Bob 155
Tufts University 12
Tulane University 33, 109, 110, 131
Tunnell, Emlen 142, 188
Turner, Clyde "Bulldog" 83, 106
Tuscarora Reservation 24
Tyler, Wendell 202–203

UCLA *see* University of California, Los Angeles
Udall, Stewart 197
Union College 8
Unitas, Johnny 1, 3, 100, 106, 134, 138, 143, 145, 160, 161, 162, 163, 175, 185, 191, 193
United Press 17, 199
United States Football League 118
University of Alabama 33, 78, 80
University of Arkansas 24, 147
University of Buffalo 24
University of California, Los Angeles 128
University of Chicago 12, 18, 19, 24, 60, 85, 109, 110, 111, 112
University of Cincinnati 159, 180
University of Dayton 36, 138
University of Florida 63
University of Georgia 7, 21
University of Illinois 18, 32, 44, 45, 61, 62, 63, 69, 110, 111, 175
University of Indiana 157
University of Iowa 13, 14, 204
University of Kansas 18
University of Kentucky 105
University of Maryland 112–113, 114
University of Massachusetts 17
University of Michigan 12, 33, 50, 61, 111, 145
University of Minnesota 23, 61, 96, 109, 112, 164
University of Missouri 17
University of Montana 76
University of Nebraska 13, 47, 54, 202
University of Nevada–Reno 129
University of North Carolina 7, 20
University of Oklahoma 33
University of Oregon 25, 76
University of Pennsylvania 8, 10, 11, 12, 15, 23, 26
University of Pittsburgh 24, 46, 49, 88, 94, 110, 113, 127, 131, 149
University of Southern California 169, 191
University of Tennessee 75
University of Tennessee–Chattanooga 189
University of Texas 33, 105
University of Utah 133

University of Virginia 25, 38, 111
University of Washington 46
University of Wisconsin 13, 118, 121
U.S. Naval Academy 10, 12, 25, 37

Van Brocklin, Norm 49, 106, 108, 114, 115, 116, 121, 157
Van Buren, Steve 87, 106, 157, 188
Van Eeghen, Mark 185
Van Tassell, Irvin 15, 17
Veeder, Paul 17
Villanova University 12, 23, 104
Villapiano, Phil 182
Voorhis, Larry 20
Voss, Tillie 48–49, 54

Wabash College 18, 69, 111
Wade, Bill 149–150
Walker, Doak 140–142
Walker, Doc 169
Walker, Herschel 186
Wallace, Charles Edgar "Blondy" 15–16, 38
Walsh, Bill 109, 138, 147, 184
Walston, Bobby 167
War Memorial Stadium 130
Ward, Arch 124
Ward, Hines 2, 143
Warfield, Paul 138
Warner, Glenn Scobie "Pop" 2, 3, 7–8, 18, 20, 21–24, 64, 127, 148
Warren, Don 169
Warren, Jimmy 182
Washburn College 12
Washington, Gene 143
Washington, Joe 169, 184
Washington, Kenny 128
Washington, D.C. 12, 197–200
Washington & Jefferson College 38, 44, 118
Washington High School 127
Washington Post 123, 197
Washington Redskins 42, 71, 76, 77, 90, 94, 96, 100, 103, 105, 106, 113, 121, 150, 164, 165–166, 169, 187, 188, 196–200, 205
Washington University 20
Waterfield, Bob 105, 107, 108, 114, 115, 116, 121
Waters, Bob 148
Waters, Charlie 184
Watterson, John Sayle 9, 11, 19
Waukesha, Wis. 13
Webster, Mike 138
The Week's Sport 7
Welch, Gibby 2, 46, 49
Welker, Wes 79
Wells, Warren 104
Wesleyan University 12, 15, 16
"West Coast Offense" 138, 147, 185, 202

248

Index

West Point Academy ("Army") 10, 12, 14, 25, 28, 30–31, 37, 46, 115
West Virginia University 38, 74, 98
West Virginia Wesleyan University 24, 38, 44
Western Interprovincial Football Union 133
Western Pennsylvania 12, 16
Westmoreland County, Pa. 16
Whalen, Jim 160
What a Game They Played 57
White, Charles 169
White, J. William 10
Whitney, Casper 6, 7, 36
Whittingham, Richard 47, 51, 57, 81, 113
Wichita State University 12
Wilkinson, Bud 109
Wilkinson, Dan "Big Daddy" 203
Williams, Carl 26
Williams, Edward Bennett 199
Williams, Dr. Harry 10
Williams, Henry L. 109
Williams, John L. 175
Williams, Mike 169
Williams College 17
Willis, Bill 125, 128, 131
Willis, Fred 183
Wilson, Billy 140, 142–143, 161
Wilson, George 84, 97, 99, 103, 104–105, 140, 141, 143, 156
Wilson, Wildcat 46
Wilson, Woodrow 26
Wilson Sporting Goods 75
Winner, Charley 139, 164
Winnipeg Blue Bombers 187
Winslow, Kellen 147, 166, 174
Witten, Jason 155, 174
Woodward, Stanley 12, 91–92
World Football League 117
Wray, J. Edward 13–14
Wright, Rayfield 180
Wrigley Field 68, 73, 85, 100
Wyche, Sam 139

Yale University 5, 6–7, 11, 12, 14, 15, 16, 17, 19, 24, 26, 27, 30, 33, 38, 60, 70, 111
Yepremian, Garo 183
Yost, Fielding "Hurry Up" 12
Young, Ricky 184
Younger, Paul "Tank" 118, 121, 130, 157
Youngstown Patricians 38

Zimmermann, Paul 32, 143, 157, 159, 160, 164, 177, 200
Zuppke, Bob 32, 44, 61, 62, 69, 110

www.ingramcontent.com/pod-product-compliance
Lightning Source LLC
Chambersburg PA
CBHW030105170426
43198CB00009B/501